MORE THAN MEETS THE EYE

POSTMILLENNIAL POP

General Editors: Karen Tongson and Henry Jenkins

More Than Meets the Eye

Special Effects and the
Fantastic Transmedia Franchise

Bob Rehak

NEW YORK UNIVERSITY PRESS
New York

NEW YORK UNIVERSITY PRESS
New York
www.nyupress.org

References to Internet websites (URLs) were accurate at the time of writing. Neither the author nor New York University Press is responsible for URLs that may have expired or changed since the manuscript was prepared.

Library of Congress Cataloging-in-Publication Data
Names: Rehak, Bob (Robert John) author.
Title: More than meets the eye : special effects and the fantastic transmedia franchise / Bob Rehak.
Description: New York : New York University Press, [2018] |
Includes bibliographical references and index.
Identifiers: LCCN 2017034127 | ISBN 9781479813155 (cl : alk. paper) |
ISBN 9781479856701 (pb : alk. paper)
Subjects: LCSH: Cinematography—Special effects. | Motion pictures—Production and direction—United States. | Blockbusters (Motion pictures) | Mass media.
Classification: LCC TR858 .R425 2018 | DDC 791.4302/4—dc23
LC record available at https://lccn.loc.gov/2017034127

New York University Press books are printed on acid-free paper, and their binding materials are chosen for strength and durability. We strive to use environmentally responsible suppliers and materials to the greatest extent possible in publishing our books.

Manufactured in the United States of America

10 9 8 7 6 5 4 3 2 1

Also available as an ebook

CONTENTS

Introduction

Seeing Past the State of the Art

At first glance, the relationship between special effects and contemporary Hollywood blockbusters might seem so straightforward as to go without saying. As of 2017, the top ten movies enjoying domestic U.S. grosses in the $500 million to $1 billion range were all pointedly spectacular productions, such as the dinosaur theme-park adventure *Jurassic World* (Colin Trevorrow, 2015) and Christopher Nolan's IMAX Batman epic *The Dark Knight* (2007); spots two and three belonged to *Avatar* (2009) and *Titanic* (1997), brainchildren of writer-director James Cameron, a "technological auteur" renowned for his cutting-edge use of visual effects technologies;[1] and two others, *The Avengers* (Joss Whedon, 2012) and *Avengers: Age of Ultron* (Joss Whedon, 2015), assembled teams of amazing superheroes to combat world-destroying villains. Number one on the list was *Star Wars: The Force Awakens* (J. J. Abrams, 2015), with *Star Wars: Episode I—The Phantom Menace* (George Lucas, 1999) and the first *Star Wars* (George Lucas, 1977) clocking in at positions eight and nine respectively.[2] If the latter trio stands out for bringing together three generations of a storytelling empire some forty years in existence, it should not escape notice that the top ten highest-grossing *franchises* are similarly dominated by special-effects-heavy properties, included four based on superhero comics (X-Men, Spider-Man, and the collective titles that make up the Marvel Cinematic Universe), along with four science fiction and fantasy properties (including Harry Potter, The Hunger Games, and Peter Jackson's Middle Earth saga).[3]

Again: it may seem self-evident that these movies' outré environments, titanic events, impossible physics, superpowered bodies, and unusual creatures are difficult if not impossible to imagine without the special effects that went into their making. In the franchise films that are its most resource-intensive tentpoles, modern blockbusters promote both explicitly and implicitly the role of digital technology in facilitating their deployment of special effects in such proliferation and sophistication. What we once, during what Michele Pierson terms the "wonder years" of its nascence,[4] labeled computer-generated imagery or CGI to distinguish it from analog forebears such as matte painting, miniature models, and stop-motion animation, has now generalized into an infinitely mutable cinema premised on less visible manifestations of the microprocessor. Film scanners that convert photochemically captured images into endlessly manipulable bitmaps; digital intermediates (DIs) that enable precise color grading and lighting; digital compositing that sandwiches near-infinite layers of separately generated elements into finished frames; and workflows of nonlinear editing and sound mixing all did their part to erode, years before the screen's colonization by virtuosic unrealities, a fundamental connection between the indexically captured materials of filmmaking and their file-based storage and recombination. Not accidently, our ways of perceiving this transformation are inflected by an overwhelming sense, for better or worse, of *currency*: look at how many of the titles mentioned above were made (or remade, reimagined, and rebooted) after the year 2000. Taken together, then, these are the defining features of what we call the state of the art: a popular culture dominated by movies whose huge budgets are part and parcel of the advanced technologies involved in their production—a smorgasbord of spectacles working at one level to immerse us in their enclosing narratives and at another to demonstrate the limitless capabilities of an entertainment industry prolix with its powers of illusion.

Against such an onslaught of manufactured visibility, this book asks what might be missing from our critical understanding of contemporary special effects—what dynamics and behaviors might be hiding, as it were, in plain sight. Answering that question, I suggest, involves seeing *past* the state of the art, moving beyond narrow conceptions of special effects as simple trickery or as symptoms of a constantly updated digital present. The four case studies presented here approach special effects instead as inherently *transmedial* constructs that play crucial, productive roles both within individual textual "homes" and across media platforms, creating and expanding the storyworlds and characters around which our systems of blockbuster entertainment—not just movies, but television, videogames, comics, and other materials—are increasingly organized. Beyond the work they do as a kind of connective tissue knitting together the texts and paratexts of convergence culture, today's special effects in fact display remarkable migratory and evolutionary behaviors of their own, providing audiences with content for borrowing, remixing, and modifying according to their own critical, creative, and social interests. This larger lifespan plays out in a double-barreled way, reflecting special effects' unusual industrial status as what Christian Metz calls "avowed machinations"—illusions that seek to "fool" us even as they invite appreciation as elaborately prepared and presented tricks.[5] By appealing to us both as memorable moments within stories and as feats of technical achievement and artistic innovation, special effects are key to understanding not just the ways in which much contemporary entertainment operates, but the larger cultural practices through which we engage what is "real" and what is "fake" in our media and, by extension, our conception of the world around us.

Just as it is important to look past the work done by special effects in individual media texts, it is also important to view them historically. Indeed, many aspects of contemporary transmedia storytelling—which, in Henry Jenkins's foundational definition, involves the coordinated unfolding of invented worlds and experiences across multiple media[6]— and the larger entertainment economy in which such narratives are embedded, came about not overnight but gradually, as first one and then another property learned to exploit the unique powers of their special effects. Only in recent years has this been done with any kind of organized logic on the part of media producers; as explored in this book, the first flowerings of truly transmedial special effects took place decades earlier, almost by accident, in the 1960s and 1970s. The evolution of special effects from the relatively limited role they played in Classical Hollywood and early television was helped along by forces falling outside traditional definitions of authorship and ownership, as fans gravitated both to the kinds of stories made possible by special effects and to effects "themselves"—the avowed machinations and the artists who made them—as objects of fascination and emulation.

The first half of this book explores media properties born in the 1960s and 1970s as a way of charting the growth of transmedial special effects and the franchise-sustaining storyworlds they made possible. In the case of Star Trek, this activity began with the establishment of design elements whose world-building capabilities were largely the result of fan labor taking place between the cancellation of the Original Series (1966–1969) and the release of *Star Trek: The Motion Picture* (1979), which marked the first significant continuation of the storyline along with its first extension into another medium, film.[7] In the case of Star Wars, by contrast, creator George Lucas exerted total control over new installments and the production of tie-ins, rendering fan contributions irrelevant—at least initially. Yet despite the narrative and industrial differences between these two sagas, both have survived to the present day and continue to thrive with the production of new installments across multiple media. Although many explanations for this longevity have been offered over the years, the role of special effects as designed elements giving consistency to individual "chapters" while exerting their own unique hold on audiences' imaginations has gone unremarked.

While Chapters 1 and 2 concern themselves with the role of special effects in building storyworlds and establishing franchise authorship, Chapters 3 and 4 consider the circulation of special effects beyond those branded territories, as elements in a larger transmedia economy, and in relation to "digitality" as both technological reality and auratic construction. Characters built in whole or in part on special effects populate our screens in performances ranging from the superpowered stars of comic-book movies to the creatures and races that make up Peter Jackson's Middle Earth trilogies *The Lord of the Rings* (2001–2003) and *The Hobbit* (2012–2014). In doing so, they draw on a long history of technologically augmented acting that comprises animated beings, monsters, aliens, and anthropomorphic animals. The ways in which such bodies reappear and evolve over time can be seen as a specific instance of a more general tendency toward migratory travel by special effects that reproduce and mutate as spectacular subunits in themselves, exemplified by *The Matrix* films (the Wachowski siblings, 1999–2003) and their signature effect, bullet time. In both cases, behaviors that seem to arise from special effects' digital nature in fact boast precedents extending back into filmmaking's "analog" era: continuities discoverable in the sedimented history of special effects manufacture but often elided in order to cement a larger narrative of digital cinema's (allegedly) game-changing break with the past.

Attending critically to the transmedial behaviors of special effects is thus essential to understanding not just how much contemporary media entertainment works, but how those operations take place in unexpected, and paradoxically unobserved, ways. Academic accounts within cinema and media studies have done a great deal to delineate and historicize special effects' techniques and meanings, but have engaged far less with the way they function outside and among traditional narrative and generic homes—at the intersectional, extensional connections among sequels and installments, at scales both larger and smaller than the two-hour feature film or one-hour TV drama, in forms both textual and paratextual. Meanwhile, transmedia studies have emphasized the importance of world-building, promotion and marketing, active audiences and fandom, and new avenues for generating and sharing media content, but overlooked the key role played by special effects in these spheres. "Transmedia storytelling," Jenkins points out, only "describes one logic for thinking about the flow of content across media."[8] He goes on to identify transmedia branding, transmedia performance, transmedia ritual, transmedia play, transmedia activism, and transmedia spectacle as other such logics, but leaves these as signposts for further investigation. This book, which exists at the intersection of studies of special effects and studies of convergence culture, answers Jenkins's hail by taking up the question of how special effects move through—and to an extent even constitute—our media networks, shaping the behavior of texts and genres as well as producers and audiences.

Theorizing Special Effects

Although special effects have been recognized as a discrete practice in film production since at least the 1920s, when the Academy of Motion Picture Arts and Sciences began to give awards in categories such as Best Engineering Effects and Best Special Effects, they did not begin to come under close academic scrutiny until 1977, with the publication of Christian Metz's "*Trucage* and the Film."[9] From today's vantage point, it is hard to ignore the felicitous (if entirely coincidental) timing of Metz's essay with the release of *Star Wars*—a movie generally credited with revitalizing the effects industry and public interest surrounding it.[10] Metz's psychoanalytic take, however, focused less on the emergence of the contemporary effects blockbuster than on the peculiar convolutions of belief and disavowal he suggests spectators undergo when confronting images they know to be unreal but provisionally accept nonetheless. Pointing out that our immersion in the screen's representations involves a complex sorting of filmic illusion into various levels of noticeability, Metz famously asserted that "all of cinema is, in some sense, a special effect," from the commonplace and unremarked techniques such as fades, dissolves, and titles to the dramatic presentation of scenes and events that invite us to appreciate them precisely as achievements of cunning artifice.

Metz's emphatically psychodynamic approach has not, by and large, been replicated in more recent academic work on special effects. But his seminal essay deserves to be labeled as such because of the key insights it introduced: insights that have been foundational, both in positive and negative ways, to the investigations that followed. First was his argument that special effects are sites where artifice and its opposite, a profilmic "truth," are most powerfully co-present for spectators, making the default mode of engaging with special effects one of division and hybridity, conflict and uncertainty. (Dan North neatly describes it as "a kind of doublethink on the part of the viewer."[11]) By suggesting that audiences neither believe nor disbelieve in special effects outright, but respond to them in a kind of fascinated hesitation, Metz opened the floor for future scholars to talk about a range of in-between (or to adopt a term from videogame studies, "half-real") spaces that would otherwise have been foreclosed to study.[12] Pierson, for example, writes about fans who dig deeply into the technical arcana behind special effects, while Jonathan Gray notes the way in which behind-the-scenes featurettes on DVD and Blu-ray function as media paratexts, shaping appreciation and interpretation of the movies with which they are packaged.[13] With analog precursors such as professional publications *American Cinematographer* (1920–present) and *Cinefex* (1980–present), and digital descendants like the promotionally celebratory visual-effects "breakdowns" and sarcastic "10 Greatest CGI Fails" videos available on YouTube and Vimeo, our ongoing attention to artifice demonstrates the point that "doublethink" is never without its share of pleasure.

Metz's other influential insight was that special effects are as much *discursive* constructs as industrial ones: that is, the way we choose to describe them profoundly shapes what we understand them to be. As in the Chinese encyclopedia discussed by Michel Foucault (a mythical taxonomy whose unruliness demonstrates the arbitrariness of all classificatory gestures), we have been conditioned to group some forms of cinematic practice under the headings of artifice, fakery, and manipulation, while excusing others as real and authentic.[14] In so doing, we call special effects into existence as identifiable entities. This is not to say that special effects are entirely constructs of language; obviously they denote specific kinds of intervention in the frame, encompassing a range of techniques that, although they have evolved over time, tend to involve the same core concepts (makeup, animation, painting) and formal characteristics (composites and layering). Still, to fully describe effects' complex operations means embracing the heterogeneity and flexibility of the term. I am not, therefore, particularly interested in the relationship between reality and its manufactured double that special effects, following North, seem invariably to highlight. Relatedly, I do not think it of great importance whether a scene was done live and "unmediatedly" before a camera or engineered by optical printers, model shops, or 3D software. To me, it makes much more sense to see these apparently opposed qualities in terms of *degrees of intervention*, following Albert J. La Valley's expansive understanding of screen illusion:

> There must be a significant and important gap between the illusion of what we see on screen and what was used to produce it. Sets, even interplanetary and futuristic ones, are at the low threshold of this discrepancy; miniatures and glass shots are in the middle range; and optically printed shots combining things of many sizes as in *King Kong* and *Star Wars* are perhaps the most discrepant and seem to call on the most sophisticated forms of special effects technology. Special effects then are a kind of continuum embracing the entire cinema, but most fully articulated in films which depict the unseen or unseeable: disaster, spectacle, fantasy, horror, and science fiction.[15]

LaValley's formulation, written in the analog era, usefully relaxes the definitional strictures that have tended to limit our discussions of special effects. As Metz suggests, there are many ways to map the manipulation of motion-picture imagery, ranging from the overly general to the overly specific. On the one hand, to describe all cinema as trickery may be philosophically provocative, but fails to explain why we consider certain classes of image as more or less "special" than others. On the other hand, categorizing special effects according to the processes by which they were achieved (e.g., distinguishing between stop-motion and digital animation, between painted matte shots and front-screen projection) may be appropriate to technical discussions or how-to articles. When it comes to questions of theory and history, however, this approach seems fine-grained to a fault, paying little attention to the plasticity and combinatorial fluidity that drive technological innovation in cinema and other media. More damningly, both taxonomic extremes reinscribe a fundamental misrecognition of the way effects acquire their semiotic identities: the assumption that special effects work only at the level of the *shot*. In truth, effects draw meaning not just locally from their constitutive elements (fragments of image composited together to simulate one unbroken take of film), but globally from their surrounding contexts (narrative, mise-en-scène, and genre).

The approach taken in this book, then, is to treat the category of special effects elastically enough to range from their traditional industrial definition as applications of technique (such as prosthetic makeup or optical and digital compositing) to any material "faked" for the production, including, for example, certain types of set design, prop construction, and costumes. Films and television shows set in the real world may score low on this metric of artifice (though this is not to say they are any less dependent on greenscreen and digital models to generate their settings). But in fantastic media franchises, whose worlds, objects, and events must be in a sense be built from scratch, the philosophical, ontological, and practical lines dividing special effects from a "real" to which they are conventionally opposed become blurred to the point of merging completely. Treating special effects in this manner may be a controversial move, given the welcome turn to technological and historical specificity in recent scholarship on special effects. But the kinds of phenomena I engage in this book take place at multiple levels, on multiple fronts, over time periods extending into years and decades, in articulations whose unpredictability requires an adaptive eye to follow. If only because our ways of attending to them shift so easily from the intensive technical detail offered by professional media to the abstract sense in which critics praise or disparage a new release's use of them, special effects must be understood both as concrete industrial practices and as discursive constructs: media "events" that are themselves always mediated, marked as artificial, by the knowledges circulating around our encounters with them. The book's four chapters delve into technical specifics where appropriate, but their larger goal is to explore what it means to live in the full realization of Metz's "cinema of special effects"—a characterization truer now than in the time of his original writing—in which all filmic narration is ultimately subsumed into visualization, or more accurately, *previsualization*.

Previz *avant la Lettre*

Engaging special effects in a transmedia context means, ironically, peering backward along the axis of time into the analog past from which they arose. By doing so, we can begin to see ways in which special effects from the start behaved differently from other elements of filmic narrative, reaching outward to other textual homes and audiences. Moving beyond the moment of special effects' initial display and impact on the viewer brings into view two phases common to all filmmaking but which bear particular importance to the genesis and circulation of effects: preproduction and postproduction. In previsualization or *previz*, motion-picture imagery is planned through a series of sketches, rough drafts, and preliminary versions. From the standpoint of special effects, this phase can be viewed as the period during which "new" cinematic texts coalesce from predecessors and influences, minting themselves as "original" in the process. Hence it is essential to the industrial logic by which movies-as-products ensure their own replication. On another level, preproduction and postproduction are interesting because of the degree to which they contribute to Hollywood's self-presentation in forms other than the end product. As Gray argues, completed feature films rarely intersect our lives in isolation. Instead, they arrive in a halo of secondary discourses: print and TV journalism, coffee-table books, trade and fan magazines, word-of-mouth, and more recently, websites, blogs, podcasts, and YouTube videos.[16] Some of these paratexts are officially sanctioned and coordinated by the marketing arm of the industry; others issue from outside the privileged inner circle, in the grassroots work of fandom. The important point is that in both cases, public awareness of the movie in question is frequently informed by materials drawn from pre- and postproduction.

It is a commonplace of new media discourse to claim that recent innovations, such as the introduction of the laserdisc, DVD, and Blu-ray formats, have made much more information about what we might call "paraproduction" available for public consumption, increasing our access by going behind the scenes of a movie to explore its conception, design, and execution. In truth, the circulation of such materials dates back to the dawn of moviemaking. Many lost films survive only through their planning materials (written scenarios, sketches or blueprints of sets) or through paraphernalia of promotion and exhibition (movie posters, lobby cards, tie-in products). One of the most famous images of early cinema—the Moon with a rocket jammed in its eye, from Georges Méliès's *A Trip to the Moon* (1902)—is frequently reproduced in the form of its associated preproduction painting, as well as the actual film frame in which it appears [Figure I.1]. In crafting his illusions, Méliès arguably produced the earliest examples of previz. Special-effects historian Christopher Finch points out that "Méliès, a frustrated cartoonist, seems to have initiated the idea of production sketches, planning many of his key scenes on paper before committing them to film."[17] The naturalistic *actualités* of Louis and Auguste Lumière required little more to produce than the placement of a *cinématographe* at a vantage point from

Figure I.1. Méliès preproduction art (left) and final image (right) for *A Trip to the Moon*.

which it could capture sixty seconds of activity occurring before it. By contrast, Méliès's screen trickery—expanding rubber heads, dancing midgets, painted backdrops, exploding Moon creatures, and cutaway submarines—necessitated planning in advance, for almost all of his illusions played on precise camera position and alignment, manipulation of depth of field, and large-scale mechanical prop effects like those in *The Merry Frolics of Satan* (1906).[18]

Méliès's illusions were but the start of a long process of incorporating special effects and their associated preproduction materials in the nascent filmmaking medium. The multiple layers of even a simple process shot require careful alignment to prevent elements from overlapping and creating distracting matte lines or soft edges. It is therefore likely that Edwin S. Porter's employment of the first "naturalistic" optical effect in *The Great Train Robbery* (1903)—to show an arriving train, seen through a window—was preplanned in order to correctly position the blacked-out areas of the matte against foreground action shot on the set of a railroad telegraph office. Over the next few years, visual effects continued to be put to work as part of an emerging narrative paradigm. In his *Missions of California* (1907), Norman O. Dawn pioneered the use of "glass shots" to extend partially built sets into full-scale vistas, a process adapted from still photography. "At one mission a row of arches had been reduced to a few piles of broken masonry. Dawn simply painted the missing arches on a sheet of glass, set the glass up in front of his camera, and, through the viewfinder, lined up the painting with the actual building, which was miraculously made whole again."[19] Glass shots remained popular for almost two decades, until they were supplanted by more sophisticated techniques such as the Schüfftan Process, a mirror-dependent illusion developed by German cinematographer Eugen Schüfftan in 1923.[20] Along with descendants such as matte paintings, front- and rear-screen projection process shots, traveling mattes generated through rotoscoping or blue- and greenscreen substitution, and most recently electronic (video) and digital compositing, special effects thus had a linked function of generating diegetic spaces and streamlining production costs. Studio effects departments labored "to create *mise-en-scène*—beautiful mountains instead of the tops of an adjacent set, multi-storied castles, and locales not available for mass transportation of hundreds of staff and players and tons of equipment."[21] These techniques depended on ever more precise mechanisms to align elements generated at different points in space and time; "standardization of precision registration around 1914 was particularly important in permitting certain special effects."[22]

This brings us to another perspective on the evolution of preproduction as a centerpiece of studio industrialization. Preproduction assisted cinema's transition from a new and experimental medium to an assembly-line-like process involving the coordination of a large labor force, working under studio supervision, resulting in productions of increasing scale and complexity. Within the production culture I am examining, certain aspects of special effects receive the bulk of public attention: the wondrous imagery they create (the "magic trick") and the nuts-and-bolts of their engineering (how that "magic" was accomplished). Yet neither dimension, I suggest, is particularly helpful in placing special effects in the larger context of a mode of production.

The fact that so many special-effects breakthroughs can be traced to advances in preproduction raises the question of how such practices reflect a longer history of Hollywood's operations—not just in the creation of "spectacle," but in the manufacture of movies more generally. As David Bordwell, Janet Staiger, and Kristin Thompson observe in *The Classical Hollywood Cinema: Film Style and Mode of Production to 1960*, special effects—along with other technological innovations such as color, sound, and widescreen—have long been as much a part of movie marketing as movie making. "Hollywood," they write, "has promoted mechanical marvels as assiduously as it has publicized stars, properties, and genres." Yet, they remind us, "there is nothing oneiric about technology; it is a concrete historical force."[23] In this sense, the creation of special effects must be considered in relation to Hollywood's mode of production. Staiger defines this concept in terms of three components that interact dynamically: labor force, means of production, and financing of production.[24] The mode of production is crucial to understanding how Hollywood both adheres to and departs from the logic of the Fordist factory system. While movies made under the studio system are undeniably products of an assembly-line-like process, they are also artistic works imprinted with the authorial signature of a director, producer, and sometimes a writer or star. This produces a tension between public conceptions of movies as art and artifact: a tension mediated in part through the discourse of special effects.

Two "descriptive and explanatory schemata related to the organization of the labor force" mentioned by Staiger are relevant to my discussion of preproduction: the specialized division of labor and a succession of different management systems.[25] It is in these areas that classical preproduction practices demonstrate their utility in the industrialization of the cinematic medium. From the perspective of labor and management, preproduction is a wide-ranging category comprising a variety of different tools for mapping, envisioning, refining, and engineering motion pictures. Each of these tools can be seen as an incremental stage in transforming an initial concept into a finished feature film. Crucially, each also functions as a form of distributed authority for coordinating the sprawling and specialized labor force involved in moviemaking. Visual materials such as costume and set designs, storyboards, and artwork are variations of the more concrete and publicly acknowledged bible for any given movie—the script—whose importance Staiger emphasizes as "a blueprint for the film":

> In the early teens a detailed script became necessary to insure efficient production and to insure that the film met a certain standard of quality defined by the industry's discourse. While pertinent before the early teens, the simultaneous diffusion of the multiple-reel film and certain stylistic options at that point placed such demands on the production crew that a precise pre-shooting plan became necessary. The script, furthermore, became more than just the mechanism to pre-check quality: it became the blueprint from which all other work was organized.[26]

The scope of preproduction expanded as movies themselves became longer and tackled more complex subject matter, eventually finding stable form in the psychologically oriented, causal narrative model that came to define the studio product. Before 1909, a casual story outline sufficed to guide production. But under the director-unit system that lasted from 1909 to 1914 and which was typified by filmmakers such as Mack Sennett and D. W. Griffith, the story outline gave way to a more detailed plan, the scenario script, assisting the studios' reorganization "into a predictable, efficient assembly system."[27] Scenario scripts allowed directors for the first time to shoot out of sequence and assemble the components of the story later, in editing, guided by the script. It also encouraged the construction of a formally unified narrative within the confines of fixed-length 1,000-foot film reels. "By preparing a script which provided narrative continuity before shooting actually started," producers ensured "complete narrative continuity and clarity despite the footage limitation."[28] This restriction fell with the introduction of the continuity script, enabling movies to leap from an average of eighteen minutes to seventy-five minutes in duration. Again, changes in narrative, stylistic, and visual form mirrored shifts in the underlying mode of production, including an increasingly prominent role for the producer, who used the "very detailed shooting script . . . to plan and budget the entire film shot-by-shot before any major set construction, crew selection, or shooting started."[29]

Preproduction continued to expand and diversify as the director-unit configuration gave way to what Staiger calls the "central producer" system, dating from approximately 1914 to 1931. The Taylorist school of scientific management influenced Hollywood's consultation with efficiency experts and its establishment of production-line practices in which paper records were increasingly used to coordinate film production. Before a single frame was shot, planning departments broke down scripts into lists of sets, wardrobes, props, and personnel such as stage hands, carpenters, and painters, in order to calculate costs and allocate resources. Of particular importance were detailed sketches of sets and costumes prepared by production departments to assist directors with their creative conception and producers with budget management. As Staiger summarizes,

> Planning the work and estimating production costs through a detailed script became a new, extensive, and early step in the labor process. This improved regularity and speed of production, use of materials, and uniformity and quality of the product. The script became a blueprint detailing the shot-by-shot breakdown of the film. Thus, it could function as a paper record to coordinate the assembly of the product shot out of order, prepared by a large number of people spread at various place through the world (location shooting, for example, to be matched to an interior in Santa Monica), and still achieve a clear, verisimilar and continuous representation of causal logic, time and space.[30]

One of the specialized departments called into existence during this time was that of art direction or production design. Dating from the teens, when theatrical holdovers such as stationary camera positions and sets with flat painted backdrops gave way to three-dimensional sets and mobile cameras, design experts prepared "pre-construction diagrams of the sets with camera set-ups precisely marked." Storyboards were born as a result of the need to consider "how a set would photograph with the camera at varying distances (an effect of closer framing and analytical editing)."[31]

The art director quickly took on an essential role in planning a film's "total visual look."[32] The first art directors came from the world of theater, including Wilfred Buckland, Joseph Urban (famous for his association with Ziegfeld Follies), Cedric Gibbons, and A. Arnold Gillespie, who, as many such figures did, soon became proficient in special-effects work.[33] Another important influence on Hollywood's growing stylistic and technical repertoire was the work of German filmmakers such as Fritz Lang and F. W. Murnau, whose "highly imaginative and dramatic art direction" required heavy use of enclosed stages. The resulting emphasis on "innovative sets, inventive approaches to cinematography, and an extensive use of special effects" drove preproduction to greater heights of sophistication and complexity.[34] According to one historian, the period to 1930 saw the steady rise of films that were "ambitious in scale and spectacle."[35] This trend culminated in a series of productions renowned for their visuals—some within the expected fantasy and science-fiction genres, such as *King Kong* (Merian C. Cooper and Ernest Schoedsack, 1933), and others in the mode of the historical epic, such as *Gone with the Wind* (Victor Fleming, 1939). Both movies made substantial use of visual effects, and both were heavily "preproduced" [Figure I.2], the former largely through drawings by stop-motion animator (and uncredited visual-effects supervisor) Willis O'Brien, the latter by William Cameron Menzies. Menzies, who received the first screen credit for "Production Design" at the request of producer David O. Selznick, was said to have "controlled the look of every scene through detailed storyboards which were rigorously adhered to."[36] In the decades that followed, storyboarding and other preproduction tools became an indispensable part of the process by which movies underwent alchemical transformation from text to screen.

Figure I.2. Art-to-shot comparisons, *King Kong* (1933).

Production designers continued to build their artistic cachet, many becoming names in their own right: Anton Grot, Ken Adams, John Barry, Dean Tavoularis, Norman Reynolds, and Anton Furst. None, perhaps, was more recognizable than Busby Berkeley, renowned for his opulent and sometimes hallucinatory musical numbers. Directors such as Alfred Hitchcock received much attention for their extensive reliance on preplanning and storyboarding, as did dedicated special-effects artisans such as Ray Harryhausen.

By revisiting the history of image production and circulation in this way, this book rethinks special effects in ways that are more specific to their industrial nature, more flexible in their understanding of what constitutes a special effect, and how those effects are taken up both discursively/affectively and within the transmission and display nodes of our complexly, ubiquitously technologized visual culture—a culture whose dominant form, the fantastic transmedia franchise, evolved hand in hand with special effects.

Special Effects and Transmedia

The traditional view is that in Classical Hollywood cinema, special effects worked either invisibly to suture viewers into diegetic and dramatic spaces, or visibly to create screen events that could not have been attained without the intervention of a technologized "magic." In today's fantastic transmedia franchise, by contrast, special effects often function in highly visible, foregrounded ways across larger, multitextual domains to create settings, characters, creatures, and events whose unreality coexists in pleasurable tension with the detail brought to their visualization. By bringing perceptual verisimilitude to fictive domains with few or no real-world referents, special effects in fantastic transmedia do more than just "fool the eye"; they also generate continuities and histories that link together the disparate texts belonging to the franchise.

According to Angela Ndalianis, blockbuster screen entertainments of the twentieth century underwent profound changes in the years leading up to the twenty-first, evolving toward technologically dispersed but narratively centralized texts whose cumulative impact is one of labyrinthine complexity and immersiveness. In Ndalianis's concept of the "neo-baroque," which anticipates by a few years Jenkins's popular codification of transmedia storytelling, the merging of media industries drove formal changes in the behaviors of media from film and video-games to comic books and theme-park rides increasingly built around shared storyworlds to be explored and experienced by actively questing audiences.[37] Along with a new emphasis on serialized storytelling, special effects are a dominant trait of the neo-baroque: "Media merge with media, genres unite to produce new hybrid forms, narratives open up and extend into new spatial and serial configurations, and special effects construct illusions that seek to collapse the frame that separates spectator from spectacle."[38]

The spectator Ndalianis identifies as the focus of this transformed blockbuster system is hardly a naïve one; neo-baroque special effects that merge "an artificial reality into the phenomenological space of the audience," she observes in a Metzian vein, "simultaneously [invite] the spectator to recognize this deception [and] to marvel at the methods employed to construct it."[39] The deception itself, however, is aimed at overwhelming audiences by "highlighting intense sensory experiences" such as kinesthesia, vertigo, and awe.[40] Placing neo-baroque special effects in a history that includes the camera obscura, panoramas, trompe l'oeil painting, and other magical "devices of wonder," Ndalianis follows a traditional genealogy of sensory immersion through technological artifice that is important for its emphasis on *affect* as a key category of special effects reception. The neo-baroque model has less to say about special effects' connection to the serialized and continuity-heavy storyworlds of fantastic media. In the case of properties such as Jurassic

Park (1993–) and the Terminator (1984–) franchises, special effects work architecturally to spatialize filmic mise-en-scène and make it available for exploration in other media such as videogames and theme-park attractions.[41] But these fundamentally immersive ends pivot on questions of spectator belief and disbelief in the experiences being created, rather than on how these experiences convey information about the story-world and its characters. The "new sensibility" of the special effects in *Star Wars*, Ndalianis writes, stems from "their spatial orientation and their depiction of objects in space in a way that produces a neo-baroque relationship between spectator and image."[42]

The genres of science fiction, fantasy, and horror point to the dependence on special effects to create and extend what I am loosely calling *fantastic transmedia*. For Ndalianis, the coevolution of genre and technology is inseparable from the rise of digital technology. "The revival of popularity in these genres coincided with the growth in special-effects companies, which themselves relied on advances in optical technology made possible by the computer revolution."[43] Julie Turnock takes a closer look at the entanglement of science fiction and the special-effects industry at a moment of significant change in her exploration of *Star Wars* and *Close Encounters of the Third Kind* (Steven Spielberg, 1978).[44] The former in particular established, for Turnock, an "expanded blockbuster" aesthetic that can be seen as the precursor to Ndalianis's neo-baroque: "Overflowing with kinetic action, taking place within a minutely detailed, intricately composed mise-en-scene, comprising an all-encompassing, expandable environment."[45] Late analog, proto-digital effects practices such as optical compositing, which multiplied the abilities of traditional optical printing and traveling-matte generation with the precision of microprocessor-driven "motion control" cinematography of miniatures, contributed unprecedented levels of depth and detail to the screen presentation of *Star Wars*'s universe, while the sheer number of effects shots—some 360, in a time when the typical science-fiction film might employ a tenth that many—and their even distribution throughout the film's running time worked to stitch together a consistent-seeming set of worlds, vehicles, structures, and creatures.[46] Turnock connects the construction and depiction of this world to the auteurist visions of the "film school generation": figures such as George Lucas, Steven Spielberg, and Francis

Ford Coppola, whose debut features were much more idiosyncratic and artistically perceived than we tend to credit nowadays.

I think Turnock is correct in attributing to *Star Wars* a breakthrough in world design as an expression of auteuristic vision and control (though her neglect of the design stage, preferring to focus on the technical and engineering, leaves out Ralph McQuarrie, Joe Johnston, and other contributing artists discussed in Chapter 2). She lays an important groundwork for understanding how techno-auteurists subsume the contributions of others. But while her history of the industry follows special-effects houses into the 1980s, she doesn't stay with the worlds themselves, providing less insight on how special effects form the interconnective tissue among media installments. If traditional film studies has mapped out essentially *negative* roles for special effects—based on their inherent falsity and deceptiveness, their ontological difference from "live action," and their alterity to narrative—the dynamics explored in this book are primarily *positive* ones: the role of special effects in building shared worlds, reminting texts and generating authorship, moving as circulatory agents, and building characters and performances that expand transmedially. In this view, special effects comprise a distinct class of imagery whose manufactured and capital-driven iconographies, yoked to fictional frameworks, grant them extraordinary reach and power. Special effects, in short, *make things possible*, and the things they make possible have worked over time to generate sprawling yet coherent franchises and the unusual characters that populate them. They do this through complex flows and circulations with short shelf lives, contributing to an overall acceleration of the evolution of visual culture in a digital era.

Chapter Preview

The cases examined in this book take place during periods when special effects and blockbuster franchises found new relationships with each other, moving forward in a mutual process that cannot be reduced to simple cause and effect. Drawing on popular and industrial documentation of special-effects manufacture, the following four chapters explore these stages in more or less chronological order, treating them as four slices through a complex, multivariable process by which the contemporary transmedia landscape was collectively forged.

Special effects and world-building are the focus of the first half of the book. The recent emergence of imaginary-world theory has added an important and timely tool to the arsenal of film and media studies—as with special effects studies, it is no accident that the language of "worlding" in videogames, experimental art, and animation has developed in step with how our media behave.[47] Considered as a matter of illustrating and giving form to unreal settings, cinematic special effects are not the only way to render imaginary worlds: videogame engines generate in realtime whole environments, from surface textures down to physics, while Dungeons & Dragons players summon a different sort of fantasy environment, one animated by cultural rather than technological ritual, in a merging of narration and roleplay. Symbolically conveyed in type, sequentially drawn in graphic novels, or colorfully painted as a pulp paperback cover, some worlds of science fiction and fantasy were mainstays of twentieth-century culture, often embodied in hero characters—Conan the Barbarian, Superman, the Lone Ranger—as recent studies in "transmedia archeology" have shown.[48] One may view the continued presence of these worlds and characters today as evidence of how flexibly forces of franchise have intertwined themselves with industries of illusion.

But while I argue for the inherently transmedial nature of post-1970s special effects, I do so from the vantage point primarily of film and television, the dominant moving-image media of the decades leading up to the flowering of the contemporary fantastic-media franchise. The first two chapters are thus a centripetal study of how the first modern special-effects-dependent storyworlds were forged, one on broadcast and syndicated television amid an avid fan movement, the other a feature film originating largely from outside the Hollywood system. Both chapters share an interest in design and designers as underreported agents in special-effects world-building; in authors and authorship within special-effects-dependent productions; and in negotiations between fans and producers around the decision-making and direction of franchises as they grow.

Chapter 1, "That Which Survives: Design Networks and Blueprint Culture between Fandom and Franchise," explores the initial genesis of *Star Trek* in the 1960s, expanding on Derek Johnson's concept of "overdesign," or the production-side profusion of detail underpinning an imaginary screen world—in this case, *Trek*'s twenty-third-century "future history"—that provides a template for shared creative collaboration.[49] Although the story of creator Gene Roddenberry's "*Wagon Train* to the stars" concept and the series "bible" that guided scriptwriters in crafting their teleplays is well known, less attention has been paid to how the contributions of multiple designers coalesced to build what was essentially an open-source universe. In the 1970s, the fandom around *Star Trek* elaborated on that storyworld through the creation of reference materials such as blueprints and technical manuals. This grassroots movement, paralleling official efforts to relaunch the franchise in the form of a new TV series and feature film, reflected that open-source ideal but came into conflict with official rights holders, suggesting an interplay of forces around the expansion and continuation of franchise storyworlds.

Those concerns recur in the preproduction and making of *Star Wars*, the focus of Chapter 2, "Used Universes and Immaculate Realities: Appropriation and Authorship in the Age of Previzualization." Exploring writer-director George Lucas's status as visionary creator of *Star Wars*, this chapter documents the contributions of production artists and visual-effects designers such as Ralph McQuarrie and John Dykstra to suggest a collaborative model similar to *Star Trek*'s. But it goes further by considering how Lucas and his team remixed a vast catalog of generic influences ranging from *Flash Gordon* serials of the 1930s to World War II films, using special effects not only to invent a fantastic fictional space but to forge originality from appropriation—a kind of transformative labor occurring at the producerly rather than fannish level. The chapter tracks this logic through the later technological and commercial evolution of the Star Wars franchise, examining how cases such as the remastered Special Editions of the late 1990s, the Prequel Trilogy of the early 2000s, the recent acquisition of Lucasfilm by Disney, and the current creation of new installments, all draw on a "previz mind-set" which, despite its strong associations with the digital, can be more logically sourced to developments in analog preproduction that occurred in the 1970s.

If the first two chapters look at special effects as creative tools—underpinning the construction and proliferation of fictive worlds on the one hand and rebranding existing texts into original properties on the other—Chapters 3 and 4 consider special effects as dynamic agents possessing their own unique itineraries within and among different media.

Chapter 3, "Chains of Evidence: Augmented Performance before and after the Digital," investigates screen acting in a technology-dominated cinema, raising questions about where—in the age of digitally assisted characters such as Gollum and Benjamin Button—the human actor ends and special effects begin. Special effects have long been used not only to augment actorly turns like Boris Karloff's in *Frankenstein* (James Whale, 1933) and Christopher Reeve's in *Superman* (Richard Donner, 1978) but to channel expressive traits from animators and technicians onto a range of drawn, constructed, and remotely operated bodies on screen. The Middle Earth trilogies *Lord of the Rings* and *The Hobbit* serve as case studies in both the star turns and stunt labor of augmented performance, connecting the earliest experimentation in stop-motion effects to the recent emergence of digital actors to show that similar processes and semiotic codes underpin these seeming technological opposites.

The most famous recent example of this phenomenon is bullet time, a visual effect appearing throughout the *Matrix* trilogy. As explored in Chapter 4, "Microgenres in Migration: Special Effects and Transmedia Travel," bullet time spread from film to film (and into television ads, videogames, and cartoons) through quotation, parody, and unauthorized appropriation. While transmedia storytelling, of which the Matrix franchise is often cited as a canonical example, emphasizes the coordination of story elements across extensions in videogames and web comics, the focus in this chapter is on larger economies of image replication. Charting the history of the special-effects techniques employed to slow down time with a moving camera—methods eventually consolidated in the supposedly unprecedented "breakthrough" of *The Matrix*—and the afterlife of bullet time as a much-lampooned cliché that eventually became an accepted part of visual culture's grammar, the chapter ultimately argues for an expanded understanding of the breakdown and recombination of generic elements through a complex interplay of technology, fandom, and producerly interests.

In all, the four chapters and the trends they highlight hinge on special effects and the specific formations of labor that generate them, each illuminating more comprehensive concerns of film and media studies: negotiations between fans and producers; authorship within the studio system; the emergence and evolution of genres; and the shifting codes of screen performance that generate dramatic characters. In this broader view of special effects as more than merely a series of tricks embedded in otherwise "unspecial" media, special effects reveal themselves as sites of profoundly transmedial activity, blending old and new in a cauldron of inherited practices and innovative methods while setting the agenda for emergent forms of production and circulation of popular texts and objects.

Seeing past the state of the art, then, is crucial to comprehending special effects, in both the forms they have assumed and will assume in the future. Special effects are always heightened, excessively noticeable elements of moviemaking; even their "invisible" uses are inevitably highlighted in the discourses that accompany a film, intriguing us after the fact with an account of how they were achieved. Such moments should be seen not as extrinsic to the special effect but part and parcel of its larger work—a further extraction of its value down the line. There exists a contiguity, that is, between the "effects" of special effects onscreen and off, summoned into existence as much by the explanatory and celebratory discourses surrounding them as by the material histories of design and manufacture on which those discourses draw. Despite this, film and media studies has insisted for the most part on treating special effects in the narrowest slice of their operations: the moment of onscreen display and the quantum state of indeterminacy they induce in the viewer, in whom indeed the questions of narrative versus spectacle, mind versus body, reality versus simulation may momentarily battle. But our traditional perspectives on these encounters—severed from the network of knowledge that is the gift and curse of contemporary media spectatorship (so informed and interpenetrated by technical knowledge, publicity discourses, as well as stardom, genre, and auteurist understandings of yore)—ignore the work done by special effects in today's networked and franchised media culture, which works to ensure that any encounter with a text is conditioned by familiarity with its forebears and siblings. Ironically, as theorists we must learn to look beyond the attention-getting glimmer of special effects to access the full truth of their existence.

1

That Which Survives

Design Networks and Blueprint Culture between Fandom and Franchise

The 2009 release of J. J. Abrams's *Star Trek* reboot marked a significant turn in the fortunes of the aging media property. The eleventh feature film in the series was the first to recast the iconic central roles of James T. Kirk, Leonard McCoy, Spock, Sulu, Uhura, and the rest of the bridge crew with younger actors, while updating the pace and tone of the story with an energetic, action-oriented approach that differed markedly from previous installments. Helmed by a professed outsider to *Trek* fandom, Abrams's "reimagining" was widely (though not unanimously) judged a success, earning the highest box-office returns of any *Trek* movie to that point, and spawning two sequels to date, *Star Trek Into Darkness* (2013) and *Star Trek Beyond* (2016). But securing a future for the franchise required more than a simple facelift. It was just as important that the fan-dubbed "NuTrek" pass the loyalty test of longtime viewers—some of whom had been devotees since the late 1960s—as it was to welcome fresh and unfamiliar audiences. The *Trek* reboot adopted multiple strategies to assure fans that it was, despite the liberties it had taken, a bona fide addition to canon. Chief among these was a time-travel plot that revolved around the creation of an alternate reality, the Kelvin Timeline, enabling the archive of previously established adventures to remain valid in both industrial and fannish imaginaries.

More important than any metanarrative contortion, however, was what the production sought to achieve on a stylistic, visual level. Key elements of the Star Trek franchise's trademark visual vocabulary, from the command insignia worn by officers and crew to the U.S.S. *Enterprise* itself, pervaded Abrams's film in modified but recognizable forms [Figure 1.1]. These elements forged links both at the level of the brand— where they marked the new movie as a member of the franchise—and

Figure 1.1. The rebooted *Enterprise* of *Star Trek* (2009), repeating the Original Series ship design with a difference.

at the level of the diegesis, where they signaled that the story's events were taking place in the same universe of "hardware" (albeit an interdimensional variant) that fans had engaged with for decades. The design allegiances connecting the rebooted *Trek* to the *Trek* of old illustrate a process that has helped make the franchise a viable transmedia presence for nearly half a century.

This chapter explores the ongoing manufacture of *Trek*-related objects and imagery in a range of media, based on what I will call a *design network*: an open-ended yet rigorously specific canon of stylistic elements infused with narrative significance. In "That Which Survives," an episode that aired in 1969 during the third season of the original *Star Trek*, Kirk and his crew encounter a computer program in the guise of the beautiful Losira (Lee Meriwether), who guards the remnants of a long-dead civilization.[1] A holographic projection, Losira manifests in as many versions as there are crewmembers, telling each, "I am for you." Her iterative nature, retaining recognizability from instance to instance while adapting to the desires and identifications of a changing audience, captures the essence of the design network: literally that which survives from one episode, series, and medium to another, organizing production, regulating difference, and ensuring brand identity in the face of potentially disruptive transitions. Simply put, it is the principle by which Star Trek manufactures more of itself—DNA of the fantastic transmedia franchise. As Heather Urbanski notes in her study of science-fiction reboots, technologies of visualization in the digital age have become important tools not just for updating but for expanding on and evolving the look of successive installments in a given franchise.[2] I would go further: special effects, understood in their broadest sense as a constellation of practical, optical, and digital techniques for bringing unreal worlds into existence, have from the start of the modern blockbuster era been essential to the establishment and growth of design networks, which together constitute a virtual universe while mediating the industrial and popular investments—linked spheres of production and reception—that maintain it.

Design networks like Star Trek's are central to the growth and maintenance of the modern hyperdiegesis: "a vast and detailed narrative space, only a fraction of which is ever directly seen or encountered within the text, but which nevertheless appears to operate according to principles of internal logic and extension."[3] In the years since Matt Hills introduced this concept in relation to cult texts, hyperdiegeses or storyworlds have become an area of fervent interest in studies of convergence culture and transmedia storytelling, which focus on the industrial production of fictions across a range of media formats, including movies, television, comic books, and games played on tabletops and computer screens.[4] The concept of sprawling fictional settings whose fundamental unreality is counterbalanced by systematic continuity is not exclusively the province of contemporary media, of course, but dates back thousands of years, from some of humankind's originary myths to its most revered works of theater and literature. Mark J. P. Wolf's *Building Imaginary Worlds* contains an appendix with hundreds of entries ranging from the Island of Atlantis in Plato's *Timaeus* in 360 BC to Jonathan Swift's satirical creations Lilliput and Brobdingnag (1726), Lewis Carroll's Wonderland (1865), Edgar Rice Burroughs's Pellucidar (1914), and William Faulkner's Yoknapatawpha County (1929).[5] With the exception of the last, most of these examples reflect the truism that alternate worlds of fiction tend to be unusual and exotic—precisely the kinds of places one does not encounter in daily reality—and hence an especially fertile ground for genres of the fantastic such as science fiction, fantasy, and horror. Our current transmedia landscape is studded with storyworlds both longstanding (Tolkien's Middle Earth) and of recent vintage (Hogwarts and environs in J. K. Rowling's Harry Potter series), the details of their settings supplied by textual description as well as artists' illustrations, maps, blueprints, and other reference materials.

Yet the activity of creating, maintaining, and expanding the story-worlds of fantastic transmedia through cartographic or encyclopedic paratexts is not just the province of the franchise's producers and owners. Audiences of design-oriented fans—in particular, members of what I call "blueprint culture"—have played a vital role in taking the materials offered by official production sources and elaborating on them to fill in gaps, explain contradictions, and connect dots, building stable, consistent frameworks from the inevitably partial and fragmentary pieces doled out by the media industry. Generally less interested in character interaction and psychological relationships than in a fictional universe's contents—biographies, geographies, political and economic systems, and most of all hardware such as buildings, vehicles, technologies, and weapons—design-oriented fans are avid students of canon (the given "facts" of the fiction). In their epistemological stance as well as in the type of textual and physical materials they create, such fans thus seem to differ from those who have been the traditional focus of fan studies, such as slash writers and video makers.[6] This difference has been codified with the labels "transformational" and "affirmational": transformational fans refashion the franchise text to reflect their own concerns and predilections, producing creative work that implicitly comments on and critiques official content, while affirmational fans seek to reinforce and elaborate on canon.[7] In suggesting the term "mimetic fandom" as a third option, Hills critically highlights the legitimizing effects of this way of categorizing fan activity, pointing out the underlying "oscillatory" movement between canonical allegiance and transformative potential in almost every mode of fannish engagement.[8]

Focusing on the case of Star Trek—in particular, its genesis as a television show in the 1960s and subsequent transformations into a fan phenomenon and film franchise in the 1970s and early 1980s—brings to light the centrality of special effects to creating a canonical storyworld and building on it over time. This occurs through economically and industrially driven dynamics of repetition and reuse, often in the form of "bottle shows" (episodes taking place mostly or entirely aboard the *Enter-prise*) that grant sustained exposure to the storyworld's most distinctive elements. Moreover, the case of Star Trek invites us to see the produc-tion and reception of those elements as an ongoing creative and critical dialogue between official and unofficial authors, working together—not always in cohesive or friendly fashion—to forge a shared, collective fic-tional property and corresponding cultural investments. Star Trek brings to light linkages among transformational, affirmational, and mimetic modes of fandom that work in perpetual, productive negotiation to shape franchise development: neither simply accepting official output in a state of mindless acquiescence, nor continually pushing back by "re-reading and rewriting" that content against the grain, but instead engag-ing with and, in a real sense, co-authoring it over time.[9] From its birth in the broadcast-television era of the 1960s to the proliferating series, re-boots, and sophisticated fan productions of its more recent incarnations in digital and streaming media, Star Trek's design network—along with the design-oriented fans who parse, contest, and contribute to it—have built a bridge between today's transmedia storytelling systems and the fledgling franchises that were its analog-era forebears.

Designing *Star Trek*, 1964–1969

The Original Series of *Star Trek* has been described as "the most suc-cessful failure in the history of television," because its relatively brief network run stands in ironic contrast to decades of persistence as a fix-ture of popular culture and revenue source for its license holders.[10] By 1991, twenty-five years after its premiere, the series had been in syndica-tion continuously, spawning feature films, spinoff series, "novels, books, videotapes, audiotapes, records, computer games, and a countless num-ber of merchandising tie-ins, [becoming] an international phenomenon. There are hundreds of *Star Trek* fan clubs and conventions around the world where fans . . . gather with others who share their interest in the program."[11] In the quarter century since then, the franchise has only continued to expand, adding new television series, feature films, video games, novels, and comics, along with sophisticated fan productions such as *Star Trek: Phase II* and *Star Trek Continues*, which I discuss later in this chapter.

Explanations of *Trek*'s popularity typically center on the show's optimistic portrayal of a future where tolerance and equality reign. As Gene Roddenberry said in 1968:

> Intolerance in the 23rd century? Improbable! If man survives that long, he will have learned to take a delight in the essential differences between men and between cultures. He will learn that differences in ideas and attitudes are a delight, part of life's exciting variety, not something to fear. It's a manifestation of the greatness that God, or whatever it is, gave us. This infinite variation and delight, this is part of the optimism we built into *Star Trek*.[12]

While noble, Roddenberry's sentiment fails to account fully for *Star Trek*'s continued ubiquity—particularly when contrasted with the many films and TV series, made with similarly progressive and humanistic messages, that *failed* to launch multimedia empires or win the loyalty of a worldwide fan movement. At least as important as ethos, storyline, and character are the elements of visual design that constitute *Trek*'s diegetic backdrop and the fabric of its future history. Publicity materials, teasers, and trailers are dominated by photographic stills and artwork featuring the series' most spectacular elements: strange planets, futuristic architecture, alien species, and the show's striking yet familiar technological home base, the *Enterprise*. The same elements anchor a collectible industry encompassing everything from toys and action figures to model rockets and Christmas ornaments. Over time, *Trek*'s visuals and the rules by which they mutate have been integral parts of the production and authentication of multimedia sequels, spinoffs, adaptations, and expansions in film, television, graphic novels, and computer games.

As Derek Johnson points out, *Trek* was always built around a principle of "overdesign," in which creator Roddenberry produced a series "bible" to guide writers in crafting stories that observed the history, technologies, and cultural norms of the invented universe.[13] Further, Johnson notes the contribution of a team of art directors and production designers to establishing the show's storyworld.[14] In tracing the franchise's movement into its contemporary incarnations, however, Johnson neglects an important factor: the role played by fans in mapping, expanding, and contributing to *Trek*'s huge design database. In fact, the output of *Star Trek*'s "legitimate" authors pales beside that of *Trek* fandom, a subculture whose attachment expresses itself not just through exhaustive familiarity with the master text but through artwork and handicraft that reproduce and extend the show's fictional setting. From the perspective of design and manufacture, *Trek* fandom has always been coextensive with *Star Trek* proper: a spectrum of identically themed creativity, but realized at differing levels of skill, resources, profitability, and legality. Toward one end of the continuum is the comparatively small, expensively produced and widely circulated cluster of texts considered Trek canon, defined on the studio-owned website *startrek. com* as "events that take place within the live action episodes and movies."[15] Toward the other end are cheaply made and narrowly circulated homegrown works of fanfic (fan fiction), as well as drawings, paintings, props, costumes, jewelry, models, and even dramatic presentations on stage, film, video, and digital media. Between these extremes lies a contested zone of manufacture in which labels like *professional* and *amateur*, *authorized* and *unauthorized*, *legitimate* and *illegitimate* roil in perpetual flux. Hence, another aspect of design networks involves this middle zone and its drama of containment and compromise between fans and producers around the production of *Trek* matèriel—a tug of war over property some consider public and others private.

Insight into what made *Trek* such a favorable medium for the development of a linked and fecund system of design can be found in Stephen E. Whitfield's *The Making of Star Trek* (*MoST*) [Figure 1.2]. Published by Ballantine Books in 1968, two years into the Original Series run, *MoST* stands as the first of its kind: an industrial anatomy of a TV series, bringing together interviews, analysis, photographs, and artwork. It spawned a new form of media tie-in—the making-of book—now a commonplace companion to high-profile movies and cult TV shows such as *Firefly* (2002), *The Lord of the Rings*, and, of course, the *Trek* spinoffs *Next Generation* (1987–1994), *Deep Space Nine* (1993–1999), *Voyager* (1995–2001), and *Enterprise* (2001–2005). The same qualities that made *Trek* an ideal candidate for the anatomization it received in *MoST* are those that later gave rise to its design network. Chief among these is the archive of visual and textual material generated during *Trek*'s design phase, which lasted from approximately 1960 to the show's launch in September 1966. What

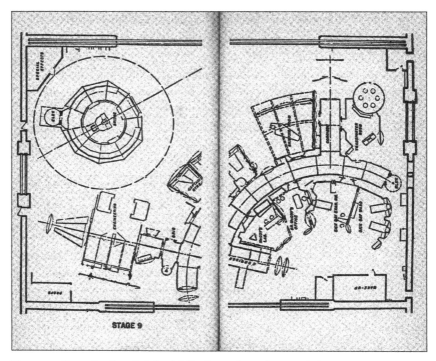

Figure 1.2. From Stephen E. Whitfield's *The Making of Star Trek* (1968), a map of Soundstage 9 showing the standing sets that make up the interior of the *Enterprise*.

was established during those six years was not so much the story of *Star Trek* as its storytelling *system*: a generative matrix within which any number of tales could theoretically be told, a studio-incubated *langue* capable of infinite acts of *parole*. It coalesced through the labor of dozens of writers, designers, and technicians—roughed out first in text documents; refined in sketches, blueprints, and paintings; constructed in the form of sets, props, costumes, makeup, and elements used in postproduction visual effects (such as miniature planets, spaceships, and star backdrops); and finally realized as images and impulses on film and videotape, broadcast over the airwaves onto TV screens.

Trek's prolonged gestation, during which Roddenberry developed the show at Desilu Studios, left in its wake a trail of documentation that Whitfield incorporated into *MoST*, presenting readers with a collage of materials culled from the show's ongoing operations. The first section,

"Birth Pangs," reprinted the *Trek* bible and showcased preproduction artwork. Part Two styled itself as "An Official Biography of the Ship and Its Crew," providing data on characters such as Kirk and Spock, as well as a detailed overview of the *Enterprise* through blueprints and special-effects stills. *MoST* included two sections of black-and-white photographs, showing different views of the *Enterprise* and its shuttlecraft, the *Galileo*; portraits of the cast in costume and makeup; walkthroughs of sets such as the bridge, sickbay, and briefing room; props such as the three-dimensional chess set, Dr. McCoy's medical instruments, and phaser weapons; portraits of the alien Balok and the Salt Vampire (fearsome visages heavily circulated in the show's promotion); and a gallery of women clad in revealing gowns, another fixture of *Trek*'s promotional iconography. Fourth-wall-violating images, by contrast, were comparatively rare: one four-page gallery of stills broke down the stages of an optical effect showing a man being disintegrated by lightning, and there were a handful of shots of directors and technical crew, actors in street clothes and makeup chairs, and angles on sets revealing lighting and camera rigs.

Thus, while *MoST* suggested by its title an exclusively behind-the-scenes account exposing *Trek*'s artifactual nature, much of the book was dedicated to below-the-threshold-of-disbelief material that treated fiction as truth: actors in full costume and makeup, ship schematics, fictional character biographies, and episode guides. Whitfield's book, that is, devoted itself as much to upholding the reality of its media object as debunking it, reinforcing rather than dispelling the impression of an extant universe. Functioning simultaneously as site of belief, knowledge resource, and revenue stream, Whitfield's making-of book presaged the struggle over limits of textual authority and legitimacy that would later shape *Star Trek*'s rebirth as a franchise in the 1970s and 1980s. Moreover, by both documenting the nuts and bolts of manufacturing a media property and treating its diegesis as history, *MoST* fueled a crucial aspect of *Star Trek*'s design-oriented fandom: the activity of reconciling gaps between the show's industrial and fictional dimensions, closing the uneven seams that separate a story from the conditions of its making.

In its framing of *Trek*'s storyworld, *MoST* can be seen as a public version of the series bible: a synopsis of the format, setting, and characters that contained everything from lists of standing sets and character histories to esoterica of astronomical terminology and twenty-third-century philosophy. Widespread sharing of these "scriptures" was integral not just to the writerly cultures of fandom that soon formed around *Trek*, but to the crafting side of those cultures reflected in fans' creation and collection of costumes, props, toys, and model kits. Consider the fact that Whitfield first came to *Trek* as an emissary from the AMT (Aluminum Model Toys) Company, maker of plastic scale-model kits, which had agreed with Roddenberry to market a model of the *Enterprise* alongside its fabrication of sets and miniatures for the show. The resulting kit sold one million units in 1967, making it AMT's most successful release to date.[16] Mere months after the series' launch, then, Hills's mimetic fandom had found its first means of making more *Trek*.

The sheer weight of documentation upon which *MoST* drew was a result of *Trek*'s narrative premise and the industrial scaffolding it necessitated. "*Everything* used on the show had to be designed from scratch," Whitfield points out. "Equipment, tools, clothing, weapons, furniture, even knives and forks—almost everything will be different two or three centuries from now."[17] It required the contributions of many artists and craftspeople to construct a diegesis whose scope ranged from vessels and hardware to uniforms and hairstyles. The introduction to a 1997 collection of production art from the Original Series captures something of this, referring to the designers as "the primary *Star Trek* crew . . . film-experienced, highly qualified visual architects charged with designing a very complicated living structure—a structure truly as complicated as the tallest skyscraper."[18] Prefiguring the varied aesthetic spaces featured in *Alien* (Ridley Scott, 1979), the *Star Wars* prequels (George Lucas, 1999–2005), and the *Lord of the Rings* and *Hobbit* trilogies (Peter Jackson, 2001–2003, 2012–2014), *Trek* wove together the work of multiple designers, each possessing a distinct stylistic signature, to craft its universe with a composite aesthetic that was convincingly varied while remaining plausibly systematic.

A key member of that team was Wah Ming Chang, who created the communicator and tricorder instruments in both motorized, lighted "hero" models and cheaper, nonfunctional versions. But Chang's influence extended beyond props, running the gamut from practical to optical effects: he built a miniature spacecraft, the Romulan cruiser seen in first-season episode "Balance of Terror," and constructed full-sized mockups of aliens such as the Salt Vampire from "The Man Trap" and Balok from "The Corbomite Maneuver."[19] (Balok's bulbous head and glaring eyes would become the standard coda to *Trek*'s end credits.) Chang also crafted the rubber mask and bodysuit for the lizardlike Gorn with which Kirk does battle in "Arena."[20] Prior to *Trek*, Chang had worked in the special-effects department at Walt Disney, as well as with producer George Pal and on the TV series *The Outer Limits* (1963–1965).[21]

Fred Phillips, the show's principal makeup artist, also had an extensive background in motion pictures, first working alongside his father on Cecil B. DeMille's *King of Kings* (1927). While Phillips's contributions to *Trek* consisted largely of "invisible" makeup used to make actors camera-ready, he also created many of the show's distinctive alien species. Looking at story outlines early in the first season, for example, Phillips made notes to himself: "Klingon—Romulan—alien races—conceptualize them—design them—make them."[22] He created iconic creatures for the first pilot, including the emerald-green Orion Slave Woman (Susan Oliver) and the cruelly manipulative Talosians, with oversized brain cases and remote-controlled veins that throbbed in rhythm with their telepathic "speech." (For added uncanniness, the Talosians were played by women but dubbed vocally by men.) One step down from the full-body constructions of Wah Chang, Phillips engineered the appearance of alien races from Andorians to Tellarites. His most famous makeup job, however, was certainly Mr. Spock, with his green-tinted skin, arched eyebrows, and pointed ears. Phillips would return to the franchise with *Star Trek: The Motion Picture* (Robert Wise, 1979), taking advantage of that production's expanded budget to redesign Klingon physiognomy in a move that proved highly controversial for design-oriented fandom.

One figure, however, dominated the show's overall design scheme. Walter "Matt" Jefferies, whose background was in aeronautical engineering and aviation history, is most often credited with originating "the physical look of the *Enterprise* and the *Star Trek* universe."[23] Credited in the first season as production designer and subsequently as art director, Jefferies's contributions covered the spectrum from *Trek*'s most iconographic physical sets to props such as the phaser and miniatures such as the D-7 Klingon Cruiser and the *Galileo* shuttlecraft. He conceived and drafted plans for every major *Enterprise* interior (including the bridge, briefing room, sickbay, engineering room, and transporter chamber); in addition, he provided numerous small electronic items (the robot "Nomad," computer consoles, and the mind-control device seen in "Spock's Brain"[24]), as well as viewscreens into which imagery was matted during preproduction. He was even responsible for small but distinctive touches like the command insignia worn on Starfleet uniforms and the Klingon flag that adorned the model cruiser.

Jefferies's best-known contribution was undoubtedly the exterior design of the *Enterprise*. Gene Roddenberry had begun the search for *Trek*'s key setting in 1964. With the goal of making the *Enterprise* distinct from other vehicles in science fiction, his first instruction to Jefferies was to avoid anything that had been done before in film or TV. "I don't want to see any trails of fire," Roddenberry said. "No streaks of smoke, no jet intakes, rocket exhaust, or anything like that. . . . I don't care how you do it, but make it look as though it's got power."[25] As Jefferies began brainstorming visual concepts, Roddenberry consulted the screenwriter and novelist Sam Peeples for assistance. Peeples's collection of pulp science-fiction digests of the 1930s and 1940s supplied numerous design inspirations in their cover art, which Roddenberry photographed for use as reference—an instance of what Chapter 2 will describe as previsualization *avant la lettre*.[26] With Roddenberry, Jefferies workshopped *Enterprise* concepts, closing in on the configuration audiences would later come to know: a saucer section attached to a cylindrical engineering hull, topped by two long engines. The final stage before approval came when Jefferies took the approved sketch to a woodworking shop at the Desilu facility and quickly assembled a mockup.[27]

Even at that juncture in *Star Trek*'s development, certain hallmarks of what would become its design network were evident. First, the *Enterprise* and ships like it are rarely sui generis, but emerge in dialectical relation to both real-world and fantasy representations of space travel: Jefferies's background in aeronautics and aviation discursively tied his *Enterprise* designs into the world of scientific possibility, incorporating influences from NASA space exploration as well as aircraft manufacturers North American and Douglas.[28] Second, remnants of early design phases remained available down the line for recuperation into diegetic history, through the work of fan artists and *Trek* producers. For example, one of Jefferies's early conceptions, topped with a sphere instead of a saucer, was later featured in a 2000 issue of *Star Trek* magazine as an "early warp vessel" called the *Daedalus* class: "One of the first designs of starship Starfleet commissioned . . . these were recognizably the prototype for most subsequent Starfleet vessels."[29] Finally, the process of development traveled through discrete media, in *Trek's* case at least three in number: the text of the series proposal, Jefferies's two-dimensional sketches and artwork, and finally the wooden mockup that enabled executives to see what the ship would look like in three dimensions. Design networks like *Star Trek's*, then, can be characterized by at least three factors: they draw on precedent (i.e., other design networks); they develop iteratively, producing at each stage a concretization that both approximates the target form and exists as a target in its own right, potentially feeding back into the network or providing nodes for new designs; and they depend for their realization on movement through a succession of different media.

Ironically, of course, all of these characteristics—marked as they are by an unruly, almost poststructuralist multiplicity and endless play of meaning—tend finally to be effaced in order to shore up the idea of the unique, standalone object: in *Trek's* case, the *Enterprise* "itself." The ship's simultaneous multiplicity and singularity can be glimpsed in the discrepancy between its on-screen identity and the special effects pipeline used to create it. Shooting miniatures of the *Enterprise* were built at three scales: a tiny model measuring just four inches, utilized for the swishing flyby shots in the show's title sequence; a thirty-three-inch version; and a highly detailed eleven-foot version. Throughout the series, these miniatures would undergo periodic revisions and upgrades (again belying their supposed finality), for example to add lighted windows and motorized warp-engine domes: tweaks that would, following the flexible and absorptive nature of design networks, later be "fanonized" in design-oriented fandom. But at the time, the cost of building the *Enterprise* miniatures, along with the other miniatures, sets, props, and costumes required to lay *Trek's* groundwork, pushed the budget for the show's initial pilot well into the red. The proposed budget for "The Cage" was $451,503; its actual cost ended up at $615,571.[30] To balance this expenditure, nearly all of the priciest elements, once established, were reused—pointing up another mechanic that helped to grow *Trek's* design network: repetition.

Serial television is, as its name implies, rooted in the principle of re-visitation. On the industrial side, a production infrastructure mobilizes to generate new content using established formal and material templates, while on the reception side, committed viewers return again and again to a show's episodes. When *Star Trek* first aired, its audience did not yet have access to the time-shifting recording and playback technologies that would later allow them to collect, scrutinize, and deconstruct the show's stylistic canon; even so, because of the broadcasting schedule set by NBC and the reruns that played when new episodes were not available, fans were exposed again and again to a science-fictional storyworld made familiar through reuse. As a weekly episodic drama with continuing characters, *Trek* broke with conventions of televised science fiction in the early 1960s, bearing more resemblance to serials of the previous decade such as *Space Patrol* and *Tom Corbett, Space Cadet* (both 1950–1955) than to contemporary anthology shows *Twilight Zone* (1959–1964) or *The Outer Limits*.

Trek's format, in fact, was intended to exploit the strengths of both the one-off anthology and the serial drama—"The first such concept," Roddenberry wrote in his initial 1964 proposal, to present "strong central lead characters plus other continuing regulars . . . while maintaining a familiar central location [and exploring] an anthology-like range of exciting human experience." That central location was, of course, the *Enterprise*: conceived as an integrated use of sets (for interiors) and optical effects (for exterior views), Roddenberry compared the vessel's diegetic function to Dodge City in *Gunsmoke* (1955–1975) and Blair General Hospital in *Dr. Kildare* (1961–1966), providing a familiar home base for every adventure.[31] Because the *Enterprise* was to appear in virtually every episode, its expense would be offset by heavy use. A similar economic logic connected both the practical and optical components of *Enterprise*'s visualization—the former "a standing set to be amortized over the life of the series. . . . designed so that all cabins, wardrooms, and passages can be redressed and doubled"; the latter, "ship miniaturization footage . . . planned for maximum use, also amortized over the life of the series."[32]

While the *Enterprise*'s hybrid ontology highlights on one level the slipperiness of distinctions between special and "nonspecial" effects, visual effects—more precisely defined as manipulations of the film frame through the compositing of layers created at different times—

also lent themselves to intensive recycling. Existing elements were shuffled and recomposed, miniatures modified, and the set of optical transformations involved in (for example) transporter dematerialization and rematerialization were standardized, almost assembly-lined, according to the demands of the production calendar. In a memo prepared prior to filming the second pilot, Roddenberry made explicit the relationship between financial logic and visual-effects reuse, tying it to a host of related cost-saving measures.

> Among our first steps will be the preparation of a *production revision* of the current script. By this we mean a quick rewrite aimed to bring photographic effects, special effects, sets, and shooting time into something that approaches practicality from a production time and budget point of view. We've already had a meeting with Darrel Anderson [of effects house Howard A. Anderson Company] and slashed deeply there; we'll be meeting with other departments immediately—and we certainly invite further comments from all affected departments at this early stage. . . . Meanwhile, Bob Justman has detailed information on which first pilot sets, effects, etc., we will be keeping and which we are discarding.[33]

Once it began to cycle, *Trek*'s production engine was defined by cost-cutting and innovation within the boundaries of a tight budget. Not that this budget was tiny; *Trek*, at $193,000 an episode, was one of the more expensive series on the airwaves at the time.[34] Nevertheless, its effects-intensive format necessitated stretching every penny, resulting in a visual style that was "often due as much to lack of money as creativity."[35] Four different special-effects providers worked on *Trek*, a decision that was made following the relatively leisurely completion of the second pilot. In the words of Howard Anderson Jr., of the effects house Howard A. Anderson Company,

> We had much more time to design and produce the effects for the pilots than we had for each episode once NBC decided to go with the series. It quickly became apparent that Desilu had to contract some of the optical work out to other houses just to get the crushing amount of effects shots done in time for airing. Sometimes we'd still be doing final composites the night before first broadcast.[36]

In addition to the Anderson Company (which also provided effects for Desilu's *I Love Lucy* [1951–1957] and *The Fugitive* [1963–1967]),[37] *Trek* employed Film Effects of Hollywood, the Westheimer Company, and Van Der Veer Photo Effects. These companies contributed most of *Trek's* trademark opticals—those effects which, in heavy rotation, were most central to establishing its backdrop of future technology: shots of the *Enterprise* orbiting planets or flying at warp speed; phaser beams and photon torpedo fire; and transporter de- and re-materialization. All four companies had worked in Hollywood's studio system, giving them "plenty of experience in class visual effects when [they] took on *Star Trek*."[38] Still, the hectic production schedule coupled with the number of effects needed placed pressure on the experienced companies to deliver. Part of the solution to this time crunch involved sharing elements. The Anderson Company, for example, provided pieces of the transporter effect to Film Effects of Hollywood, streamlining creation of those sequences: "once the timing was done," said Film Effects' Linwood Dunn, "the compositing was fairly routine."[39] The *Enterprise* miniature also traveled from one effects house to another, used whenever new elements needed to be shot against blue screen.

Production pressures also took a toll formally and narratively. As *Trek* got under way, "demands grew for shootable scripts, lower-budget shows, cheaper effects, and deliverable episodes."[40] Methods for meeting these needs took several forms, but one strategy that made a lasting impact on the design network was known as the bottle show. Even under Roddenberry's "Parallel Worlds" concept, episodes taking place outside the familiar environs of the *Enterprise* tended to drive up costs, requiring location shooting, modification of existing sets, and casting, wardrobe, and makeup for guest stars. In addition, unusual settings made it more likely that new special effects would need to be created. By contrast, bottle shows were staged mostly or entirely aboard ship, using the regular cast, standing sets, and, more often than not, the reuse of stock *Enterprise* footage. The production therefore fell into a rhythm of alternating planet shows and bottle shows, recouping time and money spent on off-ship stories.[41] A standard episode of *Trek* might take seven or eight days to shoot; one typical second-season bottle show—and one of *Trek's* most enduringly popular episodes—was "The Doomsday Machine," completed in just five.[42]

It is curious that *Trek* episodes featuring nothing new in terms of characters or settings were capable of capturing fan interest to a degree that the series' more elaborate and unusual stories could not; producers Herbert Solow and Robert Justman note that the bottle shows "were enormously compelling, as indicated by both fan reaction and the ratings."[43] One likely explanation for these episodes' popularity was the opportunity they provided fans to experience the *Enterprise* as a coherent space—to experience, by extension, *Trek*'s future history as an enclosed and internally consistent domain of its own. This seemed especially true of "The Menagerie," a two-parter that aired during *Trek*'s first season.[44] Following the completion of the series' eleventh episode, producers found themselves lacking a fresh script ready to begin filming. Facing the prospect of "an unplanned production hiatus," Justman had the brainstorm of using "The Cage"—which had never aired, despite a plan of Roddenberry's to shoot additional footage and release the unused pilot as a feature film—to pad out the season.[45] But because of the substantial changes *Trek* had undergone between first and second pilots, "The Cage" could not simply be broadcast in its existing form.

> With the singular exception of Leonard Nimoy, actors in the pilot crew and the series crew were different: There were two medical officers, two yeomen, two communications officers, two helmsmen, and Majel Barrett playing both Number One, the second in command, and Nurse Chapel. Even the production itself was different. The sets, set dressings, props, and wardrobe were more refined in the series. Even Spock's ears were more realistic.[46]

To solve this problem, Roddenberry wrote an "envelope" tale exploring Mr. Spock's relationship with Captain Christopher Pike, now horribly disfigured and confined to a wheelchair (an expedience made necessary when Jeffery Hunter, who originally played Pike, refused to reprise his role). Fearing that his former commanding officer is close to death, Spock commandeers the *Enterprise* in an attempt to return Pike to planet Talos IV, setting of "The Cage." When his crime is discovered, Spock undergoes a court martial, and as part of his defense, screens a recording of Pike's first visit to Talos IV.

This conceit solved a major problem facing *Star Trek* at that juncture. By recycling nearly seventy-eight minutes of completed footage into not one but two new episodes, "The Menagerie" allowed the production team to catch up with its script preparation and get through the rest of the first season. At the same time, it diegetically recuperated material that otherwise would never have fit into canon, explaining changes to cast, tone, and even special effects by stating that this earlier conception of *Trek* was in fact an adventure that occurred prior to Kirk's assumption of command. With "The Menagerie," *Trek*'s future history became a hall of mirrors, reflecting past, present, and future back at one another—suggesting story possibilities even more varied than those described in Roddenberry's initial proposal for "a new kind of television science fiction with all the advantages of an anthology, but none of the limitations."[47]

Limitations of a financial nature, however, would ultimately bring the original *Star Trek* to an end. The series had always been a pricey production, unable to justify its expense to a network that remained skeptical about the show's niche popularity. (The much-publicized letter-writing campaign that saved *Trek* when it faced cancellation at the end of season 2 was unable to do the same in season 3.) Further cutting into its numbers, frequent shifts in the show's timeslot made it difficult for its audience to find. In 1969, *Star Trek* went off the air. Its sets were torn down, costumes and miniatures mothballed, and film elements retired to the vaults of special-effects houses. Just around the corner, however, a rebirth awaited.

The Rise of Blueprint Culture

The first mass gathering of *Star Trek* fans took place over the weekend of January 21–23, 1972, at the Statler-Hilton Hotel in New York City. The "Star Trek Convention Committee" that planned the event anticipated an attendance of about 800 people; instead, 3,000 showed up, paying $3.50 apiece to get in. But for *Trek* fandom, the convention's value was as much symbolic as financial, proving that the show's audience was a coherent and mobilizable body. Media coverage of the 1972 convention appeared in *Variety*, the *New York Daily News*, and *TV Guide*. As word spread, conventions multiplied. According to Joan Winston, there were three such conventions in 1972; four in 1973; eight in 1974; twenty-three in 1975; and forty in 1976.[48] Science-fiction fandom predated *Star Trek*, of course, with conventions held since the 1930s; "The Menagerie," the two-part bottle show from *Trek*'s first season, had in fact won a prestigious Hugo award at the 25th World Science Fiction Convention in 1966.[49] Still, *Trek* initially received only a lukewarm reception from literate science-fiction fans of the 1960s, who tended to lump the show together with Irwin Allen productions such as *Voyage to the Bottom of the Sea* (1964–1968), *Lost in Space* (1965–1968), and *The Time Tunnel* (1966–1967). What changed between June 1969 (airdate of *Trek*'s final episode, "Turnabout Intruder"[50]) and January 1972 to turn *Star Trek* into a rallying point for thousands of fans?

The answer, in a nutshell, was syndication. When the Original Series ended, it appeared that rights to syndication and foreign TV sales were up for grabs. Gene Roddenberry briefly tried to acquire them, but could not afford Paramount's asking price of $150,000. (Struggling to support his ex-wife and family as well as his new bride, *Trek* actress Majel Barrett, Roddenberry simply did not have the means; most of his income at that point came from college lecture appearances and the sale of *Trek* merchandise through Lincoln Enterprises.) In truth, midway through the Original Series run, rebroadcast rights to *Trek* had been granted through a handshake agreement between Paramount and Kaiser Broadcasting, which owned UHF stations in Philadelphia, Boston, Cleveland, Detroit, and San Francisco. When the show went off the air, Kaiser began showing reruns at 6 P.M., based on research suggesting this was the best hour to reach *Trek*'s intended audience of young males. The new timeslot resolved *Trek*'s longstanding struggle to capture and build an audience. Further contributing to the snowballing fan base was the fact that episodes were shown every weekday. At that rate, it took approximately sixteen weeks—four months—to exhaust all seventy-nine episodes, after which the cycle began anew. *Trek* thus replayed in its entirety three times a year, for a total of six to eight complete rebroadcasts by 1972. Solow and Justman note the rising tide of *Trek* fandom (and material tie-ins) that followed as a consequence:

The show began to spawn generation after generation of Trekkers. . . . "I Grok Spock" stickers began to appear on automobile bumpers everywhere. From *Saturday Night Live* and *Mad* magazine to NASA's space shuttle *Enterprise*, the show had become a cultural phenomenon. Thousands of *Star Trek* conventions were launched everywhere and probably saved the hospitality business in the seventies: A zillion "Trekkies" (or "Trekkers") wearing pointy ears and decked out in "Federation" uniforms converged on a million Hilton hotels to cohabit with each other—strictly in a cultural sense, as far as I know.[51]

Repeated exposure to *Trek* did something more than simply generate revenue—it inspired the creation of costumes, models, decorations, documents, and other paraphernalia that simultaneously announced fans' passionate investment, charted the details of its diegetic backdrop, and made *more* of it, albeit in unauthorized and noncanonical form. Nowhere was this clearer than at the conventions. For their entrance fee, attendees entered a space characterized not only by the screening and discussing of episodes, but also material extensions of *Trek*'s universe. Some of these extensions were textual, taking the form of photocopied zines, but they also included more object-oriented activity such as costume shows, art fairs, auctions, and the "trading posts" (also known as "huckster rooms") where goods were sold. This assortment of what one reporter called "nostalgia and handicrafts" included "oil portraits of *Star Trek* heroes, handmade space-creature dolls, home-stitched *Star Trek* uniforms and models of outer-space hardware, including the *Star Trek* phaser."[52] Other big sellers included "publicity photographs and tape recordings, scripts to be auctioned, individual frames of *Star Trek* scenes rescued from the cutting-room floor and snapshots of the series taken off TV sets."[53]

Given the emphasis in these activities on the content of *Trek*'s story-world, it is surprising that discourses around *Trek*'s popularity continued to downplay the show's mise-en-scène in favor of its message. As Winston relates, "Roddenberry explained *Star Trek*'s special appeal, which is, according to him and all of the Trekkies we spoke to, entirely unrelated to the shallow glamour of rockets, ray guns and such."[54] Indeed, the "shallow glamour of rockets, ray guns and such" seems precisely what was showcased by one display at a convention that took place in February 1973, where "two guys from Poughkeepsie," Art Brumaghim and Mike McMaster, assembled a full-scale model of the bridge—the cost of building which they recouped by selling pictures taken of fans sitting in the captain's chair.[55] At the same convention, the dealers' room featured "loads and loads of tribbles," "pictures of Kirk and Spock and McCoy and Scotty and Sulu and Nurse Chapel and Uhura," and "the U.S.S. *Enterprise* in any size, shape, or form you could think of, and a few you couldn't or wouldn't."[56]

Just as Matt Jefferies had dominated the foundational visualizing of *Trek*'s storyworld, one 1970s figure in particular would dominate what was in some ways that process's obverse: blueprint culture. Although he professed not to be a *Trek* enthusiast himself, Franz Joseph Schnaubelt was the first to awaken a broad base of fans to the pleasures of charting and extending the series' diegetic backdrop. At the same time, he brought to the attention of the show's license holders the enormous profit potential of *Trek* manufacturing, first through supplementary materials that expanded on the *Trek* universe, then through relaunching *Trek* as a proto-transmedia franchise.

Schnaubelt, who went professionally by the name Franz Joseph, was born in Chicago in 1914. A designer and draftsman, he began working at the aeronautical and military research firm General Dynamics in 1941, drawing up plans of seaplanes and fighter planes. "For being a man who was vehemently opposed to war," Joseph's daughter Karen Dick writes, he "certainly worked on some of the most formidable war machinery of the '40s, '50s, and '60s."[57] Laid off in 1969, Joseph entered an early retirement that ended when his attention turned to *Trek*—not as entertainment, but as intellectual exercise. During the Original Series' run, Joseph and Karen had watched the show together, and in April 1973, he was taken by his daughter to the inaugural meeting of the San Diego branch of the Star Trek Association for Revival (S.T.A.R.).[58] The fans gathered there brought with them homemade models of *Trek* equipment such as communicators and phasers. According to Joseph, the ersatz props "were made out of cardboard, balsa wood, tape, wiring, glue, and paint and, for college kids . . . the workmanship was pretty bad any way you looked at it."[59] A former Cub Scout leader, Joseph told the amateur craftsmen he thought "they could do better."[60]

Working from more than 800 film clips amassed by Karen, he began drafting blueprints of the props, reversing a principle of architectural draftsmanship in which schematic drawings are projected into 3D views. Instead, by moving "from picture to plan" rather than from plan to picture, he inverted the process by which Matt Jefferies, a decade earlier, had designed *Trek*'s sets and spacecraft.[61] According to Joseph,

> I could take a picture of an enemy airplane and, as long as there was something on the airplane, or in the picture, that permitted me to determine the scale or make a fairly good judgment of the scale, then I would simply reverse the procedure and draw the plans of the airplane in that picture. This is what I was doing with the *Star Trek* slides. I drew the plans of the communicator, and then plans of the hand phaser and the pistol phaser.[62]

When Karen's friends saw the drawings, Joseph said, they "went wild over them. They wanted a lot more. They wanted everything. They made a whole list of stuff they wanted to see and I decided, well, I would do it if there was an interest in it."[63] Joseph realized that the fans were asking for "a 'technical' manual," and set to work drawing up a comprehensive mechanical anatomy of *Trek*'s diegetic contents [Figure 1.3].[64] From Lincoln Enterprises, the memorabilia vendor run by Roddenberry and Majel Barrett, Karen obtained a set of Jefferies's drawings of the *Enterprise*, the *Galileo* shuttlecraft, and the shuttle deck. From those sketches and those in Whitfield's *MoST*, Joseph "laid the drawing out, scaled and sized it, and made a drawing of the *Enterprise*."[65] He topped off this initial set of drawings with a pattern for the standard Starfleet uniform, again demonstrating the seamless slippage among visual effects and more concrete elements such as sets, costumes, and props.

In the course of preparing the *Star Fleet Technical Manual*, Joseph decided it would also be necessary to map the *Enterprise*'s internal layout. This was, he said, because the fan community "wanted bridge stations and other things concerned with the interior of the *Enterprise*." Since these "did not exist except in a book or in somebody's mind as a throwaway line . . . it became rather obvious that I would have to lay out the *Enterprise* far enough to get to those areas—to see whether I could make drawings."[66] This led Joseph to create what would eventually be known as the *General Plans* (blueprints of the *Enterprise*), which together with the *Technical Manual* would mark the public emergence of *Trek*'s design-oriented fan movement. Joseph's encounters with the fan community convinced him there was substantial interest in his technical drawings: a site

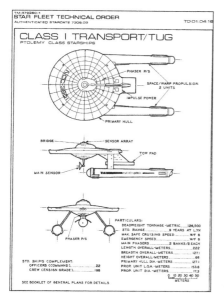
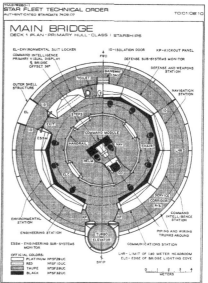

Figures 1.3a and 1.3b. Pages from Franz Joseph's *Star Fleet Technical Manual* (1975) showing a starship—the Transport/Tug—extrapolated from the Original Series, along with an overhead view of the "in-world" bridge. Compare to the bridge set shown in Figure 1.2. Figure 1.3a: Transport/Tug. Figure 1.3b: Bridge cutaway.

of potential profit as well as imaginative investment. Taking care not to step on the toes of *Trek*'s copyright holders, he had corresponded with and sent copies of his work to Paramount executives. By May 1973, only a month after the S.T.A.R. meeting that inspired the project, Rodden-berry himself gave Joseph a go-ahead, hinting that Lincoln Enterprises would market the drawings once they were completed. Months later, with a major *Trek* convention approaching, Joseph had still not received official permission to sell his work. Bypassing Roddenberry, he made a one-time deal with Paramount to sell the *Enterprise* blueprints at the 1974 Equicon convention in Los Angeles.

The 500 copies of the *General Plans* Joseph had printed sold out quickly, with requests for nearly as many additional copies taken on postcards. Paramount, which received Joseph's royalty check shortly thereafter, began negotiating for a mass-market release of both the *Plans* and the still-growing *Technical Manual*. The results exceeded all expectations. The blueprints went on sale across the nation on May 24, 1975, selling out within two hours. By May 28, 50,000 additional copies had sold, prompting Ballantine to print 100,000 more. In July the *New York Times* marveled,

> It lives! There's one publication that's been selling so furiously in book stores during recent weeks that it would be included on the list [of bestsellers] above except for one fact. It's not a book. "Star Trek Blueprints" is a set of 12 reproductions by Franz Joseph Schnaubelt showing "every foot of every level of the fabulous starship *Enterprise*." Since mid-May Ballantine Books has sold 150,000 sets, enclosed in a plastic and leatherette portfolio, at $5. This week it goes back to press for 100,000 more.[67]

The blueprints continued to sell strongly throughout the summer, reaching tenth on the paperback bestseller list and receiving a fourth printing in October. Meanwhile, interest in the *Technical Manual* was growing: at a time when a typical first printing of a *Trek*-related publication might run 20,000, Ballantine Books planned an initial run of 450,000. Both the *General Plans* and the *Technical Manual* became bestsellers.

Following a period in which he consulted on the design of tabletop wargames set in the *Trek* universe, Franz Joseph's work on the property ended.[68] His later years shadowed by prolonged illness, he died in 1994. Although his importance to the emergence of blueprint culture is inarguable, Joseph was by no means the only maker of *Trek* reference materials. In addition to the range of such work that presumably went on unremarked in viewers' bedrooms, basements, and garages, other design-oriented fans printed maps and manuals, selling them at conventions and through mail order; Geoffrey Mandel's *Starfleet Handbook* (1974), for example, featured "schematics of the phaser, communicator, tricorder, and shuttlecraft."[69] It was not until the *General Plans* and *Technical Manual* captured the attention of Roddenberry and Paramount, however, that a string of similar publications at the mass-market level followed, in some cases elevating select fan artists to the professional ranks. The *Star Fleet Medical Reference Manual*, published in 1977, featured the work of Doug Drexler, who went on to create makeup and visual effects for several of *Trek*'s spinoff series. The popularity of design-oriented fandom also arguably influenced the development of the "*Star Trek* Poster Magazine" (1976) and the *Trek* "Fotonovel" series

(1977–1978), both of which showcased *Trek*'s spectacular visual world through color reproductions of film frames.[70] This trend would eventually lead to a series of official publications such as *Mr. Scott's Guide to the Enterprise* (1987), as well as technical manuals for *The Next Generation* (1991) and *Deep Space Nine* (1998).[71] With the maturation of the personal-computer industry, software products such as the CD-ROM-based *Star Trek: The Next Generation Interactive Technical Manual* (1994) and simulation *Starship Creator* (1998) joined the lineup of paratextual reference materials aimed at a niche-within-the-niche market of design-oriented fans.

Launching the Franchise

If *Trek* license-holders' negotiated embrace of blueprint culture represented the incorporation of subculture at the mainstream—here professional—level, it was in part because the importance of design issues and storyworld consistency had emerged by then as a central logic in the franchise's successful self-reproduction.[72] As blueprint culture took root, Roddenberry and other parties were strategizing ways to extend the series. By March 1972, two months after the Statler-Hilton convention that had made headlines in *Variety*, Roddenberry "was mentioning in his correspondence possible deals for a *Star Trek* feature film, and for reviving the series on NBC."[73] The first result of these efforts, a Filmation Associates cartoon that ran on Saturday mornings, represented an economizing shortcut past the expense of pulling the original production out of mothballs or investing in an expensive and time-consuming redesign and casting. Running only one season from September 1973 to October 1974, the Filmation cartoon presaged a mid-seventies moment in which growing collective enthusiasm for *Star Trek*, along with the demonstrated ability of fandom to generate new stories (in fan fiction form) and new designs (in design-oriented reference materials) dovetailed with the goals of Paramount.

As Roddenberry developed first a motion-picture version of *Trek* entitled "The God Thing" and later a new TV series called *Phase II*, the nascent franchise faced questions similar to those that had dogged its birth ten years earlier—problems of casting, writing, and design—compounded now by tensions around the design network and its fan base. On the one hand, "seventies' *Trek*" was able to draw on an established framework of future history and, to some extent, the physical production materials left over from the sixties. But this was also a burden, for whatever form the new *Trek* took, it would have to faithful to its previous incarnation, with a contentious and demanding audience as arbiter. In a twist of fate, the same fans who had embraced *Trek*, schooling themselves in the minutiae of its diegetic backdrop, were potentially both the new production's biggest supporters and most ardent critics. The dilemma is reflected in the comments of Harold Livingston, producer of the aborted series *Star Trek Phase II*, who said he "wanted to make [*Trek*] more universal to appeal to more people. And I just didn't believe in 'the cult.'" *The cult* was a term used by Livingston and Michael Eisner to refer "to *Star Trek*'s most loyal and hardcore fans. In the seventies, few shows had such devoted followings, and production people were sometimes uneasy about how seriously those viewers took their work"—a characterization probably aimed more at affirmational, design-oriented fans than transformative ones.[74]

After the failure of several motion-picture projects to get past the story treatment phase, Paramount decided in 1977 to push ahead with its plans for a separate television network to compete with then-dominant CBS, NBC, and ABC, predicated on the assumption that a new *Trek* series would guarantee a desirable, eighteen-to-thirty-four-year-old audience. A team of creators from the Original Series began to design *Phase II*—a process that, like the cost-saving measures that allowed the design network to take root ten years before, was based as much on what to keep as what to excise or reinvent. In writing the new show's bible, Roddenberry expressed the following goals: "Give as much information as we can about the new look of the ship"; "Confirm which old props we'll still use, which have been changed, which have been eliminated"; "Same as above on opticals and process, old and new. For example, we should specify that the old-style transporter system will still be used (although we ourselves may improve the optical a little."[75]

Matt Jefferies, who returned briefly to revisit objects such as the shuttlecraft, had to leave the production due to a prior commitment to *Little House on the Prairie* (1974–1983)—but not before contributing designs for a new *Enterprise*. In discussing the refit, Jefferies recalls that Roddenberry simply wanted the starship "updated," not redesigned. Indeed,

Jefferies's classic design of saucer, lower hull, and twin nacelles remains fresh after more than three decades, still serving as the basis for the designs of the *Next Generation* starships D and E, as well as for the starship *Voyager* and the nuTrek variants.[76] NASA artist Lee Cole worked on the look of the control panels on the bridge. In the end a photocopied booklet, the *"Enterprise" Flight Manual*, was created for the cast and crew. Released in February 1978, the *Flight Manual* was described as "the first *Star Trek* Technical Manual for an ongoing *Star Trek* production," containing layouts of bridge stations and consoles, and instructions for switch operation.[77] Meanwhile, scripts were developed, sets constructed, and optical and makeup tests filmed. Perhaps encouraged by the way the production was coming together, Paramount scrapped the network to refocus on a film adaptation, and preproduction on *Phase II* gave way to preproduction on *Star Trek: The Motion Picture*. This process was far from seamless—it was soon realized that the *Enterprise* miniature created for TV would not be appropriate for the film, because "a television screen could not come close to presenting the same amount of visual detail as could a movie screen"; still, given that "all the models constructed for *Phase II* would have to be at least refinished, and quite possibly built again from scratch," it was presumably helpful to have a design network as a guide.[78]

Historically, *Star Trek: The Motion Picture* serves as one of the cautionary examples of out-of-control spending that characterized the era, such as *Apocalypse Now* (Francis Ford Coppola, 1979) and *Heaven's Gate* (Michael Cimino, 1980). All exceeded their projected budgets and resulted in pictures considered swollen, portentous, and overproduced, the product of indulgence. In *Trek*'s case, however, there was no auteur to blame—just the legend of *Star Trek* and an evolution of special-effects technology enabling more shots to be produced more quickly. Under Douglas Trumbull, who took over from Robert Abel and Associates, *Trek*'s large quantity of ambitious effects was forced through a production pipeline in the eight months leading up to the film's December release. But despite its expense and much critical drubbing, *The Motion Picture* managed to turn a profit, grossing $180 million globally and winning a lucrative $5 million deal with ABC for TV broadcasting rights.[79] Paramount's thoughts inevitably turned to a sequel. In surveying the *Trek* property's prospects, an important ingredient in the production calculus was an investment in materials that could now pay itself off—amortizing expense across installments of a movie franchise, just as the original *Enterprise* sets and miniatures had been amortized in their day.

> Paramount began to think once more about bringing out the sets it had carefully stored away after the first film wrapped. This time things would be done differently, they decided sensibly enough. This time the television arm of Paramount would produce the motion picture. This time its budget would be strictly controlled and kept to about a quarter of the final cost of the first film. This time it would be *Star Trek* as it had been in the much-loved TV series: a story about people, not technology or special effects.[80]

Apart from the cast, nearly everyone involved in *Star Trek II: The Wrath of Khan* (Nicholas Meyer, 1982) was different, from the writer, director, and producer to the special-effects team, headed now by Industrial Light and Magic. Even Gene Roddenberry was retitled "executive consultant," a position from which he no longer exercised central control over the story or the details of the *Trek* universe. Harve Bennett oversaw the movie as executive producer, brought in by Paramount based on his experience in television (including *The Six Million Dollar Man* [1974–1978]). Roddenberry took this move as "a slap in the face," according to one biographer, because "Bennett was a *television* producer with no feature experience."[81] In fact, Bennett's methods proved sound precisely because they *were* derived from a television mentality. One of his first moves, for example, was to hire Robert Sallin as producer. Sallin's work had primarily been in commercials, and he applied his knowledge of that field, especially the visual-effects aspect:

> I storyboarded everything. I had a chart made which listed, by scene, every special effect and optical effect, and I timed each one. I designed and supervised all the special effects. Mike Minor, our art director, sat up here in my office and did the storyboards. . . . When the movie was finished, the amount of deviation from the plan was very slight . . . in the first movie there were quite a few problems with the special effects. This time we came in so close to budget that you couldn't go out for a decent lunch on the difference.[82]

In addition to careful storyboarding and shot-by-shot management, several factors were responsible for *Wrath of Khan*'s success on a financial and aesthetic level (at a production cost of only $11 million, it grossed nearly $80 million domestically). First was a story carefully worked out to draw on available sets and properties, taking place mostly on board the *Enterprise* or the bridge of the *Reliant*—itself a redress of the *Enterprise* bridge. This reflected a more global reuse of elements from the first movie: sets such as the Klingon bridge served double duty in *Wrath of Khan* as the photon-torpedo bay and the transporter room aboard Space Station Regula One. That space station was the same miniature seen in orbit around Earth in the dry-dock sequence of *The Motion Picture*, turned upside down and detailed slightly differently. Footage from that lengthy sequence reappears in *Wrath of Khan*, as do several shots of Klingon cruisers from the first film's opening. Reused costumes included the spacesuits worn by Chekov (Walter Koenig) and Tyrell (Paul Winfield) on the inhospitable surface of Ceti Alpha V; the debris from the crashed spaceship they find there were first used as cargo containers in *Star Trek: The Motion Picture*.

Khan was followed by *The Search for Spock* (Leonard Nimoy, 1984) and *The Voyage Home* (Leonard Nimoy, 1986), made using similar strategies and returning substantial profits. The following year, 1987, saw the launch of *Star Trek: The Next Generation* on television, kicking off a period of franchise development across film, television, gaming, and comic-book media that has continued to this day. But in terms of grasping the underlying principles of *Trek*'s reproduction and renewal, the period through *Wrath of Khan* neatly recapitulates the franchise's birth during the 1960s. *The Motion Picture* and *Wrath of Khan*, that is, stand in roughly the same relationship to each other as do the show's two pilots, "The Cage" and "Where No Man Has Gone Before." In both cases a difficult launch—overly expensive and slow to come to fruition—was followed by a livelier, more colorful, and more audience-friendly production. As an industrial phenomenon, *Star Trek* seems destined to face daunting startup expenses, either in creating a design network or, as was the case from 1975 to 1979, in modifying those designs in systematic ways to guarantee commercial individuality while affirming its family resemblance to the rest of the franchise—

ideally to be followed by a smooth period of manufacture using the modified template.

From its crystallization in the 1960s through its development in the 1970s and onward, the activity of the design network has always involved questions of how, where, and by whom *Trek* gets made. This making brings together not just narrative, textual, economic, industrial, and commercial elements, but forces of regulation and control that enlist *Trek*'s official and unofficial creators in a complex dance of complicity and compromise. The bumpy, fits-and-starts negotiations between Franz Joseph, Gene Roddenberry, and Paramount reflect a larger tug of war between fans and industry when it comes to extending versus re-creating design elements. These tensions, and the way their stakes have changed over the decades, can be seen in more recent permutations of design-oriented fandom and its changing relationship to the twinned authorities of *Trek*-the-text and *Trek*-the-commodity.

"Get a Life" versus "It's All Real": The Joys and Sorrows of Design-Oriented Fandom

For design-oriented fans grappling with constant changes presented by the franchise's expansion and evolution, the details of visualized "Treknology" such as warp-nacelle configuration, transporter range, and the correct color of phaser beams are sites of intense negotiation over authenticity and allegiance. At the same time, it is this picky focus on accuracy and (in-universe) plausibility that frequently draws mainstream mockery of fans as obsessed with pointless fictional minutiae. Fans who pride themselves on intricate knowledge of starship design, *Trek* production history, or both are precisely the target of the December 1986 *Saturday Night Live* satire with which Henry Jenkins opens his foundational study of television fandom and participatory audiences, *Textual Poachers*.[83] In the sketch, guest host William Shatner makes an appearance at a *Trek* convention.

> When Shatner arrives, he is bombarded with questions from fans who want to know about minor characters in individual episodes (which they cite by both title and sequence number), who seem to know more about his private life than he does, and who demand such trivial information

as the combination to Kirk's safe. Finally, in incredulity and frustration, Shatner turns on the crowd: "Get a life, will you people? I mean, for crying out loud, it's just a TV show!"[84]

For Jenkins, the joke crystallizes a familiar set of stereotypes about media fans: "brainless consumers" who "devote their lives to the cultivation of worthless knowledge" such as "the combination to Kirk's safe, the number of Yeoman Rand's cabin, [and] the numerical order of the program episodes." Fans "place inappropriate importance on devalued cultural material," "are infantile, emotionally and intellectually immature," and "are unable to separate fantasy from reality."[85] Some of these traits are expressed in dialogue between the convention-goers and Shatner, while others are silently telegraphed in the sketch's set dressing and costumes—fans wear rubber Spock ears, and blueprints of the bridge and images of the *Enterprise* adorn the walls. Jenkins notes other ways in which mainstream media assists in the mockery:

> *Newsweek* provided actual photographs of real *Star Trek* fans—a bearded man ("a Trekkie with a phaser") standing before an array of commercially produced *Star Trek* merchandise; three somewhat overweight, middle-aged "Trekkies" from Starbase Houston dressed in Federation uniforms and Vulcan garb; an older woman, identified as "Grandma Trek," proudly holding a model of the Enterprise.[86]

Jenkins's exploration of the fandoms around *Star Trek*, *Beauty and the Beast* (1987–1990), and *Blake's Seven* (1978–1981) concerns itself with how fans make "texts become real" by "poaching" meanings, rewriting storylines and characters, producing new adventures set in the same diegetic universe, engaging in "filksings," and reediting episodes on videotape. But, writing in the early 1990s, he spends less time examining those aspects of fandom specifically lampooned in his examples from *Saturday Night Live* and *Newsweek*: the guileless display of manufactured items such as Vulcan makeup and costumes, phaser weapons, *Enterprise* models, and blueprints of series settings. Such artifacts, whether commercially produced or crafted purely for the pleasure of their maker, are surely an important part of making texts "real." Yet the focus in *Textual Poachers* and other early academic treatments of *Trek* fandom centers for the most part on *literary* modes of appropriation and related struggles over hegemonic meaning. Camille Bacon-Smith, for example, mentions in passing the materialities of fandom—"In general, all forms of material art serve as visible reminders of the fictional universes in which the community shares an interest"—but devotes the bulk of her study to the writing of fan fiction and the editing of videotape.[87]

As recent scholarship on materially oriented fan activities such as collecting and construction proves, there are sound reasons to broaden the definition of participatory culture to include activities like building props and model kits, drawing blueprints, making websites, and managing the vast archive of invented facts generated by a fifty-year-old storytelling franchise.[88] In part this is because such activities—and the goods they produce—interact in complex and sometimes counterintuitive ways with the interests of producers and owners, both eroding and reinforcing the aura of authenticity on which the master text's authority hinges. In part it is because such activities complicate polarizing stereotypes of fans as either cultural dupes or resistant authors. And in part it is because even within what Jenkins, adapting Pierre Bourdieu, terms the "scandalous category" of fandom, scandalous *sub*categories have always been present. If, that is, "the stereotypical conception of the fan . . . amounts to a projection of anxieties about the violation of dominant cultural hierarchies," then some *Trek* fans arguably project their own anxieties by distinguishing between "normal" fandom and its "excessive" design-oriented counterpart.[89]

The ties among merchandising, fandom, and franchise longevity have begun to be addressed in recent treatments of *Star Trek* fandom, such as Roger Nygard's somewhat tongue-in-cheek documentaries *Trekkies* (1997) and *Trekkies 2* (2004). More soberly, Jeffrey Sconce has analyzed the *Trek* phenomenon in relation to the notorious Heaven's Gate cult, many of whose members committed collective suicide in 1997:

> A recurring question in the now copious critical literature surrounding *Star Trek* concerns the basis of the show's extraordinary appeal. Why has *Star Trek* spawned such an active and invested group of viewers, many of whom are eager to attend annual conventions, dress in *Star Trek* costumes, compose fan fiction, sing "filk" songs, master the wholly imaginary language of the Klingon empire, and even don "Away Team" patches before embarking on a final exit to the final frontier?[90]

Sconce's own question suggests that *Trek*'s longevity can be at least partly understood through the very activities and artifacts hidden, like Edgar Allan Poe's purloined letter, in plain sight: going to conventions, painting pictures, drawing blueprints, constructing props, sewing costumes, speaking constructed languages ("conlangs"), and engaging in other forms of manufacture based on *Trek*'s storyworld. It is the objects and archives associated with *Trek*—the "side" industries, both official and unofficial, embroidering and giving material shape to the episodes and movies—that ever more clearly distinguish it from other media entities by mapping in material form its vast and internally coherent diegesis. Sara Gwenllian-Jones, for example, argues that *Trek*, along with other cult TV shows such as *Babylon 5* (1994–1998), *The X-Files* (1993–2002; 2016), *Xena: Warrior Princess* (1995–2001), and *Buffy the Vampire Slayer* (1997–2003), functions as a kind of virtual reality, promoting "immersive engagement with the fictional world" by "uniting what is conveyed by the text with the reader's own experiences and knowledge" and thus "facilitating a sense of vicarious presence in the imaginary environment."[91] This presence is achieved precisely through the practices of design-oriented fandom:

> Cult television fictions extend across a wide range of secondary media, untidy yet comprehensive, so that the multiple and various signs of the fictional world saturate the world of actuality from which it is imaginatively accessed. Fans are voracious consumers of spin-off texts and artifacts, surrounding themselves with signifiers of the desired virtual reality. In the process, they feed the lucrative merchandise industries that have evolved around cult television series and serialized, transmedial film franchises such as *Star Wars* and *The Crow*. Posters and photographs adorn walls; PCs display themed wallpaper, icons, and screensavers; dolls and models stand on desks; life-size cardboard cutouts of characters lurk in corners; series-related books fill shelves; CDs play sound tracks; countless screen snatches are downloaded from the web and scrutinized; recorded episodes are repeatedly viewed and closely analyzed until they are indelibly embedded in memory.[92]

Another approach emphasizing the franchise's specificity in both its mediated and material aspects can be found in Alan N. Shapiro's treatment of *Star Trek* as a Baudrillardian simulation—systematic visualizations of an imaginary future reflecting "our own twenty-first century technologies *in development*."[93] Shapiro critiques "mythological" explanations of *Trek*'s enduring appeal for failing to acknowledge industrial components of the show's reproduction. "All suffer," he writes, "from blindness to the 'recombinant' industrial reproduction of contemporary consumer culture."

> In *Star Trek*'s case, this hyper-reality or "parallel universe" is a neverending expansion of "really existing" extraterrestrial species, beloved characters, endlessly marketed paraphernalia, and endlessly refined referential details furnished by Paramount pictures and global fandom. The *Star Trek* culture industry is a profit-oriented economic and signifying system of cyber-commodities and quasi-automatic generation of products from a computer program-like code.[94]

These writers are correct that a fuller accounting of *Star Trek*'s myriad forms is the next logical phase of *Trek* studies; Shapiro in particular suggests with his invocation of a "quasi-automatic generation of products from a computer program–like code" something like the design network I have described. Yet, like Gwenllian-Jones, Sconce, and the ritually minded theorist Chris Gregory (who argues that *Trek* has attained the status of "a modern mythological system"[95]), Shapiro flirts with the same trap that has dogged *Trek* fan studies since their inception, refusing to accord the manufacture of *Trek*-related drawings and artifacts the same status as transformative literary production. In fan studies as in fandom itself, textual practices are privileged over object practices. Design-oriented materials are instead disparaged as corporate exploitation, having little to do with the true spirit of participation in *Trek*.

Shapiro, for instance, asks rhetorically, "Do individual fans love *Star Trek* due to an attachment to some piece of fetishized memorabilia that they purchased at an online auction, or because of passions that were originally stirred by a great science fictional story?"[96] The *or* in his question inserts a wedge between "authentic" responses to story—tied to the aura of some original author(ity)—and grimly "purchased" pleasures of "fetishized memorabilia." A similar taint of pimpery haunts Sconce's description of the ways in which *Trek* has opened itself to fan participation:

Star Trek is one of the few series to make available the series "story bible" to the public, providing readers with the time lines and character biographies that govern its textual universe. Paramount has also cashed in on fan interest in designing and diagramming the various ships in the Federation fleet, publishing blueprints in the days of print, and more recently issuing a CD-ROM that allows prospective ship-builders to design their own crafts. Role-playing games and Klingon language camps can help round out days and months spent in the *Star Trek* metaverse.[97]

Gregory, too, treats the abundant material and reference-oriented para-texts of *Trek* as cold-hearted merchandising schemes, claiming that "in order to maintain credibility with the fans, *Star Trek*'s designers have published intricately detailed 'plans' of the various *Enterprise*s, accompanied by 'scientific' schematics as to how the ships work."[98] The problem here is that each writer, in endeavoring to expand our conception of *Trek*'s participatory culture and the media forms on which it depends, invokes a familiar stereotype of active (fan-based) participation versus passive (corporately managed) consumption. Note, for example, the absence in critical literature of Franz Joseph and likeminded "amateurs," despite the strong likelihood that the design-oriented fan movement of the 1970s actually *gave rise to* the cascade of technical manuals, cartographic guides, and "visual encyclopedias" of characters, vessels, and weapons that now share shelf space with *Trek* novelizations on Amazon and at Barnes and Noble (where their handsomely oversized and spectacular formats make them one of the physical bookstore's few remaining anchors against virtualization). Instead, franchise-related reference materials are characterized as products of a culture industry—in Sconce's words, "cashing in on fan interest" through "endlessly marketed paraphernalia."

The contradictory sorrows and joys of design-oriented fandom are explored with surprising frankness and optimism in *Galaxy Quest* (Dean Parisot, 1999). Its story is a thinly veiled treatment of the *Star Trek* phenomenon, but rather than focusing exclusively on fans, it casts an affectionate eye on *Trek* as a business, and in so doing tells a tale of economic redemption alongside its ostensible satire. The film opens at a convention devoted to the science-fiction TV show *Galaxy Quest*.

Although the series has been off the air for years, its aging stars milk their former celebrity by squeezing into old costumes, making guest appearances, and cutting ribbons at store openings. Jason Nesmith (Tim Allen), the actor who plays the Kirk-like Captain Peter Quincy Taggert, is signing autographs when he is accosted by Brandon Wheeger (Justin Long), a teenaged "Commander Fan" who runs a club of equally gawky SF buffs. Brandon peppers Jason with questions about *Galaxy Quest*'s technical inconsistencies. Exasperated, Jason blows him off in much the same fashion as Shatner on *Saturday Night Live*:

BRANDON
Commander, as I was saying . . . In "The Quasar Dilemma," you used the auxiliary of deck b for Gamma override. But online blueprints indicate deck b is independent of the guidance matrix, so we were wondering where the error lies?

JASON
It's a television show. Okay? That's all. It's just a bunch of fake sets, and wooden props, do you understand?

BRANDON
Yes, but, we were wondering—

JASON
There IS no quantum flux and there is no auxiliary . . . There's no goddamn ship. Do you get it?[99]

As the plot unfolds, however, Jason learns that *Galaxy Quest* is in fact quite real—at least to the Thermians, an alien species who have been monitoring Earth broadcasts and interpreting the show as historical record. Drawn into actual interstellar war, Jason and the rest of the cast are forced to reinhabit their screen roles, this time for mortal stakes. In the climax, Jason calls Brandon for assistance, drawing on the young fan's intimate knowledge of the show's fictive universe—in particular, the layout of engineering ducts and hidden passageways on the starship *Protector*, through which Jason and Gwen DeMarco (Sigourney Weaver) are attempting a rescue. The sequence is revealing in its suggestion that fandom's "cultivation of worthless knowledge" is bound up in merchandised objects—and that, through a miraculous alchemy, the two can combine to bring fiction to life. As Jason and Gwen make their way through the bowels of the spaceship, Brandon is shown in his bedroom: a collector's paradise replete with *Galaxy Quest* posters, blueprints, and action figures. He sits at his desk, assembling a scale-model kit of the *Protector*, peering through a magnifying lens in order to glue a component into place. When Jason calls, Brandon at first makes a show of distancing himself from his over-the-top behavior at the convention.

JASON
Brandon, I remember you from the convention, right? . . . You had a lot
   of little technical observations about the ship, and I spoke sharply to
   you . . .

BRANDON
Yes, I know, and I want you to know I thought about what you said . . .
   I know you meant it constructively but . . .

JASON
It's okay. Listen—

BRANDON
. . . But I want you to know that I am not a complete braincase, okay? I
   understand completely that it's just a TV show. There is no ship, there
   is no Beryllium Sphere, no digital conveyor . . . I mean, obviously it's
   all just a—

JASON
It's real, Brandon. All of it, it's real.

BRANDON
(no hesitation) I knew it! . . . I KNEW it! . . .

JASON
Brandon . . . The crew and I are in trouble and we need your help.[100]

His faith restored (though we never really believed it was endangered), Brandon and his friends bring their collective knowledge to bear on Jason and Gwen's dilemma, checking blueprints, consulting episodes, and running computerized 3D flythroughs of the *Protector*'s interior. This happy synthesis of technology, belief, and media commodity is played out on a grandiose scale in the film's finale. The *Protector* crashes to Earth, touching down in a parking lot and sliding to a halt . . . on the stage of yet another *Galaxy Quest* convention. Jason and his crew emerge triumphantly before a cheering audience (one of whom turns to another and exclaims, "Great special effects!"). For these fans as for Brandon, dreams have literally *come true*; the boundary between diegesis and reality has been gloriously breached. Far from signaling a breakdown in the order of things, this validation arrives—like a spaceship bursting through the wall of a convention center—as an inevitable reward for those who always believed, deep down, that "all of it" was real.

Galaxy Quest thus inverts the message of the *Saturday Night Live* skit, redeeming fandom through a wish-fulfilling parable of relevance. But the film goes even further in bringing sociological and economic characteristics of fandom into the light. First, it quite knowingly portrays fandom's design-oriented dimension. Centered on what one *Trek* historian has called "the 'hardware' part of the science fiction formula,"[101] this most affirmational of fan modes is tied unapologetically to commerce; it disdains story and character elements except insofar as they relate to the world of the show; and it is, in stereotype at least, mostly male. The latter point is driven home in *Galaxy Quest*'s opening convention scene. Brandon and his group ask the cast questions such as "In episode nineteen, when the reactor fused, you used an element from Leopold Six to fix the quantum rockets. What was that called?" By contrast, a fan described in the screenplay as "a shy girl" hesitantly approaches Gwen to ask: "Miss DeMarco? . . . In episode fifteen, 'Mist of Delos 5'? I got the feeling you and the Commander kind of had a thing in the swamp when you were stranded together. Did you?" Shy Girl is, of course, a caricatured distillation of the predominantly female fan base found in Jenkins and Bacon-Smith, interested less in SF technology than in penumbras and radiations of romance surrounding the lead characters (though it is worth noting that Shy Girl's question smooths the unpalatable edges of slash writing by transposing homoerotic rereadings of the fictional series into traditionally heterosexual terms).

Galaxy Quest is equally forthright about the economic utility of design-oriented fandom, represented by Brandon's bedroom with its wall-to-wall posters and action figures. As argued above in relation to the AMT *Enterprise* model, the side industry of *Star Trek* collectibles is as old as the show itself: a trend that began in the late 1960s and exploded in the 1970s through the licensing of print and photo novels, toys, games, costumes, posters, and comics—merchandising at times indistinguishable from (an admittedly loose form of) transmedia storytelling. *Galaxy Quest* recapitulates this expansionist trajectory in its conclusion, showing scenes from an upcoming "Galaxy Quest" movie adaptation; riding a wave of renewed interest, the show has reinvented itself on the big screen, revitalizing the actors' careers and providing audiences with a fresh supply of "historical records" to delight in.

By connecting the fan community's accumulation of knowledge and collectibles to the commercial vitality of a media franchise, *Galaxy Quest* reminds us that *Trek* model kits and blueprints have always been more than simple marketing tools (though they are definitely that as well). As Bacon-Smith writes, objects constitute a means of imaginative access to the franchise's diegetic universe, using "art to re-create the narrative world in a variety of concrete forms and images."[102] Jonathan Gray strikes a similar note in his analysis of toys and games related to the *Star Wars* universe, which offer "audiences the prospect of stepping into that world and exploring it."[103] Objects spawned by design networks also quite literally give shape to two forces that operate in tension with each other: on one hand, the fan's desire to know/possess/produce more of the master text, and on the other, the producers' desire to profit from and regulate this type of participation. *Galaxy Quest*'s treatment of design-oriented fan activity illustrates how design networks can serve as sites of discursive struggle over who ultimately "owns" a media text through mastery of knowledge about it—as seen in the clash of viewpoints between Brandon and Jason—while paradoxically serving as a mechanism to manage fan practices, as when Brandon's potentially disruptive command of canon becomes, in a distant metaphor for commodification, the key to conscripting him into a supporting role that saves and prolongs the life of the official text. For all that they seem to offer fans a path into the exploration, critique, and extension of canon, design networks are subject to asymmetrical power dynamics that seek to define and regulate how participation in those networks should take place.

Another aspect of design networks' instability can be found in their polymorphous productivity, in that any number of artifacts can be manufactured by any number of creators—in any number of media—from a given template. This principle underlies *Galaxy Quest*'s many reifications of the starship *Protector*: in the cheap-looking model used on the TV series, contrasted with the more detailed movie miniature glimpsed in the closing "preview"; in the form of model kits, blueprints, and 3D programs belonging to Brandon and the fan club; and in the functioning *Protector* built by the gullible Thermians—itself yet another copy, based on the aliens' study of reruns. Finally, widening our perspective to Hollywood's production context, we can add the physical models, computer graphics, and full-scale props used to create the visual effects in *Galaxy Quest* (the Dreamworks production) itself. Though its story is driven by the idea that studio fakery conceals a deeper truth, the movie ultimately seems to prove that any notion of a unique *Protector*, when scrutinized closely, dissolves into a sea of substitutes and approximations. This ever-expanding multiplicity points to the generational engine at the heart of any successful transmedia franchise, in which—to invert Ferdinand de Saussure's assertion that in language there are only differences without positive terms—"versioning" drives the creation and circulation of additional textual forms and their associated physical realizations.[104]

The many lives of *Protector* parallel the many lives of the *Enterprise*, produced in thousands of instances within *Star Trek*'s production-consumption ecosystem. Every version of the fictional starship, from a clay model fashioned in a third-grader's art class to a wooden mockup devised in preproduction, from a motion-controlled miniature built by optical-effects houses for bluescreen composition to a digital asset designed in 3D animation software, exists as a realization of a certain blueprint—that is plain enough. A more subtle point is that none of them is ultimately more authentic than any other, save in how they are discursively framed through the actions of corporate makers and fan builders. The *Enterprise*, like the larger fictional universe it anchors, has never existed except as a composite of effects trickery, still frames on film reels, and the endless recirculation of video broadcasts. Yet the notion persists that a "real" *Enterprise* or *Protector* can be found at a particular juncture on the TV or movie screen—apparently unified despite the many objects, images, and processes that work in conjunction to generate its auratic glow of singularity.

The real difference between the Jefferies and Abrams *Enterprise*s, then, is a matter of ideology as much as anything else, fraught with all the complexity that term implies. The undecidability of this difference is precisely the site of ongoing negotiation between *Trek*'s industrial and cultural aspects, as well as a set of coordinates by which to map the franchise's rise and fall. Before its 2009 reboot, *Trek* had started to fade from the public eye: the final pre-Abrams movie, *Nemesis* (Stuart Baird, 2002), performed poorly at the box office, and the last remaining TV series, *Enterprise*, went off the air in 2005 after only four seasons. *Galaxy Quest* itself is evidence of this: the film dances along the edges of *Trek*'s design network, flirting with copyright infringement but never mentioning its inspiration by name, secure in the knowledge that audiences will get the joke.[105] It marks a fundamental shift in the nature of *Trek* fandom, which began in the 1970s as an underground movement, became well-known enough in the 1980s to be ridiculed by *SNL* and studied by academics, then matured during the 1990s into a commercial foundation solid enough to get the $45 million *Galaxy Quest* greenlit.

The reality, of course, is that the coevolution of franchise and fandom has not been nearly so linear. Just as junk DNA remains atavistically present in our genetic code, pockets of grassroots design-oriented fandom persist. Franz Joseph's role in bridging fannish and industrial investment in *Star Trek*'s design network and *Galaxy Quest*'s representation of that relationship occur at very different moments in the overall history of fandom and its discursive place within industry articulations of brand value. Despite its canny acknowledgment of design-oriented fandom's existence, then, *Galaxy Quest* ultimately elides the complexities and power differentials that define it; by treating fans as fans and producers as producers, it keeps everyone tidily within their established roles in the media ecology. As Alan McKee points out in his essay "How to Tell the Difference between Production and Consumption," this perspective ends up reinscribing a production/consumption binary that reception theory and cultural studies have devoted much effort to unraveling in recent years.[106] For McKee, the opposition reveals underlying economic and moral values that structure the interpretation of fan culture:

> [Traditional fan studies] repeatedly make the distinction between the work of fans and that of the industry, insisting that these are quite different—again, binary opposite—forms of cultural production. Fans do not have an industry—or if they do, it is a "mini-industry" or a "cottage industry." . . . For example, in this account, fans do not produce in order to make a profit; indeed, fan production is characterized by "a distaste toward making a profit." Similarly, fan production is more open and democratic in organization.[107]

McKee confronts and attempts to dismantle this opposition through an analysis of British *Doctor Who* fandom, noting the generational movement of many fans into professional roles, and pointing out that producers themselves often possess backgrounds as fully credentialed fans. Discussing Gary Russell, former secretary of a fan organization called the Doctor Who Appreciation Society, who became a *Doctor Who* novelist and CD-ROM producer for the BBC, McKee writes, "The question is a simple one—at what point did Russell stop being powerless? When did he stop being a fan and start being a producer? Can he be a producer, in the media itself—indeed, in the mainstream—and still be a fan?"[108]

McKee goes on to argue that a better classificatory system for official/unofficial production involves canonicity, that is, the degree to which a given story is collectively believed to be part of the "real" metatext, or merely apocryphal. He cites one respondent to an online survey about what is and isn't canon: "One post suggesting that 'Everything with *Doctor Who* on it is canon' was met with the response, 'Even the underpants?'; these underpants became an important symbol in this debate about policing the boundaries of *Doctor Who* canonicity. All posters agree that there must be limits."[109]

Here McKee skates past an interesting point—one that is perhaps more germane to *Star Trek* than to *Doctor Who*. For while underpants decorated with Captain Kirk's command insignia might not count in anyone's eyes as canonical, what about that same insignia sewn onto a velour shirt and worn at a convention—or on the set of a new *Trek* production? Clearly there are differences between a doodled *Enterprise* in a loose-leaf notebook, a more polished but still handmade schematic done in a fine arts class, a blueprint photocopied and circulated through mail order, an STL file downloadable from Thingiverse for use in a 3D printer, and the digital assets of spacecraft used in *Star Trek Beyond*—but, to paraphrase McKee, at what point did the insignia, the drawing, the object become canonical?

Such questions take on new force in light of a trend in design-oriented fan creation dating back to Super-8 fan films of the 1970s but taking hold as a more widespread phenomenon in the first decades of the 2000s: the production and distribution of new episodes of *Trek*, and stories set in the *Trek* universe, outside the ambit of Paramount. In 2004, a collective of fans based in upstate New York began releasing full-length episodes of a series entitled *Star Trek: New Voyages* (later renamed *Star Trek: Phase II*). Filmed on exacting re-creations of the bridge and other *Enterprise* sets, using faithful facsimiles of the original costumes, props, and music, *Phase II* marks a commitment to making more *Trek* according to the design specifications laid out in the sixties. As the production's official FAQ explains,

> The new show will be the continuing voyages of Captain Kirk and the crew of the U.S.S. Enterprise, NCC-1701 as seen in the 1966–69 television series, *Star Trek*. The series was cancelled after its third season. We are restarting the series as if it were in its fourth year. . . . The costumes, sets and props will be those seen in the original series of *Star Trek*. Some of the props, sets and costumes will be updated to reflect the changes planned for *Star Trek Phase II*, the aborted series that would have featured the original cast in the late 1970's.[110]

Special effects generated by computer recreate Jefferies's original design for the *Enterprise*, as well as numerous other vessels derived from Franz Joseph's extrapolations. Continuity in design is matched by continuity in narrative, with scripts making enthusiastic use of established players Kirk, Spock, and McCoy, as well as the lesser-known but no less canonical Captain Pike and Transporter Chief Kyle. The presentation of these characters, like that of the rest of *Trek*'s future history, is resolutely unironic. The producers write,

> [We] feel that Kirk, Spock, McCoy and the rest should be treated as "classic" characters like Willy Loman from Death of a Salesman, Gandalf from Lord of the Rings or even Hamlet, Othello or Romeo. Many actors have and can play the roles, each offering a different interpretation of said character. Though the character is the same, the interpretation of the actor is what's in question. We feel that the crew of the Enterprise has more to teach us about life and each other than has been explored to date. We also feel the new actors can add to the legend in a believable and contemporary way. Yes, some may have a problem separating [William] Shatner from Kirk—all we ask is that you give it a try and see whether Kirk and the crew still have something to say to you.[111]

The same performative sentiment might well be applied to the production in general: "inhabited" by a team of writers, directors, and technicians who, while not among the original creators Roddenberry, Jefferies, Chang, Phillips, and Theiss, stay true to the industrial roles those men established. Indeed, the episodes themselves could be said to "play the part" of the Original Series texts, though *Phase II* episodes are downloaded or torrented rather than broadcast or streamed by network providers. And in a final inversion of the expected hierarchy, the *Phase II* project is attracting writers and actors from *Trek*'s many incarnations—among them Walter Koenig, Grace Lee Whitney, Tim Russ, and Eugene Roddenberry Jr. (son of Gene)—who reprise their roles onscreen and off as part of this new "enterprise." Soon enough, it seems clear, even William Shatner might find it tempting or profitable to reprise the role of Kirk in a *Phase II* episode. If and when he does so, it will neatly mirror the arc of Tim Allen's Jason Nesmith/ Captain Taggert: an actor finding a new industrial home within fandom's realized fantasy, changing his tune from "Get a life" to "It's all real." Within the design network, differences between fans and professionals, original work and surgically precise homage, blend to the point of disappearance—reminding us, perhaps, that such differences were never essential and unchanging, but the result of highly contingent configurations of culture, technology, and capital.

Conclusion: The Continuing Voyages

Of course, *Phase II* is but one instance of how the Star Trek franchise continues to ramify across media, propelled not just by audiences but by communities of creators working along the spectrum from authorized to unauthorized. Web series like *Star Trek Continues* (2013–present) or films such as *Prelude to Axanar* (Christian Gossett, 2014) extend existing Kirk-Spock-McCoy versions of *Trek* or expand into fresh territory with new crews and starships, yet each proceeds from a production base of extensive and meticulous material creation: settings such as the *Enterprise* bridge, costumes such as Starfleet uniforms, props such as communicators and tricorders, and prosthetic makeup appliances such as pointed Vulcan ears or Klingon forehead ridges. This exacting physical mise-en-scène is matched by digital visual effects that portray starships and planets in outer space, shimmering transporter dematerializations, and the luminous blasts of phaser beams. However, the same elements that grant authenticity to fan productions also run the risk of infringing on Paramount's intellectual property: in 2015, CBS and Paramount brought suit against the makers of *Axanar* for their use of copyrighted material such as settings, characters, and spacecraft. Perhaps not coincidentally, this legal action occurred as the company was developing its own new TV series, *Star Trek Discovery*, set to launch in 2017.

Approaching *Star Trek* through the design of its storyworld rather than through the lens of its stories, characters, or message, we come to a better understanding of "that which survives" from one transmedia incarnation to another. McKee suggests that in engaging the vast array of texts and products generated by a franchise across multiple decades, it is wise to resist any easy distinction between authentic versus inauthentic, original versus unoriginal, or authorized versus unauthorized forms—except insofar as we can approach those classifications as the culturally and legally constructed categories they are. In the struggle to establish canonicity, all participants have a shot, as well as a stake; legally recognized authors and owners are capable of missteps that lose them the faith of the fan base, while fans—especially in an era of low-priced production equipment and the many-to-many distribution channels of the Internet—are capable of making artwork that parallels or supplants the status of the "official" version. Special effects organized by design networks mark the terrain on which this tug-of-war continues. In the design network we find a way of explaining not only the forces that generate more *Trek* but those that regulate and limit that generation. Ultimately, we glimpse an important truth about media franchises that operate, like *Trek*, at scales and durations far exceeding traditional categories of film and television studies: the inseparability of fans and producers, texts and objects, one *Enterprise* and another.

By contributing the most distinctive created elements of a media property, special effects are the cornerstones of design networks, which in turn anchor the visual, narrative, and formal "family resemblances" knitting together the myriad texts and paratexts of the fantastic transmedia franchise. At the same time, by providing a space where the creative contributions of fans vie with content of official producers, growing the franchise's fictional universe in uneven fits and starts rather than the smoothly controlled trajectory of corporate planning, design networks also highlight the shared and negotiated nature of franchise authorship. The next chapter turns to another long-running fantastic transmedia franchise, *Star Wars*, exploring the origins of its special-effects-dependent universe at the hands of multiple creators—and by extension, the relationship of special effects to questions of authorship, originality, and authenticity.

Used Universes and Immaculate Realities

Appropriation and Authorship in the Age of Previzualization

A defining characteristic of the successful fantastic transmedia franchise is that it branches out widely both in space—through the sheer proliferation of texts, images, sounds, and objects subsumed under its brand—and in time, as installments are replayed and serial chapters accumulate. As a result, generational forces inevitably affect how such properties are crafted by creators and evaluated by audiences over the years. The case of *Star Trek* discussed in the previous chapter demonstrates some of the forms these tensions can take, as the characteristic design system from which an imaginary world is built also becomes a site of interplay between fans and legal rights holders who must negotiate the storyworld's openness to exploration by both authorized and unauthorized creators. But in the case of another popular, profitable, and long-lived franchise—one whose launch, eleven years after *Trek's*, triggered an explosion in science-fiction and fantasy filmmaking, special-effects-dependent blockbusters in particular—issues of authorship and control take on a very different form.

With the acquisition of Lucasfilm in 2012, the Walt Disney Company became the steward of a huge trove of narrative and stylistic content ripe for further expansion: not just the first three films of the "Original Trilogy"—*A New Hope* (George Lucas, 1977), *The Empire Strikes Back* (Irvin Kershner, 1980), and *Return of the Jedi* (Richard Marquand, 1983)—but the prequels *The Phantom Menace* (George Lucas, 1999), *Attack of the Clones* (George Lucas, 2002), and *Revenge of the Sith* (George Lucas, 2005). Reflecting the industrial and cultural changes they themselves helped bring about, these six feature films were in turn merely tentpoles of an even larger "Expanded Universe" elaborated in a variety of media including video games, comics, and television series, along with less narratively structured (if just as brand-identified) physical content like toys, model kits, and action figures. Yet until the Disney acquisition, the transmedial growth of *Star Wars* had played out under the sole jurisdiction of George Lucas, the writer/director/producer who entered 1970s Hollywood as a relative outsider—a young and independent member of the so-called film school generation whose approach to filmmaking, as Julie Turnock notes, hinged on the application of then-advanced special-effects technology to bring out the more visionary aspects of science-fiction cinema.[1] Disney's acquisition marked the return of this spirit to Lucas's empire with the help of J. J. Abrams, taking on the challenge of updating and reinvigorating the franchise much as he had done with *Star Trek* (2009). Abrams's *The Force Awakens*, released in 2015, marked the dawn of a new era for *Star Wars*, with a host of follow-up films put quickly into production, including *Rogue One* (Gareth Edwards, 2016), *The Last Jedi* (Rian Johnson, 2017) and a feature based on the adventures of a young Han Solo.

By opening the floodgates in this way, Disney seemingly resolved a longstanding concern regarding Lucas's overbearing control of the property he originated. These tensions centered on the soundness of Lucas's decisions in guiding the production of new installments while revising existing chapters. Although undeniably popular and capable of holding its audience across generational lines (as parents introduced children to the fictional property they themselves grew up with), *Star Wars* has also received fan backlash over the years for its willingness to toy with its own history through revisions of key texts—such as the alterations and additions to the Original Trilogy in the 1997 "Special Editions"—and through Lucas's choice to retroactively examine Darth Vader's origin story in the prequels, rather than moving forward (as *The Force Awakens* would do) with characters and situations established in the first trio of films. Even with directors like Abrams, Gareth Edwards, and Rian Johnson bringing fresh blood to the franchise, however, *Star Wars* is destined to remain George Lucas's creation, largely because of strategies Lucas developed in the 1970s while preparing the movie that started it all. Extending from the realm of financing and merchandising deals to the assembly of a screenplay from well-established precedents to the workflow for visualizing his science-fictional universe, Lucas sought through his visionary brand to reconfigure the functions that authorship had until then served among industry professionals and filmgoers.

In expanding the control that director-producers can exert over their artistic "product," he created the severest imaginable reaction against the open source, co-creative culture at the heart of *Star Trek*'s design network from the decade prior.

The rise of the science-fiction blockbuster is usually described in terms of technological breakthroughs in image manufacture: the motion-control cameras to shoot opticals for *Star Wars* and *Close Encounters of the Third Kind* (Steven Spielberg, 1977); the traveling mattes and miniature cityscapes of *Superman* (Richard Donner, 1978) and *Blade Runner* (Ridley Scott, 1982); and, since the early 1990s, the creation of imagery through computer graphics in films such as *Jurassic Park* (Steven Spielberg, 1993), *Independence Day* (Roland Emmerich, 1996), and *The Perfect Storm* (Wolfgang Petersen, 2000). In order to fully understand recent trends in the fantastic transmedia franchise, however, we must take into account two factors often overlooked in the analog/digital dichotomy. First is the evolution of behind-the-scenes managerial methods and technologies to coordinate the design and planning (not just the final execution) of special effects. Second is the slippery, sometimes counterintuitive relationship between old and new—the traditional and the cutting-edge—within that evolution. Both factors play a crucial role in Lucas's mode of authorship, the composite nature of which is evident in the period of history just prior to the release of the first *Star Wars* on May 25, 1977. During that time, Lucas took two of Classical Hollywood's venerable techniques for planning feature films—concept art and storyboarding—and transformed them into formidable organizational tools that enabled the top-down coordination of labor across a range of production fronts including location shoots in Tunisia, soundstage work in England, and the special-effects facility Industrial Light & Magic (ILM) in California. In doing so, he refined a preproduction methodology, previsualization, in which whole shots and sequences are conceived, engineered, and finalized through a series of approximations.

Since the 1970s, "previz" has become a standard tool for mapping out complex imagery in advance, as well as planning how that imagery will be integrated into footage produced by other means. Previz assists in the consolidation of control (by producer, director, or studio) over a large and specialized labor force. But equally important from the perspective of intellectual property, previz often marks the point at which one creator's work is stripped of its protected status and reassigned to the purview of another. It is, in other words, a phase in which distinctions blur not only between "rough" and "final" but between "original" and "copy," "authentic" and "fake." Along with the larger history of preproduction from which it descended, previz suggests much about how the movie industry routinely valorizes certain versions as singular and unique while relegating others to the half-light of rough drafts and rip-offs, the flawed and incomplete—regulating the visibility and invisibility of its texts while simultaneously regulating the visibility and invisibility of labor.

The first part of this chapter examines the previsualization of the 1977 *Star Wars*, focusing on two figures—Ralph McQuarrie and John Dykstra—whose stylistic and technological innovations were smoothly married to Lucas's authorial brand. The discussion then turns to Lucas's wholesale adoption of digital methodology at all levels of production, from planning and shooting to editing, postproduction, and exhibition. Arguing that these technologies are less important than the philosophy that drives their use, the chapter ends by considering the case of the Special Editions to illustrate what I call the "previz mind-set" and emerging tensions over textual ownership in the transmedia era.

Previsualizing *Star Wars*, 1974–1977

In the famous conclusion to the first *Star Wars*, Rebel forces strike at the Death Star, flying their X-Wing fighters down a long trench in hopes of shooting proton torpedoes into a vulnerable exhaust port and setting off a destructive chain reaction. The sequence begins with pilots donning fight gear and boarding their spacecraft. Soon, in combat around the moon-sized battle station, they engage with TIE fighters, some dogfights ending in victory, some in fiery defeat. Luke Skywalker (Mark Hamill) maneuvers into position for a trench run with Darth Vader on his tail, urged by the ghostly voice of Obi-Wan Kenobi (Alec Guinness) to switch off his targeting computer and "Use the Force." With a last-minute assist from Han Solo (Harrison Ford), the attack succeeds, and the Death Star explodes in a thunderclap of sparks. The briskly paced sequence lasts approximately twelve minutes and contains the bulk of *Star Wars*'s substantial-for-the-time 360 optical effects shots. With its hard-driving, kinetic quality, the Death Star battle has become one of the iconic set pieces of science-fiction film.

The ostensible author of this sequence is writer and director George Lucas, who featured the Death Star assault early in his screenplay drafts, evidence that—unlike much of the rest of the story, which evolved radically in the writing—the battle had always been an integral part of his "vision." To accept Lucas's authorship wholesale, however, is to neglect the contributions of editors Paul Hirsch and Marcia Lucas (the director's wife), who assembled the sequence over a period of months; or that of editor Richard Chew, who made the key suggestion to cross-cut between two different lines of action, one following the space dog-fight, the other showing the Rebel base on Yavin IV, where Princess Leia (Carrie Fisher) and other mission planners listen with strained faces to the pilots' radio chatter.[2] (Originally, the screenplay called for two distinct attacks on the Death Star, the first of which was unsuccessful.) As Chew reports, "I had the idea that if we could put Princess Leia in jeopardy and then simultaneously have Luke try to destroy the Death Star in order to save her and the Rebels, it would just provide much more tension to the ending. Originally, these were not simultaneous events; they were separate."[3]

But there is another layer of authorship underneath that of Lucas and his editors—or for that matter the small army of model makers, rotoscope artists, and camera operators at ILM, the department Lucas established to provide *Star Wars* with its special effects. Much of the action in the Death Star sequence was planned and based on a moving storyboard or "animatic" stitched together out of World War II movies. This film reel functioned not just as a reference, but as a rough draft of the sequence. It also marked the emergence of a newly precise method of planning motion-picture imagery. Along with Lucas's reliance on preproduction artwork and storyboards, the reel of World War II movies suggests much about the changing nature of cinematic authorship, particularly in regard to the visually spectacular school of filmmaking pioneered by Lucas, Steven Spielberg, Robert Zemeckis, James Cameron, and other director-producers coming out of the 1970s and 1980s whose movies are typified by the heavy use of sophisticated technology. Although the creative output of what Chuck Tryon calls the "technological auteurs" is often framed by discourses of game-changing originality, it is precisely in the conception and execution of special effects that such filmmakers mint innovation from precedent.[4]

It has never been a secret, of course, that *Star Wars* sprang from many sources. On the contrary, Lucas admits drawing on a trove of cultural texts in conceiving the film. These include black-and-white science-fiction serials such as *Flash Gordon* (Frederick Stephani, 1936) and *Buck Rogers* (Forde Beebe and Saul A. Goodkind, 1939); swashbuckling pirate movies *Captain Blood* (Michael Curtiz, 1935) and *The Sea Hawk* (Michael Curtiz, 1940); and the Akira Kurosawa film *Hidden Fortress* (1958). Omnivorous intertextuality has long been a refrain in Lucas's self-publicity, as is evident in the words of authorized biographer Dale Pollock:

> Lucas used Ming, the evil ruler of Mongo in the Flash Gordon books, as another model for his emperor. Alex Raymond's *Iron Men of Mongo* describes a five-foot-tall metal man of dusky copper color who is a trained servant and speaks in polite phrases. From *John Carter on Mars* came banthas, beasts of burden in *Star Wars*; Lucas also incorporated into his early screenplay drafts huge flying birds described by Edgar Rice Burroughs. George watched scores of old films, from *Forbidden Planet* to *The Day the World Ended*, and read contemporary sci-fi novels like *Dune* by Frank Herbert and E. E. "Doc" Smith's *Lensman* saga.[5]

Far from undermining our pleasure in *Star Wars*, this catalog strives to establish the film's generic and commercial pedigree, suggesting that its originality—and hence its value—inheres not in narrative invention but in the agile reworking of predecessor texts. What we might call a *discourse of influences* portrays *Star Wars* as a palimpsest of the twentieth century's science-fiction dreams, tying it to popular and profitable ancestors and positioning it at a particular rung (not too high, not too low) on the hierarchy of taste.

A better-known way in which *Star Wars* is based on a preexisting reservoir of ideas is its much-publicized association with archetypes and the collective unconscious. Tied to Lucas's involvement with religious and anthropological scholar Joseph Campbell, this perspective explains *Star Wars* as the umpteenth iteration of a millennia-old "hero's journey," a pattern prevalent in the storytelling traditions of diverse cultures around the world. According to this template, a young hero (Luke

Skywalker) receives a call to action (Princess Leia's holographic plea for assistance). He undergoes a series of initiation trials (losing his parent-figures, rescuing the princess), accompanied by helpful companions including a wise mentor (Obi-Wan Kenobi), a trickster (Han Solo), and "animal" familiars (Chewbacca and the droids R2-D2 and C3PO). In the end, the hero triumphs in a final battle (the destruction of the Death Star) against an evil nemesis (Darth Vader).

But where does a discourse of influences leave the "real" author? Whether by accident or intention, George Lucas has constructed for himself a realm of plagiarism without penalty. The paradoxical nature of this space shows in the oxymoronic explanations of his creative process. Becoming "a voracious science-fiction reader, devouring Isaac Asimov's contemporary novels and classic sci-fi authors like Edgar Rice Burroughs and Alex Raymond," Pollock states, "Lucas was building *Star Wars* from scratch."[6] At another point the same writer asserts that Lucas "looked *everywhere* for ideas for *Star Wars*, which is at the same time derivative and original."[7] The fan website *Star Wars Origins* details Lucas's borrowings, from Tolkien's *Lord of the Rings* to *Ben Hur* (William Wyler, 1959), but its mode of appreciation is resolutely unironic:

> Every storyteller wants to connect with people as deeply as Lucas did with *Star Wars*, and everyone had access to the same raw materials. If the process was really so obvious and simple, wouldn't every story be just as good? . . . The question is never *where* Lucas found his inspirations, but rather *how* he wove them together with such intelligence, insight and compassion. What gives a story the power to touch us? How does the imagination *work*?[8]

This interpretation seeks to resolve a dialectic between invention and derivation that characterizes the work of many contemporary filmmakers. But the same dialectic has been present in Lucas's work from the start. In film school at the University of Southern California, he flirted with experimental techniques; his first student film, *Look at Life* (1965), was a one-minute photographic collage, "a rapid-cut barrage of seemingly disparate images" captured from a single issue of *Life* magazine.[9] The follow-up, a forbiddingly austere portrayal of a totalitarian future entitled *THX 1138 4EB* (1967), would serve as the foundation for his first theatrical feature, *THX-1138* (1971). At that stage Lucas seemed a willfully obscure filmmaker. However, throughout the early 1970s he began developing more accessible projects, including the 1950s coming-of-age story *American Graffiti* (1973); *Radioland Murders*, a screwball comedy set in the 1940s;[10] a Vietnam movie;[11] and the cliffhanger-structured thriller *The Adventures of Indiana Smith*. All of these would eventually get made: *Radioland Murders* (Mel Smith, 1994) was quickly forgotten following its release, with Lucas producing and co-writing, while Francis Ford Coppola filmed *Apocalypse Now* (1979). The other project, of course, became *Raiders of the Lost Ark* (Steven Spielberg, 1980).[12] Despite the varying fortunes of these projects, all could be described as strong genre concepts, heavy on narrative conventions and iconography borrowed from different decades, and filtered, as always, through film: not ideas for stories, but ideas for *movies of* stories.

Retrospectives on Lucas have attempted by various methods to locate a unified authorial signature writ large across his first three movies (*THX 1138*, *American Graffiti*, and *Star Wars*). One argument they offer is that Lucas was making "immaculate realities"—a term borrowed from Kurosawa to denote "a flawless evocation of an entirely imagined society."[13] Another reads Campbellian archetypes into *THX* and *American Graffiti*. From the evidence, however, the explanation is probably simpler, and, on an industrial level, more sensible: Lucas sought to make movies based on other movies he had seen. Each of his projects had precedents in the archives of popular and cinephilic culture, offering ample iconographic scaffolding on which to build; *THX-1138*, for example, was strongly influenced by *Alphaville* (Jean-Luc Godard, 1965) and the icier extremes of the French New Wave. With his highly quotational style, Lucas thus took part in the "massive, widespread changes within some of the most fundamental categories of filmmaking and film criticism" identified by Jim Collins in his study of postmodern genres and auteurs.[14] According to Collins, textual hybridity has come to serve as an artistic signature in its own right: "The primacy of quotation likewise troubles the category of auteur, since cinematic authorship now obviously needs to be reconceptualized in reference to directors whose 'personal vision' is articulated in terms of their ability to reconfigure generic artifacts as eclectically, but also as individually, as possible."[15]

But something sets Lucas's auteurism apart from that of Zemeckis, Tim Burton, and other filmmakers discussed by Collins. While auteurs of the 1990s used quotation to forge recognizable styles of their own, Lucas's use of quotation seems to have taken place at a more fundamental level, assembling movies out of earlier productions in a frank and guileless fashion. Evidence for this can be found in the previsualization practices that are the focus of this chapter: initially in planning the Original Trilogy, and later in designing the prequels. The previsualization mind-set pioneered by Lucas results in a particular attitude toward existing texts, treating them less as inspirations than as rough drafts for future productions.

In its unadulterated form, adherence to an existing template results not in a new text but something else entirely—the remake. The kernel of *Star Wars* was not, in fact, an original story but an adaptation of *Flash Gordon*, the 1930s serial cliffhanger and comic book. Becoming interested in the project following the release of *THX-1138*, Lucas met with King Features, owners of the rights to Alex Raymond's vintage comic strip. Already Lucas saw the nascent project as, in some sense, the assemblage of a movie already made in bits and pieces, waited to be culled from history. What he called his "movie comic-book" would incorporate elements of Edgar Rice Burroughs's Barsoom novels (1912–1948) and Frank Herbert's *Dune* series (1965–1985), but would be "shot in a style inspired by old Hollywood action films."[16] Disappointed to learn that producer Dino De Laurentiis had already purchased the rights to *Flash Gordon*, Lucas decided he "could make up a character as easily as Alex Raymond," and set to work conceiving "a contemporary action fantasy" built around "your basic superhero in outer space."[17]

It may seem strange, then, that early drafts of *Star Wars* met with trouble precisely because they seemed to *lack* precedent—even the most basic cinematic contours and narrative signposts that would convince others to collaborate artistically or financially in the project. Lucas's thirteen-page plot summary, completed in May 1973, met with mixed reactions from his agent and lawyer, who found its mix of SF and fantasy elements bewildering.[18] Prospective funders were equally skeptical: United Artists rejected the project, asserting it "would cost a fortune, with no guarantee that the special effects could be done."[19] Evidently Lucas learned his lesson, for by the time he met with Twentieth

Century Fox, he had started to anchor his ideas in concrete references, illustrating the story treatment with pictures cut from magazines and comic books—a foreshadowing of what would become previsualization.[20] According to Pollock, Fox executive Alan Ladd Jr. appreciated *Star Wars*'s connection to movies of yesteryear, a connection that he perceived in terms of his own past as a descendent of Hollywood's aristocracy: "Lucas described *Star Wars* as an amalgam of *Buck Rogers* and *Captain Blood* and *The Sea Hawk*, two Errol Flynn swashbucklers. Ladd had grown up with the people who starred in and made these movies and was willing to take a chance on Lucas."[21] This chance took the form of a $150,000 deal: Lucas would get $50,000 to write the film and $100,000 to direct.[22] (*Star Wars* itself was initially budgeted at $3.5 million, an "intentionally low" figure reflecting the studio's doubt that such a proposal, with its demanding special effects, could be rendered onscreen.[23]) Armed with these funds and profits from *American Graffiti*, Lucas began to develop the project in earnest, engaging in copious research while whittling the story outline into a coherent script. What he ended up with was, in the words of one biographer, "an esoteric world that only [Lucas] understood."[24] By summer 1974, the rough draft of what was then called *The Star Wars* ran 132 baffling pages. According to fellow director Michael Ritchie, to whom Lucas showed the draft, "It was very difficult to tell what the man was talking about."[25] Another friend, Hal Barwood, said the script "started off in horrible shape. . . . It was hard to discern there was a movie there. It was both kind of futuristic and funny and endearing and exciting all at once, but that combination of possibilities just didn't dawn on us reading these words on the page."[26]

Perhaps thinking back to his use of comic-book panels to sell the story treatment to Twentieth Century Fox, Lucas acknowledged that "the concepts and characters he was devising were so bizarre that it was very difficult for anyone else to visualize them." So he turned to a professional artist, Ralph McQuarrie, to portray *The Star Wars* in concrete visuals.[27] McQuarrie was an industrial artist for Boeing Aircraft who came to prominence in Hollywood circles in the late 1960s when he created illustrations of space flight for CBS's coverage of the Moon landings. Lucas hired him to paint "concept artwork" based on a handful of key images.[28]

It is fair to say that without McQuarrie's paintings, *Star Wars* would not have been made—or would at least have been a very different film. "George spent his money wisely on *Star Wars* by developing the art," according to Lucasfilm production assistant Miki Herman. "Ralph McQuarrie's paintings sold the movie to Fox."[29] The paintings' primary value was in leapfrogging past the limitations of time and budget to bring back images from *Star Wars'* own future, its spectacular "money shots." Executed in opaque gouache and acrylic in a cinematically widescreen aspect ratio, the art envisioned in arresting ways the central settings, character looks, and action beats of Lucas's screenplay. Studio backers were all too pleased to find order amid the chaos; they were particularly reassured by the guarantee that the planned effects would be both technically achievable and splendidly unlike anything that had come before. Lucas "wanted the pictures to be idealist," according to McQuarrie. "In other words, don't worry about how things are going to get done or how difficult it might be to produce them—just do them how you'd like them to be."[30] Compared to the probable expense of producing the special effects they called for, the paintings cost nothing; yet that very lack of expense suggested that the images could be delivered on time and on budget. With the paintings, Lucas "wanted people to look and say, 'Gee, that looks great, just like something on the screen.'"[31]

McQuarrie's artwork also helped to organize the production side of *Star Wars*. They defined the look of different characters as well as designs for costumes, settings, props, spaceships, planetary environments, and alien beings. McQuarrie is credited, for example, with originating key aspects of the film's iconography, including Darth Vader's breathing mask, the Jedi light sabers, the desert planet Tatooine with its two suns, R2-D2's "three legs, a round swivel top on his cylindrical metal body, and a squat demeanor,"[32] and certain spaceships. His designs helped lend the film its air of being a "used universe"—Lucas's term for the scuffed and careworn quality of his retrograde future. More important, McQuarrie's paintings provided a concrete reference point for the growing staff of casting directors, costume and set designers, storyboard artists, and special-effects craftspeople coming on board as ILM expanded. At higher levels, the artwork functioned as a collaborative archive, enabling heads of design teams to view, assess, and modify designs. At lower levels, the paintings coordinated the labor of draftsmen and model makers, providing a template for maintaining consistency in their output. Joe Johnston, credited with effects illustration and design, was responsible for creating the extensive storyboards for *Star Wars*. "A lot of people ask me if I was the creator of the Star Wars spaceships, and I really wasn't," he has said. "Everyone else's imagination was kind of funneled through mine and Ralph McQuarrie's."[33] Similarly, John Stears, special production mechanical effects supervisor, stated, "We had superb production illustrations by Ralph McQuarrie, and . . . the film adhered closely to them. A lot of the credit is due McQuarrie, as the look of the picture was due to him."[34] Several shots in *Star Wars* duplicate almost exactly their corresponding preproduction art, suggesting that McQuarrie's paintings acted as ersatz finished frames, which were then reverse-engineered by the production team, who built them from the ground up [Figure 2.1].

Although McQuarrie went on to provide artwork for sequels *The Empire Strikes Back* and *Return of the Jedi*, he expressed disappointment that his work for Lucas did not receive more credit in its own right ("I wonder if I haven't been ripped off," he is quoted as saying. "But then, why should George pay me any more than he had to? He's a pretty cool businessman").[35] Many of the commonly cited examples of *Star Wars'* incorporation of existing designs and motifs have their roots in McQuarrie's artwork. He based the look of C-3PO on the robot Maria in *Metropolis* (Fritz Lang, 1927). An even more significant contribution is the signature shot from near the end of the film: the Rebel ceremony in which Luke Skywalker and his companions receive medals from Princess Leia. Frequently described as recycling the starkly symmetrical "mass ornament" of Nazi ranks from Leni Riefenstahl's *Triumph of the Will* (1935), the shot in *Star Wars* can be traced to McQuarrie through his preproduction painting, reproduced onscreen almost identically, albeit in reverse angle. McQuarrie also contributed several matte paintings to the *Star Wars* films, literally inscribing his artwork into the movie. Standing somewhere between design concept and finished frame, these images mark transitional layers within an unfolding transmedia system—here understood not just in terms of narrative networks but their related paratextual extensions, which encompass behind-the-scenes information.

Previz abounds in such intermediate objects—sketches, blueprints, crude models and maquettes, film tests, outtakes, work prints—weird hybrids seldom discussed in studies of film production, which devote

Figure 2.1. Ralph McQuarrie's preproduction art from *Star Wars* (1977) of the *Millennium Falcon*'s capture and the completed shot based on it. Figure 2.1a: McQuarrie painting of *Falcon*'s capture. Figure 2.1b: Shot of *Millennium Falcon* being captured by Death Star.

attention and analysis to more stable, neatly classifiable forms. Yet the materials of previz deserve theorization precisely because they fill in the hidden interstices of production, marking incremental transformations from paper to screen and encompassing the totality of filmic manufacture. It is as though the production of motion pictures takes place on a darkened stage with spotlights illuminating a few select nodes of creation to celebrate: in this corner, a director; in another, a writer and screenplay; and at the center, the final print distributed to theaters and rental/streaming markets, which serves thereafter as the nucleus of popular, journalistic, and academic discourse about the film. Within this metaphor, bringing up the house lights reveals that the stage is in fact crowded with materials and personnel whose work, while essential to the production, must be effaced in order to maintain an orderly cosmology of creation. This industrial mythology is anchored by the unifying figure of the film director.

Which is not to say that previsualization (or the preproduction phase that is its larger backdrop) receives no public attention. Indeed, these technical activities and their associated narratives and imagery fuel a highly visible side industry of publication pitched to audiences fascinated with the process of making movies. As the example of Stephen E. Whitfield's *The Making of Star Trek* (1968) in Chapter 2 demonstrates, making-of books and later phenomena such as behind-the-scenes documentaries and director's commentaries are nothing new, and have to some extent been the focus of academic scrutiny for their role in what Steve Neale terms cinema's "inter-textual relay."

> The institutionalized public discourse of the press, television and radio often plays an important part in the construction of [movies' public] images. So, too, do the "unofficial," "word of mouth" discourses of everyday life. But a key role is also played by the discourse of the industry itself, especially in the earliest phases of a film's public circulation, and in particular by those sectors of the industry concerned with publicity and marketing: distribution, exhibition, studio marketing departments, and so on.[36]

The making-of mania was particularly intense around *Star Wars*, echoing in discursive form the many tie-in objects—toys, model kits, pajamas, posters—that served not just to promote the film but, as Jonathan Gray argues, to render its storyworld a space for imaginative expansion during the long years separating the releases of the Original Trilogy.[37] As part of the film's promotion in 1977, Ballantine Books released an oversized portfolio of McQuarrie's paintings, along with *The Art of Star Wars*, a book reprinting Lucas's screenplay alongside preproduction art, storyboards, and movie stills.[38] Dovetailing with the mainstream eruption of *Star Trek*'s blueprint culture (also published by Ballantine Books) discussed in Chapter 1, these publications provide snapshots of an evolving production, freezing them like *Jurassic Park*'s prehistoric insects in amber: a glimpse of Luke Skywalker as a woman; a McQuarrie painting of Han Solo as a Chewbacca-like monster; a scene or snippet of dialogue that failed to make the final cut. The material record of previz, riddled with gaps on their way to being closed, offers not just a glimpse of possibilities that might have been, but a relatively unvarnished perspective on the logics of appropriation and suppression by which Hollywood attempts to close a circle of authorial singularity and originality around its products. Perhaps because of its very in-betweenness, previz records moments at which forces of ideological regulation are at their most contested and unstable. The promotional use of previsualization materials might therefore be seen as a clever strategy of containment, drawing attention to the protean metamorphosis of visual-effects design in order ultimately to reinscribe it within the techno-auteur's all-encompassing "vision."

Originality is even more at stake in the second important instance of *Star Wars* previz: the recycling of footage from World War II movies to map action sequences in advance [Figure 2.2]. Planning of this type is crucial in contemporary visual effects work, for which many separate pieces have to combined. Elements in a single shot are composited synchronically, but the shots themselves must then be set in diachronic relationship with others—everything must be edited together in correct order, each cut timed effectively. Static production art like McQuarrie's doesn't do the trick; storyboards are only a marginal improvement. What is needed is a moving storyboard. This was especially important

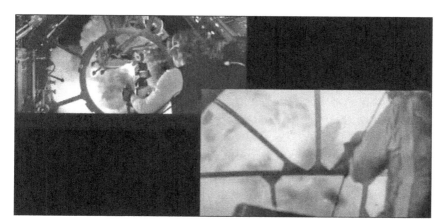

Figure 2.2. Animatics drawn from World War II movies served as guides for the manufacture and editing of visual effects shots.

in constructing the types of sequence that anchored *Star Wars* from its earliest conception: space battles, featuring small, maneuverable craft moving at high speeds and captured in short, dynamic shots with a moving camera, intercut with live-action imagery (closeups of actors, reaction shots, dialogue).

Lucas "wanted spaceships that were operated like cars," according to Gary Kurtz. "People turned them on, drove them somewhere, and didn't talk about what an unusual thing they were doing."[39] Lucas was emphatic about the need to realize onscreen fast-moving space battles, claiming "I had some images in mind [but] I'd never seen a space battle. I'd seen flying around in serials like *Flash Gordon*, but they were really dopey. And in *2001*, it was slow. Very, very brilliant, but not what I was interested in. I wanted to see this incredible aerial ballet in outer space."[40] The traveling-matte systems used in previous films were susceptible to minor deviations in camera movement and suffered from imprecise matting techniques, forcing space travel scenes to be filmed in sluggish, static-camera setups. With Gary Kurtz, Lucas shopped the project around to special-effects professionals, including Douglas Trumbull and stop-motion animator Jim Danforth—both of whom begged off when Lucas made it clear that he intended to oversee shot-by-shot production, rather than leaving creation of those sequences in the hands of the professionals.[41] John Dykstra, a young engineer and special-effects assistant who had worked on *2001* and Trumbull's *Silent Running* (1972), agreed to take on the challenge of producing a record number of effects shots according to Lucas's particular vision of "a new kind of space travel on screen." In July 1975, Industrial Light & Magic was created in an abandoned warehouse in Van Nuys. A subsidiary of Lucasfilm, ILM would handle the bulk of the special-effects shots needed for *Star Wars*, farming some work to other effects houses in L.A.

As part of the pitch to effects technicians that eventually led to the hiring of John Dykstra, Lucas, "always happier if he could show rather than explain,"[42] cut together a 16 millimeter print consisting of excerpts from documentary and fiction films set in World War II and the Korean War.[43] Source texts included *Battle of Britain* (Guy Hamilton, 1969), *The Bridges at Toko-Ri* (Mark Robson, 1955), *The Dam Busters* (Michael Anderson, 1955), and *Tora! Tora! Tora!* (Richard Fleischer, Toshio Masuda, and Kinji Fukasaku, 1970), among others.

This footage of aerial combat, which intercut exterior shots of diving and swooping planes with closeups of pilots in their cockpits and
ground crew monitoring the action, became a template in at least two
major set pieces of *Star Wars*. One was the "gunport sequence" in which
Han Solo and Luke Skywalker, escaping the Death Star, use turret lasers
aboard the *Millennium Falcon* to pick off attacking TIE fighters. The second was the assault on the Death Star described earlier: the final battle
epitomizing the film's overwhelming impression of speed, achieved not
only through dynamic optical-effects shots, but also by the rapid inter-
cutting of those shots with live-action footage. As a writer in *Sight and
Sound* summed it up:

> The Death Star trench sequence was unthinkable in its day not simply
> because of the effects technology but because of the very way it moved;
> while this was remarkable in cinema as a whole, it was doubly so in terms
> of science fiction, where—as in *Star Trek*—a space battle would previ-
> ously involve two near-static spaceships firing occasional beams of thick
> yellow light at each other. Lucas's instructions to the ILM effects people
> were to try to make the trench run as exciting as the car chase from *The
> French Connection* (William Friedkin, 1974). . . . The Death Star run re-
> mains, in spite of all its imitators, a hugely tense, fraught, frantic, exciting
> sequence, staggeringly well edited and utterly compulsive.[44]

Like McQuarrie's artwork, the dogfight footage served multiple functions in advancing *Star Wars* toward a finished film. Its primary use
was as a guide for Dykstra and the ILM team in generating shots. More
importantly, it served as a kind of action plan, first in shooting live-
action inserts—actors firing their guns, reacting to explosions, etc.—and
later in the editing process guiding the assembly of rough cuts and final
prints. (Indeed, early screenings featured the unadulterated black-and-
white dogfight footage from the fifties and sixties spliced with material
shot by Lucas at Elstree Studios, putting the old films to work as placeholders.) With the World War II footage, "Lucas had planned *Star Wars*
right down to the second."[45] Shot by shot, swooping and diving aircraft
were replaced by X-Wings and TIE fighters, so that, in essence, Lucas
"preshot and edited the climactic sequence of *Star Wars* months before
he began filming the movie."[46]

The biggest hurdle Dykstra faced was that, on paper, the action sequences were nothing but a bland succession of shot descriptions—as opaque in their way as Lucas's confused early story treatments. "The most difficult problem was translating the material that was going to appear in the film, from the written script into a visual dynamic," Dykstra has said. "This included the continuity that had to be controlled with regard to where the lasers appeared, what ship cut with what ship, the pacing of the scene, etc."[47] By providing ILM with a more specific kind of storyboard, the old movies enabled Lucas to exert precise control not just over the assembly of the film, but over the daily labor of the effects house. This control was part of an extensive planning infrastructure by which nearly every frame of *Star Wars* was previsualized in static or moving form. According to the effects illustrator Joe Johnston,

> When I first started on *Star Wars* in August 1975, I began by storyboarding the main battle sequence using the 16mm footage that George Lucas had compiled from World War II dogfights. . . . I must have watched it ten times on a movieola just to get an idea of the action. Then I would take it shot by shot and try to interpret the movements of the Jap Zeros and Mustangs into X-wings and T.I.E. fighters. That was kind of fun. All in all, there were probably one thousand storyboard drawings that were done. At one time, I had three assistants helping me on storyboards, almost three sets of 350 board scenes. We kept redoing them, changing shots and adding shots. I ended up redrawing all the boards that had been done! The storyboard took well over a year altogether, on and off.[48]

In the decades that followed, previsualization practices would be put to use in ever greater quantity and sophistication by ILM and other effects companies that took their lead from Lucasfilm. For *The Empire Strikes Back*, the battle in the snowy landscape of Hoth was first drawn on index cards and animated through a flip-book technique. In *Return of the Jedi*, the chase through the forests of Endor was precomposed and edited on videotape, using models of the speeder-bikes manipulated on puppeteer's sticks, with dolls perched in the driver's seat. It was during this period that the moving storyboard acquired its moniker of *animatic*. Defined by the *Encyclopedia of Movie Special Effects* as "a series of animated images used to represent special effects elements during the preproduction or production phases of a movie," animatics are now commonplace in the industry.[49] Although crude stop-motion anima-tion was used as late as 1993 to previsualize the raptors-in-the-kitchen sequence of *Jurassic Park*, digital previz become the norm starting in the early 1990s, with the use of architectural rendering programs to build virtual sets, populate them with virtual actors (initially little more than stick figures), and "film" action using virtual cameras.[50] The first film to employ digital previz to plan *every* shot—not just the visual effects—was *The Phantom Menace*.

Lucas was by no means operating in a vacuum when he put Ralph McQuarrie's art and the World War II dogfights to work as design tem-plates for *Star Wars*. Instead, he drew upon a longstanding logic of the Hollywood film industry, in which movies are brought into existence in stages—through a series of translations, often in different media—culminating in a finished feature film. Yet it would be inaccurate to claim that the conception and design of *Star Wars* did nothing to change the way in which movies are made. On the most basic level, Lucas's strategies of previsualization resulted in the invention of a powerful managerial tool. In its formalization of the filmic "rough draft," the animatic constitutes a gen-uine innovation in preproduction methodology. Animatics represent the quick and relatively cheap creation of a proto- or pseudocinematic object in which diachronic as well as synchronic relationships can be established well in advance of shooting. That is, while static storyboards and artwork map out basic composition and framing, animatics allow filmmakers to experiment with and adjust a given sequence's editing and rhythm. They enable a greater degree of synchronization among elements shot at dif-ferent times and places, enhancing Classical Hollywood's construction of continuity and diegetic realism. (The example of *Star Wars* demonstrates how essential this fine-grained continuity is to the diegetic integration of visual effects.) In addition, animatics provide explicit illustrations of cam-era movements that were previously indicated only by shorthand, such as a horizontal arrow to indicate a panning motion. In semiotic terms, animatics might be said to shift the register of cinematic preplanning from the iconic to something approximating the indexical.

Another of Lucas's preproduction innovations was to refine the process by which movies incorporate cultural precursors, placing them in new contexts and assigning them new meanings. If the animatic represented a more precise way of mapping moving imagery, it also provided a means of transposing complex generic traits from one storytelling environment to another. Film scholarship has often noted genre's composite and hybrid nature, arguing against the existence of "pure" genre. Collins claims that major films of recent decades have demonstrated an eclectic "hybridity of conventions that works at cross-purposes with the traditional notion of genre as a stable, integrated set of narrative and stylistic conventions."[51] While I do not wish to rehearse in detail the stances and schisms of genre theory here (Neale, for example, critiques Collins and other theorists of postmodern media, pointing out that "allusion, pastiche, and hybridity are not the same thing, nor are they as extensive or as exclusive to New Hollywood as is sometimes implied"[52]), I would point out that the animatic supplies a helpful missing link in the chain of citation whereby stylistic and narrative conventions find new generic homes. What traveled through the interstitial agency of the dogfight animatic was a kind of generic template, a 1950s armature over which Lucas and his crew stretched a 1970s skin. Using the old footage as a master plan for shooting and editing, the Death Star battle rephrased in science-fiction terms the venerable grammar of war movies, recycling an immediately recognizable iconographic system and revitalizing its clichés.

Such wholesale borrowings were hardly unique to or originated by *Star Wars*. But developments in previsualization in the 1970s pushed cinematic borrowing in the direction of larger syntagmatic clusters through the translation of lengthy strings of generic code such as battle sequences. Indeed, it could be argued that while industrial moviemaking has always involved borrowing, previsualization "freezes" the process for public pleasure and critical scrutiny, preserving archaeological evidence of the migration of elements. It does this by calling into existence a liminal cinematic object with both technological and discursive dimensions. Previz materials are technological insofar as they function as rough drafts; they can be seen as an engineering stage, a prototype. And they are discursive insofar as they function ideologically to suppress the "original" status of a previously authored object and transmute it into raw material for a new work.

Previz, then, performs a kind of industrial rendition, forcibly removing textual elements from their residence on a privately owned preserve and returning them to the public domain. Even as the more extreme aspects of Lucas's appropriative practice were made palatable by the animatic's conversion into a "clean" visualization tool through the use of video mockups and 3D software, a basic mechanism of effacement remains at its heart. Previsualization, like preproduction in general, functions as a foundry in which authorship is melted down and reformed into new shapes, making the work of many into the work of one. An unstable and contested space of creation, its excesses are nowhere clearer than in the mind-set that has come increasingly to the fore in Lucas's recent output—particularly in remaking his own early work.

A "Level of Finish" Issue: The Vicissitudes of Digital Authorship

Prior to the Disney sale, George Lucas's career could be roughly divided into two periods, each anchored by a trio of movies and an associated authorial/managerial style defined through the use of technology. The first extends from his time at USC through the release of *Return of the Jedi* in 1983. During these years Lucas underwent a transformation from maverick to mogul, crafting several of the top-grossing films of all time, including not only the original *Star Wars* trilogy but *Raiders of the Lost Ark*, which he executive produced and co-wrote. In the decade and a half that followed, he consolidated his position as head of Lucasfilm, producing other directors' movies but doing little filmmaking of his own. Instead, Lucas invested heavily in the development of an extensive digital filmmaking infrastructure, which put computers to work at all stages of production. More than anything else, digital filmmaking defines the second phase of Lucas's career, culminating in the release of the prequels. But there is another, more liminal trilogy to consider—one whose status as a separate and original work is far more troubled. The Special Editions were revised versions of *A New Hope*, *The Empire Strikes Back*, and *Return of the Jedi* released just weeks apart in the first months of 1997. The issues raised by the Special Editions reveal not just a growing gap between Lucas and his audience, but an authorial philosophy that stems in equal parts from his infatuation with digital filmmaking and what I will call a *previsualization mind-set*.

In order to understand the linked philosophies of digital filmmaking and previz, it is helpful to review the origins of Lucas's technologized mode of authorship. Following the completion of *Empire*, a separate division at ILM was founded for the research and development of digital filmmaking tools. This unit produced most of the signature breakthroughs in digital visual effects throughout the 1980s and early 1990s, notably the Genesis planet animation in *Star Trek II: The Wrath of Khan* (Nicholas Meyer, 1982) and the stained-glass knight in *Young Sherlock Holmes* (Barry Levinson, 1985). The first motion-picture "morph" appeared in the Lucas-produced *Willow* (Ron Howard, 1988). All were brief, stand-alone sequences, reflecting the high cost and steep computational demands of even limited CGI. As will be discussed in the next chapter on augmented performance, by the early 1990s digital imagery was creating celebrated wonders such as the T-1000 in *Terminator 2: Judgment Day* (James Cameron, 1991) and the dinosaurs in *Jurassic Park*. It is worth noting that the narrative integration of these characters was achieved with techniques directly descended from the dogfight reel used in 1976: precisely timed and carefully planned through animatics, snippets of digital effects were deftly intercut with live-action footage based on more traditional effects work such as prosthetic makeup appliances and full-sized animatronic puppets. Nevertheless, ILM's digital turn marked the flowering of what many academic writers have described as a renaissance in special effects.[53]

Lucas's interest in digital technology, however, was never exclusively, or even primarily, visual in orientation. Rather, his use of computers seems to be based on an agenda to expand the pre- and postproduction toolset available to filmmakers—and by implication the control that director-producers can exert over their artistic "product." In public statements, Lucas has distanced himself from questions of image creation, avowing a desire to bring advanced technology to bear on other tiers of the production process. His lack of interest in the graphical output of computers is apparent in his willingness to sell off what was undoubtedly the most successful spinoff of ILM's computer division, Pixar. (This company, after a series of highly successful short cartoons such as *Luxo Jr.* [John Lasseter, 1986], *Tin Toy* [John Lasseter, 1988], and *Knick Knack* [John Lasseter, 1989], produced the first full-length digitally animated feature, *Toy Story*, in 1995, and has gone on to become the flagship for commercially and critically successful digital animation.) According to *Cinefex*, which headlined him in 2005 as "The Godfather of Digital Cinema," Lucas was never as "entranced by the possibilities of the third dimension" as the Pixar team.[54] Instead, he remained focused on his original priorities of developing a scanner for film input and output, a digital printer, and 2D graphics applications—tools enabling film to be digitized, manipulated within the computer, and then transferred back to film. While these are essential stages in the engineering of visual effects, Lucas's goals had as much to do with the exigencies of editing and sound design as with the production of imagery. As he remarked,

> I wanted to develop a digital editing system. I'm an editor, and I thought digital postproduction would really change the way we make movies— especially in the way we finish them. So I was pushing for that. I know that once we could get an image into the computer, we could really manipulate it in extraordinary ways. . . . Doing just pure computer animation wasn't on the agenda.[55]

For Lucas, the value of digital technology is the fundamental changes it enables in the production process. He describes himself as experimenting "with lots of different production techniques and different ways of using digital technology—not just in the special effects area, but all over the picture in terms of how we manage time and money." He goes on to assert that "my whole intent has been to make the making of a film more facile so I can better utilize my resources to tell bigger stories in quicker and more interesting ways."[56]

In characterizing his relationship to the digital, then, Lucas seeks to stand outside of it. Rather than fetishizing the tools or the results, he fetishizes instead the process of tool use itself. He positions himself as a driver of innovation, one who summons into existence the means to accomplish his ends:

> When you start out making movies you're trying to get the largest vision with what amounts to a limited amount of resources. So it's a constant struggle to add more colors to the palette, and the way you get more colors is to spend huge amounts of money. But at some level there are colors you can't get because no amount of money will get you there. With *Star Wars* we were basically off the color palette. The technology did not exist to pan and move with miniatures, but that's what the story was. I wanted to tell this story, but the color only existed in theory.[57]

Thus John Dykstra's development of the microprocessor-driven motion-control camera is tied inseparably, in Lucas's account, to the impetus that Lucas himself provided: the World War II animatic whose dynamic shot plan required a breakthrough in camera design. In another sense, however, Dykstra's creation works as a smokescreen to cover up a subtler if equally profound shift in production methodologies. At the heart of Lucas's philosophy is the co-optation of other people's labor—the establishment of artistic ownership over another's innovation. It is a common dialectic in Hollywood history; David Bordwell refers to it as the *artist/inventor couplet*, a pairing that "generates a dialogic model of the causes of technological change."[58]

> Technology defines a horizon of possibilities. The filmmaker may either accept these constraints and work within them, or the filmmaker may innovate, for whatever reason (craving for novelty, the challenge of overcoming obstacles, etc.). When the artist demands an innovation, the technician responds. . . . Horizon of possibilities, artistic innovation, technological implementation: these stages define the shuttling pattern that [V. F.] Perkins calls "a constant two-way traffic between science and style, technology and technique."[59]

In the legal and cultural discourses of industrial technology, authors and inventors remain sharply distinct. But the example of *Star Wars*'s previsualization demonstrates that gray areas form when the definition of "industrial technologies" expands to include the diffuse and ephemeral worlds of design and artwork. Viewed this way, Lucas's continual pushing of the envelope is at the same time a process of continual appropriation: Dykstra's camera is like McQuarrie's designs, which are in turn like the aerial combat sequences from fifty-odd films of the 1940s and 1950s. Paradoxically, the authored status of each of these artifacts remains intact (the camera is named the Dykstraflex, not the Lucasflex) even as the significance of that work is refashioned in service of an overweening supervisory "vision."

In order to exist as an author—as a brand—Lucas's authorship ultimately represents just such an exercise of vision. This can be seen in the ways in which he has been positioned discursively around his own texts. Alongside the expected shots in documentaries of Lucas directing actors on location or standing around in the background of production activity, he is frequently shown examining models, storyboards, and makeup tests, bestowing approval on some designs and not to others. For some, this portrayal of Lucas marks the ebbing of a certain magic, a fading connection between film and filmmaker. (As Will Brooker writes, "Seeing Lucas looking over someone's shoulder at a wire-frame computer model of Jar-Jar rotating on a screen doesn't carry the same buzz."[60]) Auteurist aura aside, these representations reflect Lucas's shift from outsider to insider, from independent director to big-wig producer. As the scale of his movies exploded, so did his role as author. Spread thin by redistribution over a wide array of labors, his authorial aura is therefore in need of continual reinforcement. Somewhat in the fashion of Walt Disney, Lucas has established himself as a second-order auteur, an overseer of others' creativity, even while he maintains a role as director of his own movies. His "vision" finds its structural counterpart in the phase of production that precedes the actual appearance of a text: a before-the-fact or not-quite-real production, a phase of authorship without authorship.

Preproduction's role in Lucas's recent output is epitomized in the behind-the-scenes story of *Attack of the Clones*. Released in 2002, *Clones* continues the story of Anakin Skywalker, the man who will become Luke and Leia's father—and whose fall to the dark side turns him into Darth Vader. Lucas wrote the *Clones* screenplay in conversation with his design team, a staff working at Skywalker Ranch. According to Jody Duncan, "Lucas fed the design effort with developing script ideas and took inspiration for the script from the evolving designs"—again showing the degree to which his work emerges from the seamless compositing of other peoples' creative labor.[61] These designs took shape in many different media, including traditional and digital paintings, sculpted maquettes, and models of settings realized in solid form as well as virtual 3D maps. All, however, passed at some point through the digital pipeline, allowing them to be assembled into animatics, and from there into entire sequences of the finished motion picture. As mentioned before, Lucas's previous film, *The Phantom Menace*, had been the first in which every shot was previsualized; *Clones* was the first to be shot entirely with high-definition digital cameras, its takes stored on a hard drive rather than on reels of film.

But the aspect of Lucas's process that received the most attention was his use of the digital backlot: filming actors against blue- or green-screens amid minimal props and set dressings, filling in the bulk of the movie's environments through computer-generated imagery. Not incidentally, this allowed the *Clones* production to continue tweaking and adjusting performances, settings, and narrative long after principal photography had ended. This process was exemplified in the late addition of an action sequence set amid the rolling conveyer belts and flying sparks of a droid factory. As "the film continued to evolve," Duncan writes, "Lucas and [Ben] Burtt [were] adding new material and deleting extraneous material. Each of the cuts was more refined than the one preceding it, featuring fewer animatics or videomatics placeholders."[62] Recalling early screenings of *A New Hope* in which the black-and-white dogfight footage literally stood in for uncompleted ILM effects shots, the gradual emergence of *Attack of the Clones*'s final version from successively finer animatic "polishings" is proof that, for Lucas, the boundary between animatic and finished movie has blurred to the point of irrelevance. In many ways it is as though his filmmaking has become nothing *but* preproduction and the digital methodologies associated with it. For the previz mind-set, pre- and postproduction merge, crowding out the middle chapter—production—that was formerly considered the most crucial phase of a movie's manufacture.

***

The profound implications of this shift, however, were actually established long before *Clones* or the other prequels. While the technological impetus for the 1997 Special Editions stemmed from research and development for the prequels, publicity around the new versions trumpeted them as primarily an artistic endeavor, answering Lucas's desire to fulfill the aesthetic goals with which he began in the 1970s. In an interview with *Cinefex*, he stated:

> What I'm doing, I think, is what a lot of painters do, and some writers do—which is to go back and repaint or rewrite. Go into any artist's studio and you'll find lots of paintings on the wall that look completely finished and completely fine. And the artist will say, "Well, I'm leaving them there because I'm not happy with them." If I had been an artist and a painter, and I had done *Star Wars*, I would have probably left it on the wall, because I wasn't happy with it, even at the time. Everybody else was saying,

"This is great! Didn't it turn out great?" And I would say: "No. I had to compromise. It didn't turn out the way I wanted. It fell short of what I wanted it to be."[63]

The Special Editions contained numerous modifications: the restoration of deleted scenes, alterations to dialogue, and an overall cleanup of image quality and sound. What drew most attention, however, were changes to the special effects. Several sequences featured digital additions to the 1977 footage, and any shot deemed unacceptable by 1997 standards was simply replaced with a digital do-over [Figure 2.3]. As Michele Pierson observes, the Special Editions were by no means the first films in the science-fiction genre to undergo alteration and rerelease. *Close Encounters of the Third Kind, E.T.: The Extraterrestrial, Aliens*

Figure 2.3. Original 1977 visual effects versus their digital replacements in the 1997 Special Edition of *A New Hope*. Figure 2.3a: Bluescreen miniature shot of X-Wings. Figure 2.3b: Digitally generated X-Wings.

(James Cameron, 1986), *The Abyss* (James Cameron, 1989), and other movies were granted "special editions" on the prestigious early 1990s home-viewing format of laserdisks.[64] Yet, as Pierson goes on to note, "what is interesting about the [Special Editions'] new visual effects imagery is not in the end how it actually turned out but the fact that it became the focus for so much media scrutiny and public debate."[65] What made the Special Editions "special," in fact, was their overwriting of the earlier films—replacing the original versions outright rather than providing an alternative cut—coupled with the fact that Lucas refused to make available the unaltered Original Trilogy. This embargo reflects his sense of ownership over the films (asked in an interview whether he expected "any backlash from fans who might resent your tampering with a classic," Lucas replied, "I don't know. It's my classic.") and by implication his control over the experiences of *Star Wars*' viewing audience.[66]

In his study of fan response to changes in the Special Editions, Brooker finds it significant that "viewers refuse to accept George Lucas's conception of the reworked trilogy over their own."[67] The standard complaint on Internet message boards and fan sites was that "George Lucas raped my childhood," with commentators lamenting that they had been robbed of their beloved memories. And Brooker himself, writing about the release of the Original Trilogy on DVD in 2004, takes Lucas to task for supplanting the crude but real pleasures of his early work with glossy new imagery. Invoking André Bazin, Brooker argues that none of the "CGI set dressing that now decorates [the] original footage" measures up to the objective reality captured by Lucas's camera in the 1970s.

> It's hard not to agree with the conservative notion that "realism" lies in a concrete, physical truth that the camera records, and to hanker for this old-fashioned approach to cinema. In fact, to hanker for cinema itself or what cinema used to mean: for a set with the solid noises of footsteps and chairs scraping, with lightsabers covered in reflective tape and whirring from a handle motor, with aliens who, even if dressed in cheap fright masks, had a solid presence and took up space on the set.[68]

This characterization follows a common line of reasoning regarding digital special effects: that by effectively destroying cinema's connection to a profilmic referent, they have achieved only hollow and synthetic spectacle. "The CGI additions to the movie can never convince us in the same way, because some deep-seated instinct within us rejects them as fundamentally unreal," Brooker continues.

> Despite the skills of the Special Edition animators, their creation could not duplicate organic movement or physical environment to the precise extent that would allow the viewer to accept them wholesale as real; there is always an awkwardness about a landspeeder's bounce, an artificial sheen to a creature's hide, a figure's stilted stride, a flatness or falseness in the visual planes.[69]

A problem with such assertions is that they invoke a too-easy notion of realism, failing to take into account the gradations and varieties of realism that shape the critique. In other words, there is something incoherent in a perspective that validates one set of images (those in the original *A New Hope*) as "realistic" by contrasting them with an "unrealistic" other. Both the 1977 and 1997 *Star Wars* movies, after all, consist of manufactured, manipulated imagery, whether achieved through old-school matte paintings or state-of-the-art CGI; both, that is, are fundamentally unreal. Our assessment of their convincing quality (or lack of it) must therefore be based on historical contingencies of viewing, and in the case of *Star Wars* specifically, nostalgia for a remembered object—a piece of the past now "lost" due to its maker's absolute control over distribution and recording.[70]

With the Special Editions, Lucas did nothing more or less than convert his original films into previsualizations—treating them as rough drafts, temporary placeholders for a more sophisticated future rendering. His approach suggests that in the previz mindset, no text can ever truly be completed, but instead remains open for touch-up and revision. This philosophy is reflected in the words of one Lucasfilm executive speaking about deleted scenes on the *Revenge of the Sith* DVD, calling them "a little discompleted. . . . It's kind of a level of finish issue. Some are completed, some are at various stages."[71] In industrial terms, the original version of *Star Wars* now stands in approximately the same relationship to its 1997 "descendant" as the World War II movies and Ralph McQuarrie's artwork did to the 1977 films.

One wonders whether Lucas—or his analogs at Disney—will continue to swap out frames and sequences in future releases of the Original and Prequel Trilogies. He has already done so in the 2004 DVD release, revising a scene in which Han Solo confronts the bounty hunter Greedo in the Mos Eisley cantina. The original cut has Solo sneakily shooting Greedo with a gun concealed under a table. The 1997 version alters the blaster shot's timing, implying that Greedo got the drop on the otherwise streetwise Solo, forcing him to shoot defensively—a particular point of outrage among fans. The 2004 edition, however, refines the timing once again, making Han's and Greedo's shots overlap. This, along with other on-second-thought changes such as Luke's scream as he falls from Darth Vader's clutches in *The Empire Strikes Back* (1980: no scream, 1997: scream, 2004: no scream) have prompted fans to complain the Lucas is playing fast and loose with the established characterizations of the renegade smuggler and the young Jedi-in-training. Ironically, the changes imply an uncertainty in Lucas's authorial intention even as they reinforce his control over the text. As Brooker observes, "It sometimes becomes hard to believe that Lucas does have a consistent vision of the way the films should look or even how they should sound. . . . It also strongly implies that there is no single pure vision motivating Lucas's alterations."[72]

At stake here is something more than the realism or lack of it in special effects from one era to another. Rather, it is the perception of authenticity mediated through the authorial aura that Lucas projects, like a flickering hologram, onto his properties. The waning of that aura—the fear that there is "no single pure vision"—is what motivates fans to break ranks with Lucas's master plan, choosing the 1977 original (whose status as "original" Lucas himself has retroactively called into existence through his present-day tinkering) precisely because it is *not* timeless, but instead bound into the historical-material context of each audience member's initial encounter with it. The contested nature of *Star Wars'* transcendent atemporality has resulted in a kind of civil war between Lucas and his audience, two parties who would each claim *Star Wars* as their own.

This is not to suggest that fans have allowed themselves to be excluded from creating work based on *Star Wars*, or that Lucas has reduced that participation to purely merchandise-driven ends. Along with substantial communities of cosplayers and amateur model builders who bring the franchise to material life, there stands a long tradition of fan films set in the *Star Wars* universe. Some of these productions have been directly sanctioned by Lucas, such as the Star Wars Fan Movie Challenge (2002–2012), which over its decade of existence moved from allowing only parodies and mockumentaries to including fan fiction, so long as it was free of sexually explicit content, profanity, and excessive violence. Further from Lucas's oversight but still tolerated is *Star Wars Uncut* (2010), which invited fans to contribute fifteen-second versions of shots from the first film, the result a shot-for-shot remake in a crazy quilt of amateur approximations. Recalling the blueprint culture and fan film tradition around *Star Trek* discussed in Chapter 1, fan expansions of *Star Wars* treat its equally enormous design network as fertile soil in which to cultivate their own affirmational offshoots. With their strong echo of the appropriative practices through which Lucas assembled his 1977 film, as well as the way they downscale and roll back the technologically advanced, resource-intensive models they emulate, grassroots *Star Wars* productions emblematize, in inverted form, the previz mind-set: reflecting in rough draft the Special Editions' burnishes and flourishes.

The structural tension between these tendencies—Lucas's desire to control his creation versus that creation's inherently composite, extensible nature—seems to have been both resolved and inflamed by the Disney acquisition. Speaking to Charlie Rose in December 2015 following the successful release of *The Force Awakens*, Lucas expressed an ambivalence bordering on bitterness at the fate of his property and the storylines he had envisioned for future installments:

> [Disney] looked at the stories, and they said, "We want to make something for the fans." They decided they didn't want to use those stories, they decided they were going to do their own thing. . . . They weren't that keen to have me involved anyway—but if I get in there, I'm just going to cause trouble, because they're not going to do what I want them to do. And I don't have the control to do that anymore, and all I would do is muck everything up. And so I said, "OK, I will go my way, and I'll let them go their way."[73]

Controversially likening the sale to a transaction with "white slavers" before later modifying his comments, Lucas's evolving relationship to

Disney's *Star Wars* may foreshadow the legal and aesthetic challenges future generations of filmmakers and media artists will face as their creative work diffuses through the labyrinthine capillaries of blockbuster entertainment systems.

Conclusion: The Folklore of a Nation

> When a movie has become part of the folklore of a nation, the borders between the movie and the nation cease to exist. The movie becomes a fable; then it becomes a metaphor. Then it becomes a catchphrase, a joke, a shortcut. It becomes *a way not to think*, and all the details of the movie, everything that made it stick in people's minds, that brought it to life not just on the screen but in the imagination of the people at large, no matter how few or many those details might be, dissolve.[74]

Greil Marcus wrote this about *The Manchurian Candidate* (John Frankenheimer, 1962), a movie whose aura emanated in part from its rarely seen status—after the shooting of John F. Kennedy in 1963, the assassination thriller vanished from theatrical circulation, not to be released again widely until 1988.[75] It may therefore seem odd to apply Marcus's words to *Star Wars*, a multimedia franchise more than forty years in existence, whose impact on the global entertainment industry has made it an omnipresence in popular culture: the very antithesis of a *film maudit*. Yet the surface differences between the two movies should not blind us to a key property that they share. Like *The Manchurian Candidate*, the place of *Star Wars* in our collective imaginary seems secured less by simple numbers than by its reputation—the way that it, too, has become "part of the folklore of [our] nation."

But if the *Star Wars* franchise possesses a folklore beyond the archetypal content of its narrative, surely it is an industrial one: a mythology of the movies themselves, a simplified "way not to think" about vexed questions of authorship and originality, labor and technology. Consider the ways in which *Star Wars* has been used to characterize both the utopian and dystopian sides of the industry. Some explain the blockbuster success of the 1977 film in terms of the nostalgic pleasures it delivered to audiences, restoring "fun" to popular entertainment at a time when

America—enervated by the Vietnam War and the Nixon administration's abuses of power—was seeking escape. "*Star Wars* rediscovered the appeal of the classic American movie: the basic theme of good guy versus bad guy that had been tapped by every film star from Charlie Chaplin to John Wayne," writes Dale Pollock, going on to note other ways in which the movie functioned as a combination time machine and editing bay, splicing bright frames of an innocent and specifically cinematic past into the decaying print of seventies ideology.

> Lucas displayed in *Star Wars* something that had been missing in American movies for decades. Luke Skywalker triumphed in the end, Darth Vader was foiled, and audiences felt good. It was the same brand of optimism that Frank Capra captured in *Mr. Smith Goes to Washington* and *It's a Wonderful Life*. Lucas made a movie about winners, not losers, a prescription that brought great relief to movie audiences.[76]

Others condemned *Star Wars* for launching a wave of high-concept, action-oriented, special-effects-laden, heavily promoted blockbusters and for inaugurating a "cinema of effects" based on sensation, spectacle, and speed.[77] Thomas Schatz writes that *Star Wars*—in contrast to the character-driven *Godfather* series (Francis Ford Coppola, 1972–1990)—exemplified "films that are increasingly plot-driven, increasingly visceral, kinetic, and fast-paced, increasingly 'fantastic' (and thus apolitical), and increasingly targeted at younger audiences."[78] Peter Biskind's analysis, while more far-reaching, is similarly concerned with the fate of art and politics when technique and technology co-opt cinema's radical potential:

> Lucas's genius was to strip away the Marxist ideology of a master of editing like Eisenstein, or the critical irony of an avant-garde filmmaker like Bruce Conner, and wed their montage technique to American pulp. *Star Wars* pioneered the cinema of moments, of images, of sensory stimuli increasingly divorced from story, which is why it translates so well into video games. Indeed, the movie leapt ahead—through hyperspace, if you will—to the '80s and '90s, the era of non-narrative music videos, and VCRs, which allowed users to view film in a non-narrative way, surfing the action beats with fast-forward.[79]

Despite their apparent opposition, these accounts share certain traits. They both tell stories of what all movies are, on a deep level, "about"— nostalgic escape versus high-tech commercialism—and hence reveal a structure of belief about the medium. They also share the notion that *Star Wars*, in a certain sense, makes history disappear, arresting and reworking the operations of time and memory. In one view, the film turns its back on the present and returns us to an edenic pop-culture past. In another, *Star Wars* unmoors movies from cultural and political reference, substituting a "fast-forward" aesthetics built of spectacle and technological bravura. Whichever characterization one chooses— nostalgic or futuristic, throwback or breakthrough—our sense of *Star Wars* as being rooted in a specific historical context is undermined by the insistent invocation of golden ages or far-flung futures. What we might call a choreographed forgetting is in fact the most "special" of the movie's many special effects.

The first film's air of being simultaneously very old and very new, "used" and at the same time "immaculate," reflects at its heart a basic tension over modern transmedia authorship. In one sense, the 1977 *Star Wars* seems to lack a single creator, being merely the latest iteration of storytelling motifs as old as human culture—or alternatively, the latest recycling of ideas and images from a century of pop culture. To say a film has many authors is another way of saying it has none. But the sense of "universal authorship" is balanced by an equally sweeping interpretation that places one figure—George Lucas—at the center of everything *Star Wars*. For evidence, one need look no further than Lucas's effort, in 2003, to have the Director's Guild change the credits for *The Empire Strikes Back* and *Return of the Jedi* so that he could share director credit with Irvin Kershner and Richard Marquand respectively. If there is a divine agency at the center of *Star Wars's* industrial folklore, it is Lucas, and one goal of this chapter has been to come to a better understanding of the philosophy and practices that make up his technologized mode of authorship.

Lucas's logic of preproduction provides a way to understand his commitment to technological advances in filmmaking. He has long been considered the kind of filmmaker who dances on the cutting edge of technology, like other techno-auteurs such as Cameron, Zemeckis, Joe

Dante, and to some extent Francis Ford Coppola (who himself is considered a pioneer of previsualization methods in films such as *One from the Heart* [1982] and *The Outsiders* [1983]). Like Zemeckis and Coppola, Lucas's "futurist" production practices seem strangely at odds with his equally strong dedication to nostalgic material. (Zemeckis is a good example of this; his *Back to the Future* [1985] employed special effects to travel in time to the 1950s, while his digitally animated *Polar Express* [2004] was much publicized for the performance capture used to illustrate a children's book whose period details are also drawn from the fifties.) Unlike them, however, Lucas's mid-career output centered on revisiting his previous movies. He continued to tweak and rework the Original Trilogy, while the prequels filled in gaps of *Star Wars* prehistory, rather than forging ahead into new territory (as many fans had pleaded) or breaking away from the *Star Wars* universe entirely (as Lucas, who has often professed a wish to return to his roots as an experimental filmmaker, claims to want). He seems, in short, trapped in his own past, even as he pushes into the future.

Perhaps these are symptoms of a previz mind-set—one that refuses to see any text as closed or inviolate, and consequently is drawn into endless revision and refinement, hypnotized by the possibilities of a text's "becoming." Perhaps they are symptoms of a digital mind-set, in which all texts are merely firmware updates of others, rendered in higher or lower resolution: *Star Wars 1.0, 2.0,* and so on. Or perhaps previz and digitality are related in ways that we are only beginning to see, as an emergent transmedia studies begins to reveal, in finer detail, both the unique predilections and inherited tendencies of this phenomenon. In any case, I want to suggest by way of closing that Lucas's strategies may bear fruit that even he could not have foreseen. When future generations encounter his work, they will be likely to do so unimpeded by the objections and frustrations that characterize Lucas's contemporary audience. With Disney's resumption of new *Star Wars* episodes, fans who resisted the changes in their beloved 1970s trilogy are being superseded by audiences for whom the proper order of the first six *Star Wars* films will always have been 1, 2, 3, 4, 5, 6, rather than (as it appears from our vantage point in history) 4, 5, 6, 1, 2, 3. For tomorrow's viewers, the leaden and derivative prequels—far from representing a corruption of some original artistic flowering—will lead *into* that flowering, pulling an "immaculate reality" of Lucas's authorship from the "used universe" his later years created. In this way, Lucas might be said to have created a scenario that endlessly restages his own birth as an auteur—reminting himself, even after death, as an original, erasing analog history to substitute instead a pleasing digital myth of authorship.

3

Chains of Evidence

Augmented Performance before and after the Digital

If all of cinema, as Christian Metz asserts, is in some sense a special effect, one place where this manifests most obviously is in the augmented performers who increasingly populate our screens.[1] By augmented performers, I mean those whose presence on screen depends in part or whole on special effects: most recently, characters celebrated as much for the technological achievements they represent as for the emotional believability and psychological depth of the acting on display. Sonny (Alan Tudyk), the titular lead of *I, Robot* (Alex Proyas, 2004), Dr. Manhattan (Billy Crudup) in *Watchmen* (Zack Snyder, 2009), and the resurrected corpses of Peter Cushing (as Grand Moff Tarkin) and a young Carrie Fisher (as Princess Leia Organa) in *Rogue One* (Gareth Edwards, 2016) all speak powerfully of the way special effects continue to be pushed in ways that encroach on being human—a concern that, as Lisa Bode observes, has become intertwined with the apparent demise of photochemical, film-reel cinema and its replacement by a digital substitute.[2] In addition to Bode, synthespians have been read astutely by Dan North, Angela Ndalianis, Lisa Purse, and others as figures who trouble the foundational indexicality of cinema.[3] Less noticed has been the way in which such bodies, because of their unique nature, travel across media to become as integral to fantastic franchises as the material hardware and branded status of their storyworlds discussed in Chapters 1 and 2.

These intersecting tendencies of augmented performers—their ever-growing prominence on screen and the way they extend across transmedia franchises—are perhaps most evident in the Marvel Cinematic Universe (MCU), born officially with the release of Jon Favreau's *Iron Man* in 2008. The launch of the MCU marked an accelerated production of superhero content across an array of movies, videogames, and comics imagined in serialized and branching form, integrated by tightly intertextual narratives and a consistent, persistent world. Unlike the Star Wars universe, it was neither composed of mythological rethinkings of a nostalgicized pop culture archive, nor much like the Star Trek universe's ship-in-a-bottle Federation in miniature. The diegesis anchoring the MCU was much more like ours, mapped onto the present moment and hence running in historical "realtime," with one exception: the physical reality of superheroes. Based on contemporary digital methodologies that effectively mesh the control afforded by animation with the aleatory liveness and emotive weight of unmediated human acting, many of these characters are obvious creations of special effects—Hulk, Iron Man, and the Vision—while erasures of wirework and stunt double replacement operate less obtrusively to contribute the unusual skills and physicalities of Black Widow, Hawkeye, and Captain America. In both cases, the bodies hide something in plain sight, inviting and deflecting attention in equal measure. Chief among the latter elisions is a clear history of the augmented performer's predecessors and tributaries in analog media such as cinema and television.

Augmented screen performance has always depended not just on the magical technologies at play within it, but on the perceived presence of a human force, an individual personality, that speaks "through" the special effects. Such performances reach back to a panoply of tricks and techniques born of the analog era, including the full-body mechanical armor worn by C-3PO (Anthony Daniels) in *Star Wars* (George Lucas, 1977), the stop-motion-animated ED-209 in *Robocop* (Paul Verhoeven, 1987), the demonic-possession makeup worn by Linda Blair in *The Exorcist* (William Friedkin, 1973), the giant monster suit of *Gojira* (Ishirō Honda, 1954), and Jack Pierce's iconic monster makeup creations in the classic Universal horror films of the 1930s and 1940s. Like superheroes, monsters and aliens and fantasy races are bodies we encounter already knowing and accepting as uncanny: they mitigate certain problems of acceptance by presenting themselves as already artificial—or better, as partly artificial and partly real, their hybridity as overbearingly visible as a fetish. Like all modern special effects, their hybridity and uncanniness are read in overdetermined fashion as digital, or as posing the "problem" of the digital. Yet like the invented worlds explored in Chapters 1 and 2, the artificial bodies that lend these spaces their all-important qualities of empathy and parasociality are rooted in an analog past. They partake in three histories simultaneously: animation, puppetry, and ghost projection; cuts and doubles and substitutions; and live, affective, believable performance. Viewed as phenomena of the present, the hypernoticeable special effects body may indeed elide awareness of the many other visual interventions at work all in our media environment, from the Oculus Rift and its promise of augmented reality, to digital makeup applied in realtime to smooth the blemishes of age. Viewed historically, however, they are about the continued forging of a "chain of evidence" by which special effects have always alchemicalized performance.

This chapter explores the origins of the contemporary special-effects body in animation, stop motion, prosthetics, and animatronics, using an approach focused on performance pipelined through the body as a generator and guarantor of authenticity. It argues that although we have passed a point where such bodies, perhaps due to their very number, are greatly commented on as achievements in themselves, they continue to invite appreciation as objects laden with import about the digital/analog shift. (In fact, they may never be free of this fundamental significatory freight.) Understanding such bodies involves thinking about how they have been put together, as we peer closely at their manufacture in part to feel awed, in positive and negative senses of the word, at the technological magic of such characters. But as this more visible drama of the special-effects body plays out, we may think less about the process by which such bodies live on over time, reproducing across texts. The fascinatory horizon promised by the augmented performer is, like the other phenomena examined in this book, anchored in a long and evolving set of practices—indeed, one of the oldest "animating" principles of cinema itself: the illusion of life. But bodies produced through special effects have an additional quality of liveliness about them, for they work across time to extend the performative lifespans of their characters, a durative dimension related closely to their propensity for transmedial travel.

Sheep and Goats: Approaching Performance through Special Effects

Special effects are often described as "performing" in some way: in moments of engineered spectacle such as the early-cinema attraction, which play self-consciously on cinema's power to manipulate reality; within certain film genres where they stage fantastic events and provide iconography demanded by convention; and as aggressive showstoppers in themselves, rupturing the orderly flow of narrative by bursting forth as a kind of spectacular insurrection. But these understandings are quite different from the kind of performances we usually talk about in relation to movies—in a word, *performers*: characters expressing emotions, framed by a story that imparts meaning to their behaviors, choices, and desires. Special effects may at first seem antithetical to our conception of acting, which has come, at least in traditional filmmaking, to mean the impression of actual emotional life and importance of accepting the narrative world as (provisionally) real. At a more fundamental level, performers tie the screen world to its profilmic source, constantly announcing the existence of real people whose actions were, at some point in space and time, captured by objective mechanisms such as cameras and sound equipment. There is Dorothy Gale, the farm girl transported by twister from Kansas to a magical land, but behind Dorothy there is Judy Garland, the young Hollywood star, who plays her—and behind both there is Frances Gumm, born in 1922 in Grand Rapids, Minnesota. Tripling the already dual identities of an acting situation, what we accept as authentic performance underscores our belief in an entire medium. By this standard, special effects that break the connection between screen and reality, representing things that never actually took place in quite the way they appear to, seem to belong to another register entirely.

But in contemplating the hybridity of Garland's Dorothy, we should not forget that *The Wizard of Oz* (Victor Fleming, 1939) is also populated by all manner of creatures whose presence and behavior consists, in part or whole, of trompe l'oeil. One hundred and twenty-four dwarfs in heavy costume and makeup play the Munchkins of Munchkinland,[4] while still others wear monkey suits (complete with battery-operated flapping wings) and fly on wire riggings.[5] In long shots, the Witch's army of henchmen is "played" by miniature rubber dolls, six inches long, suspended from piano wire. Talking apple trees, manufactured from chicken wire, foam rubber, and liquid latex, are manipulated from within by members of the prop department.[6] Witches' entrances and exits are assisted by pyrotechnic explosions and superimposed glowing

CHAINS OF EVIDENCE | 111

bubbles. Like the fearsome, large-craniumed visage of the Wizard of Oz "himself" (actually a model, filmed in advance and rear-projected onto a cloud of steam[7]), these performances all have a dual nature: they are eye-catching illusions, but also characters within a story, inhabitants of a diegetic world. And like the Wizard, in back of each stands "a man behind a curtain"—or, more accurately, a crew of artists and technicians, designers and engineers, whose off-stage activity translates into the presence of fantastic characters.

At first glance, such performers seem simple to distinguish from the human beings with whom they interact. We do not consider flying monkeys to be the same kind of characters as the Tin Man (Jack Haley), the Scarecrow (Ray Bolger), or the Cowardly Lion (Bert Lahr), even though all three achieve their screen identities with the help of similarly elaborate costumes: silver paste, buckram, and leather; straw bundles and a rubber mask painted to look like burlap; a lion-skin bodysuit complete with clawed mittens.[8] Talking trees are clearly a kind of machination, while the Wicked Witch is just as clearly a real person—Margaret Hamilton—wearing "a false nose, a jutting chin, and a horribly ugly wart with large black hairs protruding from it," in addition to which she is covered with green paint.[9] Despite the artifice that undergirds nearly every performance in *The Wizard of Oz*, we have little trouble drawing a line between illusion and actor, technology and talent. In drawing that line, however, we collude in a particular understanding of the cinematic medium as divided between that which is real and that which is artificial, using special effects—in this case, performance—as a measuring stick.

The limits of such classificatory schemes are even more strained in the case of Peter Jackson's Middle Earth movies, consisting of the trilogies *The Lord of the Rings* (2001–2003) and *The Hobbit* (2012–2014). These six films, based on J. R. R. Tolkien's fantasy saga, boast among their large casts not a single performance untouched in some way by visual or practical special effects. The films' setting, Middle Earth, is populated by numerous inhuman races, including Hobbits, Elves, Dwarves, Orcs, Goblins, Ents, and Trolls. In some cases, human beings play these roles, wearing heavy makeup and prosthetics; in others, computer-generated figures perform the parts; in still others, animatronic puppets take the stage. The wizard Gandalf (Ian McKellen) towers over the Hobbit Frodo

(Elijah Wood), requiring both actors to be continually resized through a battery of techniques that include forced perspective, duplicate sets and props built to different scales, body doubles, and bluescreen compositing. Huge armies collide on the battlefield, each warrior an artificially intelligent digital "agent" following its own set of environmental cues, responding to simulated sights and sounds in its vicinity. The distinctions grow even more subtle: from one shot to another, a character might be replaced by a digital stunt double, or a human double with the original actor's face digitally painted onto his head. (At times the double takes over mid-frame, substituted without a cut and match-moved precisely to the original actor's position.) The movements of Cave Trolls are based on motion-capture of Jackson and channeled through animators, while digital soldiers draw on fighting styles performed by combat experts and programmed into a menu of behavioral selections.

Amid this chaos of borrowings, translations, substitutions, and simulations, we may still cling to the idea that certain performances in *The Lord of the Rings* and *The Hobbit* are real while others remain mere tricks. As with *The Wizard of Oz*, we consider Gandalf to be performed by Ian McKellen, while his evil nemesis Sauron, a fiery eyeball at the top of a black tower, is just as surely the result of special effects. And while the artists at New Zealand's WETA who created the vicious Balrog might receive awards for technical excellence, the Balrog itself is unlikely to be nominated for Best Supporting Actor. One performance in the Middle Earth films that did receive serious Oscar buzz, however, stands out as perfectly suspended between actorly turn and special effect: Gollum, the emaciated wretch whose desire to possess the Ring of Power drives him through a complex character arc. Gollum begins *The Lord of the Rings* as a malevolent mystery, becomes for a time the troubled traveling companion of protagonists Frodo and Sam, and finally betrays his friends (and concludes the story) in an ecstatic act of self-immolation. Gollum's psychological and affective multidimensionality parallels the complex layers of manufacture that went into his performance. At Gollum's core is a well-publicized performance by Andy Serkis, who provides the creature's voice and also physically acted out many of his actions, both on location with other actors and alone on a motion-capture stage. Gollum's exterior is a blatantly uncanny design digitally overlaid on Serkis's performance. But it would be a mistake to say simply that Serkis provided the raw material and that software did the rest, for Gollum's performance sprang just as much from drawn and painted illustrations, clay sculptures, and frame-by-frame animation of the Disney variety, encompassing a range of old-school and cutting-edge technologies and evolving in continual dialogue with Serkis, Jackson, and the films' screenwriters.

Gollum is a useful test case for thinking about the creation of characters through special effects, not because he resolves the technology-versus-performer debate, but because his problematically hybridized nature reveals the shaky premise on which the debate is built. When scrutinized closely, that is, no special-effects performance is completely free of expressive traits—or else it could hardly be called a performance. All of these traits come of necessity from somewhere (i.e., are performed by someone, whether it is a voice actor, an animator, a modelmaker, or other artists and technicians). Similarly, no natural performance is without its ingredient of artifice, if only in the sense that photographic technology and cinematographic grammar combine to present the illusion of a real person on screen. Gollum, in short, provides a means of deconstructing our conventional wisdom about performance and authenticity, and hence about the way movies themselves deliver the world to us.

Although otherwise far afield from my discussion, the famous scale developed by the sex researcher Alfred Kinsey is helpful here as a conceptual tool. Writing about statistical differences in sexual orientation, Kinsey argues that "the world is not to be divided into sheep and goats. It is a fundamental of taxonomy that nature rarely deals with discrete categories. . . . The living world is a continuum in each and every one of its aspects."[10] In place of these ironclad distinctions, Kinsey proposes a sliding scale, ranging from 0 ("Exclusively Heterosexual") to 6 ("Exclusively Homosexual"), on which most people show up as a blending of characteristics. Similarly, I propose that one way to understand performance in light of special effects is through a sliding scale of artificiality, one sensitive to the specific materials, personnel, and skills that go into bringing a given character "to life." An actor wearing a false nose might rank as a 1 or a 2 ("Mostly Natural"), while a creature achieved through stop-motion animation might clock in at a 5 or a 6 ("Mostly Artificial"), depending on the degree to which the performance has been augmented by means not exclusively within the actor's own physical body. But while these examples mark clear "limit cases" of augmented performance, it is harder to categorize acting turns like those of Boris Karloff in *Frankenstein* (James Whale, 1933), Christopher Reeve in *Superman* (Richard Donner, 1978), John Hurt in *The Elephant Man* (David Lynch, 1980), and Jeremy Irons in *Dead Ringers* (David Cronenberg, 1988) without taking into account the prosthetic makeup, bluescreen traveling mattes, and digital compositing that gave these performances their expressive and aesthetic impact. The challenge is to map out a theory of augmented performance while avoiding the Manichean trap of dividing the screen into real people and clever tricks—into sheep and goats.

A History of Augmented Performance

From the moment the medium of cinema emerged, special effects have been used in a range of registers and levels of noticeability to augment, and even to build from the ground up, movie performances. Stop-motion and animatronic constructs such as King Kong and E.T., besides lending their names to the films in which they appeared, gave convincing and emotionally moving performances that turned them into global icons. "Famous monsters" anchor innumerable cinematic narratives, including the froglike Martians and their manta-ray spacecraft in *The War of the Worlds* (Byron Haskin, 1953), the insatiable jelly of *The Blob* (Irvin Yeaworth, 1958), the shark in *Jaws* (Steven Spielberg, 1975), the biomechanical xenomorph in *Alien* (Ridley Scott, 1979), and the giant snake in *Anaconda* (Luis Llosa, 1997). In cartoon form, characters such as Mickey Mouse and Donald Duck—combinations of hand-painted cels, voice performance, and bodily forms borrowed equally from animal and human references—have long been screen fixtures. My purpose in this section is to explore the roots of augmented performance by examining the ways in which expressive attributes (character, emotion, psychology, and agency) have been "encoded" into the appearance and activity of artificial screen bodies. This encoding can be read as a kind of *transferred performance* in which the labor of special-effects designers and craftspeople speaks through the conduit of the technological body. As a consequence, discourses around augmented performance often foreground the technical personnel involved in their creation. This suggests a kind of parallel "star system" of effects labor arising as though to fill the gap left by the artificial performer's erasure of human reference—the sense, that is, of a single actor tied to the production of a fantastic screen body.

The earliest augmented performance recorded on film was created four months before Louis and Auguste Lumière first demonstrated their *cinématographe* to a Paris audience:

> On 28 August 1895, camera operator Alfred Clarke filmed a re-creation of the execution of Mary, Queen of Scots at the Edison studio in New Jersey. To create the illusion of a royal beheading, Clarke first filmed the Queen as she knelt before the executioner. After the axe was raised, the camera was stopped so that the actress could leave the scene and be replaced by a dummy. When filming resumed, the axe was dropped and the Queen's head appeared to be separated from its shoulders.[11]

Clarke's relatively primitive act of substitution predated by more than a year Georges Méliès's accidental "discovery," in the Place de l'Opéra, of the *arrêt* or "stop-action" trick.[12] As James Naremore points out, it was the first special effect; it also marked the birth of a cinematic practice of optical and mechanical manipulation to augment human performance—in this case delegating what would otherwise have been a lethal decapitation onto a submissive and deformable alternate: a body that was also a technology.[13] Exotic and exceptional though it may seem, the use of trickery to "place actors in settings that [are] too distant, too dangerous, or otherwise impractical," or, alternatively, to create beings whose diegetic existence constitutes "a magical, supernatural, or otherwise physically impossible feat" has long been a standard tool in cinema's repertoire.[14] The history of augmented performance is thus coextensive with that of special effects and of the cinematic medium itself. It might not be far-fetched to suggest that all three share an essential principle: using illusion to impart life to that which is lifeless, whether in feigning natural processes, crafting mechanisms that gesture and emote, or giving apparent motion to a succession of still images.

That the emerging medium so quickly pressed artificial performers into service is less surprising when one considers the tradition of magic shows out of which early cinema grew. Erik Barnouw's *The Magician and the Cinema* explores this connection in detail,[15] while Michele Pierson, in her study of the discourses and cultures surrounding illusionistic entertainment, identifies an even wider array of nineteenth-century public amusements that "enchanted audiences with their wonder-working special effects."[16] These included "phantasmagoria and magic shows, pantomime, exhibitions of new technologies, and science lectures and exhibitions."[17] Although many of these precursor forms featured animated bodies such as ghosts, animals, and automatons—as well as inanimate "stand-ins" capable of being levitated or sawn in half—augmented performance itself has not received much academic attention as an element distinct from (or perhaps marking the apogee of) precinematic spectacle. One exception is Matthew Solomon's essay "Twenty-five Heads under One Hat," which examines the tradition of "quick-change" by professional illusionists. These showmen, Solomon explains, "Specialized in adeptly performed transformations such as quick-change artistry, the rapid alteration of character through costume changes; chapeaugraphy, the manipulation of a piece of felt to form different hats; and shadowgraphy, the use of the hands to create human and animal figures in a beam of light."[18] Solomon goes on to argue that, while the art of quick-change enjoyed a brief vogue in pre-1900s film, "performed metamorphoses seem to have been largely superseded by technological transformations in film not long after the turn of the century."[19] Dependent as they were on real time—the impact of their performance a function of speed and unbroken flow—the "protean artists" at the heart of Solomon's study may indeed have encountered competition from optical magic, that is, special effects. Duration was fragmented by the camera's ability to shoot discontinuously, and its ability to skew spatial relationships by staging action at varying distances from the lens enabled impossible scenes and actions to be composited in-camera. These two hallmarks of the medium, more than anything else, sundered the contract of authenticity that formerly had bound theatrical performers to their audiences.

But Solomon may be too quick in arguing that optical effects "superseded" performed metamorphoses. A more inclusive model would describe the complex interaction between levels and layers of trickery that evolved in the first decade of film. As live feats of quick-change mutated within the new medium, filmgoers witnessed attractions like

Indian Rubber Head (1902), in which Méliès used a split-screen matte to duplicate himself.

> The viewer sees Méliès in the role of a scientist, placing a duplicate of his own head on a table and beginning to inflate it with a bellows. An assistant takes over and enthusiastically pumps air into the head, which grows enormous, pulling distended faces until finally exploding. The disembodied head was added in the second exposure, and enlarged by wheeling Méliès closer to the camera in a specially constructed carriage.[20]

Renowned as the first master of special effects, Méliès employed a range of methods, many of them adapted from magic shows at his own Théâtre Robert-Houdin, to craft and populate his "artificially arranged scenes."[21] These included working automata, superimposed flying fairies, and, as mentioned in the Introduction, one of the most widely recognized images from the era: the pie-faced Man in the Moon, squinting around a rocket shell stuck in its eye.[22]

The aesthetic and technical elements of early cinema's lifelike artifice demonstrated a lineage going back even earlier than the magic shows and phantasmagoria explored by Barnouw and Pierson. Many were descendants of the large-scale automata—"machines that seemed to move spontaneously and of their own volition"—that originated in Alexandria, Egypt, and enjoyed a resurgence during the seventeenth and eighteenth centuries. As described in Barbara Maria Stafford and Frances Terpak's *Devices of Wonder*, the most popular automata included a flute player, a drummer, and various waterfowl, all of which performed actions that simulated the beings on which they were based. (A duck built by Jacques de Vaucanson in the 1730s "paddled in the water, shook its head and neck, greedily took grain from an outstretched hand, made motions of drinking and digesting, and marvelled its audience most of all by expelling suitably colored pellets as droppings."[23]) In 1848, the French magician Jean-Eugène Robert-Houdin built a mechanical trapeze artist with whom he interacted during shows. Actually operated by an offstage assistant through pistons and wires, the trapezist Antonio Diavolo indirectly prefigured the team-coordinated animatronic creatures of late twentieth-century films.[24]

As the fledgling medium of cinema was digesting and assimilating its forbears in the theatrical, magical, and mechanical arts, optical tricks unique to film were being used in combination with those arts to put new kinds of artificial bodies on the screen. Two lines of development dominated the period from 1900 to 1920: hand-drawn animation and its three-dimensional counterpart, stop-motion animation. As these forms evolved, they produced very different kinds of imagery, which were put to use in very different genres. Yet the techniques and principles at their heart were the same: manipulating whatever was in front of the camera one frame at a time, resulting in fluid motion when the film was run through a projector.

From the start, animation concerned itself with imparting lifelike motion and recognizable behavioral characteristics to unusual bodies. As Donald Crafton observes in his study of the form's early years, "The first animated films were concerned with making objects appear to move with a mysterious life of their own."[25] In 1906, J. Stuart Blackton produced comical stick figures that sprang to life after being drawn by an artist's hand (pictured within the frame), while the French caricaturist Émile Cohl created a series of stick-figure films between 1908 and 1910.[26] Cohl's work in particular—"surreal animations, in which fantastic drawings metamorphosed into one another with no apparent logic"—gestured toward the quick-change artists of whom Solomon writes.[27] But the first animator to produce a "star" character was Winsor McCay, a print cartoonist known for the *Little Nemo* series that ran in the *New York Herald* from 1905 to 1926. McCay's *Gertie the Dinosaur* (1914) was "the first [cartoon] to feature a character with a personality."[28] In public screenings, McCay would stand before the screen on which his animated brontosaurus was being projected, interacting with the artwork in a carefully timed routine. This teamwork brought Gertie's character into sharp comic relief through a kind of living dialectic. Describing a typical presentation by McCay and his "lovable but cantankerous creature," Crafton writes: "The brontosaurus emerges, shy at first and aware of the audience, but she quickly warms up to the performance. Her personality is a cross between a trained circus elephant and a frisky puppy. Gertie is tame, but not domesticated. She even snaps at McCay when he tries to get her to salute the audience."[29] Adding to the sense of Gertie as a living being were traits of physical mass and dimensionality:

Gertie's ponderous weight is suggested as she shifts rhythmically back and forth on her feet. When she kneels to drink, the ground sags beneath her enormous mass. We see her abdominal muscles work to suck in the water, as her stomach slowly expands. The up-and-down rhythm of her breathing can be seen when she lies on her side. Anthropomorphic qualities contribute to her personality, as when she daintily scratches an itch with the tip of her agile tail. In minutes McCay convinces the audience that he has resurrected a tangible and lovable animal—a triumphant moment for the animator as life giver.[30]

Drawn as flat artwork, then filmed as a succession of still frames, attributes of both physical and psychological realism were carefully built into Gertie (who "even shed tears when admonished by McCay"[31]). This encoding constitutes an early example of the chain of evidence tying artificial bodies to real-world reference—a practice that would, in decades to come, take on increasingly complex form through technologies such as rotoscoping and motion capture.

By the 1920s, a new hand-drawn star had arisen: Felix the Cat, created by Otto Messmer and Pat Sullivan. Appearing in a series of films as well as printed comic strips and in the form of dolls and other tie-ins, Felix was, by 1926, "perhaps the most popular screen character, living or animated, except [Charlie] Chaplin."[32] Crafton points out that Felix's appeal stemmed less from some revolutionary property of the animation involved (which was actually rather crude and jerky) than from the character's identity, expressed over a body of work:

> Only by viewing dozens of Felix films does one come to understand that Felix's special attraction arose not from the clever gags (although they were very important), but primarily from the consistency and individuality of the character. Unavoidably one sees Felix as a living being. Felix . . . is an index of a real personality. After meeting Otto Messmer, one realizes that the personality is that of the creator.[33]

This discourse of the animator-as-actor—giving a performance through the medium of an artificial body—was even more prominent in the other strand of early animation, stop motion, which made use of the *arrêt* to impart movement to objects, evolving its own set of protocols, creators, and stars. Méliès experimented with dimensional animation in an 1898 advertisement, making wooden blocks stack themselves into the name of a company. Over the next decade, multiple filmmakers (including Blackton, who also worked in hand-drawn animation) produced short films featuring moving toys, dancing dolls, and, in 1907, six marching teddy bears for Edwin S. Porter's *The Teddy Bears*. But in a preview of the shift in digital imaging that would take place ninety years later, the animation of toys soon gave way to the animation of more explicitly anthropomorphic bodies.[34] In 1913, Willis O'Brien crafted two miniature boxers out of clay and used stop-motion techniques to stage a prizefight between them. He moved on to short (one- to five-minute) animations of apemen, cavemen, and dinosaurs, using articulated puppets "crudely fashioned from wooden skeletons with soft clay bodies."[35] Refining his models as well as the painstaking and time-consuming labor by which they were given motion, he contributed special effects of "living" dinosaurs to *The Lost World* (Harry O. Hoyt, 1925). The unexpected financial success of *Lost World* led O'Brien to spend many years developing an even more dinosaur-intensive production called *Creation*, which never got made. However, many of its key sequences (and even some of its models) were salvaged when they were incorporated into Merian C. Cooper and Ernest Schoedsack's 1933 production of *King Kong*.[36]

Described as "one of the best-known characters ever produced by the Hollywood cinema, and a figure repeatedly activated in art and mass culture, both in the United States and abroad,"[37] King Kong was in actuality a pair of miniatures (or perhaps three; the record is spotty), crafted from cotton, latex rubber, and rabbit fur over an articulated armature of steel and aluminum [Figure 3.1]. The Kong puppets were designed and constructed by Marcel Delgado and animated by O'Brien, who is credited in most accounts with Kong's performance and responsibility for the overall ingenuity of the film's special effects. Originally, the story concept had called only for a "Giant Terror Gorilla" to be featured in a handful of battle scenes in the midst of a story about a New York actress's rescue from a primitive jungle island.[38] But as artwork, engineering designs, and animated test footage accumulated, producers began to shape the narrative around the gorilla as a main character. This was in part due to their growing confidence that

Figure 3.1. Willis O'Brien animating *King Kong* (1933). Publicity stills such as this worked discursively to secure the direct, performative relationship between animator and model.

Delgado's mechanism was sophisticated enough to generate the range of emotions and behaviors necessary to a complex character:

> Holes were drilled into the aluminum skull and threaded with thin, bendable wires. Lips, eyebrows, and a nose made from rubber were then attached to these wires. When the features were moved into different positions, the wires would hold them in place, which allowed the animators to create Kong's facial expressions. Eyeballs made of glass were set into sockets in the skull. Delgado painted liquid latex over the skull and features to create Kong's face, which was then detailed with bits of cotton that were also painted with liquid latex. Finally, Delgado glued strips of pruned rabbit fur to Kong's body to create his pelt, which was then smoothed down with glycerin.[39]

Kong's fur was constantly disarrayed during miniature photography by O'Brien's hands as they pushed and pulled the armature, building the body's motion in tiny increments. The result, when the finished film was shown, was a constant rippling of the coat, as though blown by a wind. This side effect of the animation process became part of Kong's overall characterization, however, when an executive at RKO, watching test footage, exclaimed that "Kong is angry—his fur is bristling!"[40] This suggests that even unplanned accidents of Kong's manufactured nature were retroactively read, by sympathetic audiences, as details of the character's psychology and inner life.

Kong bore Willis O'Brien's fingerprints in another, more figurative sense. In animating the gorilla, O'Brien left a signature of himself in the form of expressive behaviors—tics, emotions, and bits of business—that add up to make Kong a unique screen presence. "O'Brien's sense of humor," according to visual effects supervisor Randy Cook, who worked on Peter Jackson's 2005 update of *King Kong*, "is part of what imbued Kong with his personality, which is so important and sets him apart from being just an unimaginative rampaging monster."[41] Using an affectionate nickname for her husband, O'Brien's wife has said that "*King Kong* was Obie. It was his personality. I could just see Obie in Kong's every movement, every gesture."[42] Several scenes in the film seem to embody O'Brien's predilections and sense of drama. A battle between Kong and a tyrannosaurus features feints and sucker punches that speak of the animator's background as a pugilist. More central to Kong's impact are moments of humor and pathos, such as the "elasmosaur sequence" set in a misty cave where Kong sets down Ann Darrow (Fay Wray), just before being attacked by a snakelike creature. In order to show Kong being caught unaware, O'Brien had to find a logical reason for the gorilla's distraction. Cook comments,

> The next cut is Kong with his back turned. So O'Brien staged something that motivated his being turned away. You can't really see it unless you stop-frame it, but what it is is he's bending down, and with pinky extended, he's picking a flower and smelling it. And assumedly, he's going to be giving it to Ann. . . . It's not even something for the audience to notice, it's just something for the actor—or in this case, Kong—to use as motivation.[43]

Along with the performance of the stop-motion model itself, several other elements contribute to Kong's illusion of life. Elaborate sound design gives the animated gorilla an impression of mass and momentum as it crashes through the jungle; sound engineers distorted and remixed animal roars to provide Kong's voice. (A hallmark of augmented performance, organic sources have been used since the advent of synchronized sound to boost the authenticity of artificial bodies, from the vocal talent used in cartoons to more subtle examples such as dumping dog food from a can to create the squishy sounds of the shapeshifting robot in *Terminator 2: Judgment Day* [James Cameron, 1991].) Visually, a number of innovative techniques blended Kong with live-action elements. Traveling mattes placed actors into the same frame with the model; previously filmed footage of actors was projected onto small screens, cunningly framed with foliage, on the tabletop "stage" where Kong performed. Finally, rear-projection screens were used extensively so that actors could react in precisely timed ways to the animated Kong and other creatures—scrambling away from Kong's grasping fingers, or tossing a grenade, which then explodes in front of a stampeding dinosaur. Much like McCay's preplanned exchanges with Gertie, the synthesis of human and animated life within a theatrical frame lent verisimilitude to the artificial body.

Special-effects-based performances continued to evolve over the following decades, with the characters created by stage- and movie-craft finding new dramatic and generic homes. The 1930s and 1940s saw an almost machinic generation of fantastic bodies in the work of Universal Studios. Overseen by producer Carl Laemmle Jr., this output included *Frankenstein, Dracula* (Tod Browning, 1931), *The Mummy* (Karl Freund, 1932), *The Invisible Man* (James Whale, 1933), and *The Wolf Man* (George Waggner, 1941). In these films and their chains of sequels, elaborate makeup and occasional optical effects augmented human performers in the title roles: lap dissolves and makeup changes assisted Lon Chaney Jr.'s transformation into the Wolf Man, while Claude Rains's Invisible Man was achieved by filming the actor separately with his head and hands wrapped in black velvet, then matting the footage onto a background plate to show a headless suit of clothes moving around the room. As a result of this shared workload between performer and effects, the public identity of the Universal monsters tended to remain anchored in the actors who played them, such as Rains, Chaney, and Karloff.

This would change with the advent of the 1950s "creature features." During a period when the movie industry sought through spectacular means to recapture an audience drifting toward television, artificially performed roles were dramatically circumscribed by the cost and difficulty of their production. The more exotic a screen body, the less screen time it occupied, with a corresponding lack of depth in characterization. Hence, augmented performances tended to be confined to nonspeaking parts, often those of monsters or predators. The actors inside the suits—or the offstage technicians who manipulated the claws and tentacles—received less attention, while the spectacular creatures paradoxically assumed prominent positions on posters and publicity materials. Rubber suits, full-sized puppets, and heavy makeup created monsters who popped out at intervals to menace their prey in movies such as *The Thing from Another World* (Christian Nyby, 1951), *Creature from the Black Lagoon* (Jack Arnold, 1954), *This Island Earth* (Joseph M. Newman and Jack Arnold, 1955), *Kronos* (Kurt Neumann, 1957), and *It! The Terror from Beyond Space* (Edward L. Cahn, 1958). Sometimes the performance was entirely given by a mechanism or a special effect, such as the giant ants in *Them!* (Gordon Douglas, 1954) or the Id monster in *Forbidden Planet* (Fred M. Wilcox, 1956)—the latter using cel animation to produce a glowing, crackling creature of pure mental energy that became visible only when interacting with force-field fences and blaster bolts.

The 1950s cycle in augmented performance centered emphatically on the science-fiction genre. Horror films were at that point undergoing a literal form of domestication in which monstrosity was made all the more terrible for being unseen, half-glimpsed, or disguised as ordinary human appearance. Part of a larger turn toward psychological horror that saw its exemplar in *Psycho* (Alfred Hitchcock, 1960), this meant that "monsters" like the pod people in *Invasion of the Body Snatchers* (Don Siegel, 1956) could root their uncanniness in what we might call "augmented augmented performance": that is, a kind of acting in which outwardly normal appearances are offset by dehumanized, mechanical behavior. By contrast, science fiction, with its thematic emphasis on technology, made it possible for the same notion of mechanization to manifest explicitly in robot and android characters such as Gort in *The Day the Earth Stood Still* (Robert Wise, 1951), Tobor in *Tobor the Great* (Lee Sholem, 1954), and *Forbidden Planet*'s Robby the Robot, discussed at greater length in the next chapter. All three were played by men encased in suits of varying mechanical sophistication—nearly robots or cyborgs themselves.

But if technological limitations robbed artificial performers of the fifties from the psychological complexity they had enjoyed at Universal in the thirties and forties, the same technologies were evolving to allow the mute (or inarticulate) monster to compensate in facial or bodily expressiveness for what was missing in dialogue and nuanced interaction with the rest of the cast. One of the better-known creators of this type of augmented performance was Ray Harryhausen, whose career spanned from the 1950s to his death in 2013. Through the puppets he manipulated frame by frame, Harryhausen greatly expanded the function and generic place of characters created with stop-motion animation. An early fan of *King Kong* and protégé of Willis O'Brien, Harryhausen consolidated the idea of the animator as a kind of performer, "acting" through the intermediary of an articulated puppet. His analysis of the process by which the animator's traits are transmuted into convincing performance is worth quoting at length:

> I did discover [from taking acting classes] that acting was important to understanding emotions and reactions, which I went on to instill in my models. I have always wanted audiences to feel sorry for the creatures when they are being destroyed. . . . When working on *Mighty Joe Young*, I would strive for compassion in the creature, and would sit like a gorilla on the floor, acting out key scenes and timing each movement with a stopwatch. How long it would take to move my arms from one point to another, trying to synchronize it so that it looked natural and convey emotion when it came to converting the action into the animated model. The ability to instill character into creatures, no matter how alien the creature, is a key element of the animator's art. A movement of the hand, a turn of the head, the furrowing of a brow at the correct moment, these were all acted out before animation began, and all were due in some part to those teachers who attempted to teach me the finer points of acting.[44]

Starting with ultimately sympathetic monsters such as the giant octopus in *It Came from Beneath the Sea* (Robert Gordon, 1955) and the Venusian "Ymir" in *20 Million Miles to Earth* (Nathan H. Juran, 1957), Harryhausen went on to found a type of mythological adventure film in which the fantastic beings of legend were entirely performed through stop-motion animation: *The Seventh Voyage of Sinbad* (Nathan H. Juran, 1958), *Jason and the Argonauts* (Don Chaffey, 1963), *The Golden Voyage of Sinbad* (Gordon Hessler, 1974), *Sinbad and the Eye of the Tiger* (Sam Wanamaker, 1977), and *Clash of the Titans* (Desmond Davis, 1981). Like O'Brien before him, Harryhausen's innovations were not confined to the artificial bodies he created, but included methods of blending those bodies with live-action plates and actors. He is credited specifically with the development of a process called DynaMation, in which a combination of rear projection and mattes are used to "sandwich" stop-motion puppets into previously filmed footage.

Special effects continued to drive unique performances into the 1970s and early 1980s, for the most part extending techniques developed in previous decades, but using them in quantities made possible by changes in budgetary priorities as well as growing sophistication in preproduction planning, as discussed in the Introduction and Chapter 2. The various aliens and droids in *Star Wars*, for example, were the product of costuming, propmaking, and prosthetic makeup, while the title characters in *Alien*, *E.T.: The Extraterrestrial* (Steven Spielberg, 1982), and *The Thing* (John Carpenter, 1982) combined advanced techniques (pneumatically operated animatronic robots) with old chestnuts (people in rubber suits). Some of the decade's "armored bodies," such as Peter Weller's cyborg policeman in *Robocop*, were simply actors encased in heavy appliances, while the title role of *The Terminator* (James Cameron, 1984) was played by an assemblage of people and techniques. These included a human actor (Arnold Schwarzenegger); a steel "endoskeleton" head and torso designed by Stan Winston as a full-sized marionette and shot from the waist up; an articulated metal armature, two feet tall, stop-motion-animated for shots in which the entire endoskeleton appears; and a series of intermediate stages between fully fleshed and completely robotic Terminator created by making detailed lifemasks of Schwarzenegger with metal and circuitry showing through holes in the plastic skin.[45] The many constituents of the Terminator role were stitched together into a coherent whole not just through editing, but through the sharing of physical traits from one performing agent to another—another instance of what I have called the chain of evidence. In a scene near the film's climax, for example, the robot Terminator's leg is crushed. To maintain continuity, the technician wearing the torso rig on his shoulders walked with a limp so that, in the words of Winston, "his movements would generate up through the puppet. That made it move more organically, and less like a puppet bouncing up and down."[46]

The Dawn of Digital Performance

Cameron's 1991 sequel, *Terminator 2: Judgment Day*, received much attention for its use of digitally produced imagery to create the shape-shifting T-1000 (Robert Patrick). While it is important to note that only three minutes of actual computer graphics were intercut with more traditional effects work to create the character, it is equally true that *Terminator 2*, along with *Jurassic Park* (1993), marked the point at which computers became a viable means—in public imagination as well as industrial reality—of augmenting performance. As discussed in the previous chapter on previsualization and digital filmmaking, the main application of specifically computer-generated effects had initially been confined to mise-en-scène, creating environments in *Tron* (Steven Lisberger, 1982) and spaceships in *The Last Starfighter* (Nick Castle, 1984). A stained-glass knight, generally credited as the first computer-generated character, appeared in *Young Sherlock Holmes* (Barry Levinson, 1985) in a performance that lasted only a few seconds. But a decade later, digital technology had advanced (and cheapened) to the point where a lead character, speaking dialogue and interacting substantively with the rest of the cast, could be played entirely through digital animation, as in the title role of *Casper* (Brad Silberling, 1995).

Yet if one principle holds true for all of these examples, from morphing assassins to friendly ghosts, it is not that they sprang whole from the computer, leapfrogging past the need for real-world reference, but just the opposite. The panes of stained glass that make up the knight in *Young Sherlock Holmes*, for example, were rendered first as a physical matte painting by ILM artist Chris Evans, then scanned into the computer and manipulated.[47] The T-1000's silver surface was wrapped around a shape and motions provided by actor Robert Patrick, and the digital dinosaurs of *Jurassic Park* began their lives as sculpted maquettes whose anatomy and surface texture were scanned by laser and converted into a digital armature. The same sculptures functioned as templates for the animatronic dinosaurs with which the computer-generated creatures were intercut. In this way, the physical nature of maquettes and other reference materials simultaneously helps to unify a creature's onscreen appearances—preventing small variations in design from disrupting the illusion of a singular entity—and the labor that goes into that body's construction, coordinating the work of multiple artists at a special-effects house. As Rickett writes, "Sculpting is perhaps the most crucial stage of bringing an animatronic character to life." He goes on to quote one effects professional, Alec Gillis: "Every little detail, each skin blemish or hairline wrinkle that is created during the sculpt will be transferred to the final piece. . . . A good sculpture can make so much difference. This is where a character is really created."[48] In this sense, digital characters are tied not only to objects and movements in the real world but also to the processes by which augmented performances have been constructed over the course of more than a century of cinema. Animatronic robots, stop-motion-animated armatures, and computer-generated "skins" are all based on the premise of lifelike design: a rendering that begins with drawings and paintings, proceeds through realization in solid three-dimensional objects, and ends up as an image on film. Stephen Prince argues that computer-generated images should be understood in terms of the "perceptual and social correspondences" that tie such imagery to reality in non-indexical ways.[49] In his model, digital and other types of artificial characters can be granted a measure of overall plausibility through cunningly implanted fragments of realistic behavior. Despite the audience's knowledge that a character does not exist in life, Prince writes, "even unreal images can be perceptually realistic."

> A perceptually realistic image is one which structurally corresponds to the viewer's audiovisual experience of three-dimensional space. Perceptually realistic images correspond to this experience because filmmakers build them to do so. Such images display a nested hierarchy of cues which organize the display of light, color, texture, movement, and sound in ways that correspond to with the viewer's own understanding of these phenomena in everyday life.[50]

Prince's goal is to find a way around the problem apparently posed by digital imagery, namely the production of images that have no real-world referent. He cites as one example the pseudopod in *The Abyss* (James Cameron, 1989), a "slithery underwater creature" that "began as a wire-frame model in the computer [so that] no profilmic referent existed to ground the indexicality of the image."[51] While Prince is correct in his assertion that the pseudopod was never literally photographed or captured by the camera in the straightforward manner that, say, Ed Harris and Mary Elizabeth Mastrantonio were in the same film, he neglects the numerous "profilmic referents" that gave shape and character to the pseudopod, including drawings and maquettes made by designers at effects house Digital Domain.

More problematically, Prince devotes much of his analysis to the creation of digital performers (as opposed to digital environments), yet never brings up the question of performance as such, instead staying quite literally on the surface. The plausibility of a character's inclusion within the narrative, for Prince, hinges on our sense that the performer is physically—as opposed to psychologically—present.

> When the velociraptors hunt the children inside the park's kitchen at the climax of *Jurassic Park*, the film's viewer sees their movements reflected on the gleaming metal surfaces of tables and cookware. These reflections anchor the creatures inside Cartesian space and perceptual reality and provide a bridge between live-action and computer generated environments.[52]

Other aspects of what Prince calls the "anchoring process" include surface texture, "bone and joint rotation," and the rendering of hair. He flirts with the notion that these tasks of simulation and "information capture" ideally add up to a performance—"Human and animal movement cannot look mechanical and be convincing; it must be expressive of mood and affect"[53]—but his emphasis on the physics of appearance rules out discussion of more subtle codes, such as those animating McCay's Gertie, by which psychological and emotional realism is achieved by special-effects-based characters.

All of this is to suggest that augmented performance may be best understood in terms of the practices by which a figure onscreen, regardless of its origin, is imbued with the most fundamental ingredient of character—expressive behavior. The power to emote is achieved through the careful transfer of recognizable traits from real-world references onto artificial bodies. This chain, whether it originates in the hand of an animator, the actor beneath the prosthetic makeup, or the computer programmer, is the most basic "special effect" involved in augmented performance, and provides a common rubric for analyzing image manufacture in a number of different subdisciplines of cinema: cel and stop-motion animation, puppetry and animatronics, makeup, and cinematography, to name a few. In addition, the protocols of augmented performance extend along the breadth of cinema's history, uniting in principle the work of many different creators and technologies in many different decades.

Both of these principles—the chain of evidence and the mixture of past and present so common to special-effects work—are evident in *The Lord of the Rings*. Populated by all manner of inhuman species, the trilogy's standout example of augmented performance is Gollum, a misshapen, froglike creature driven to murder by his desire to own the titular "Ring of Power." I now turn to a discussion of Gollum's performance: a creation involving not just special effects and CGI, but other levels of film craft: acting, screenwriting, directing, and editing. All combine to create in Gollum what some have called a breakthrough performance in digital acting—though, as I will later suggest, this claim may be misleading.

The volumes that collectively constitute *The Lord of the Rings—The Fellowship of the Ring*, *The Two Towers*, and *The Return of the King*—were written over a period from 1937 to 1949 and published between 1954 and 1955. But it would be almost half a century before the trilogy was successfully adapted in motion-picture form. One reason for this was author J. R. R. Tolkien's reluctance to part with the rights, intent as he was on maintaining the integrity of his sprawling epic against an industry notoriously quick to bowdlerize and oversimplify. But another check on *Lord of the Rings*'s dispersion through the media ecosystem was undoubtedly the technical challenge of visually realizing the trilogy's elaborate world of Middle Earth and its large and varied cast of Hobbits, Elves, Orcs, Goblins, Ents, Trolls, and wizards. Even beyond its magical and mythical central players, the text posed an additional challenge to screenwriters and production designers with its many set pieces involving clashes between enormous armies of good and evil.

A literal cast of thousands would be needed to convincingly bring the books to life.

Yet it was just this desire—to bring the story and its characters to life—that fueled efforts like those of the Beatles, who during the 1960s tried to acquire the rights to the trilogy. The British band envisioned themselves in the roles of the four figures at the heart of the narrative: Paul McCartney as Frodo, Ringo Starr as Sam, George Harrison as the wizard Gandalf, and John Lennon as Gollum, the tale's most tragic and complicated figure.[54] Other unsuccessful attempts were made by filmmakers with styles as diverse as Walt Disney and Stanley Kubrick. John Boorman developed a script in the 1970s, but finally found the project too big to accomplish, settling for the smaller in scale (though similarly themed) *Excalibur* in 1981. In 1978, Ralph Bakshi released an animated version of *The Lord of the Rings*. The film was significant not because it was a success—it pleased almost no one, least of all Tolkien's legion of fans—but because of the way in which Bakshi solved the problem of casting. In his previous movies *Fritz the Cat* (1972), *Heavy Traffic* (1973), and *Wizards* (1977), he had experimented with rotoscoping, a technique in which animated imagery is traced or painted over live-action footage. This primitive form of motion capture, which can be traced back at least as far as Dave Fleischer's Betty Boop cartoons of the 1920s, results in an uncanny class of figures that blend fluid and recognizably "human" movement and gestures with explicitly "inhuman" surfaces. For his *Lord of the Rings*, Bakshi relied heavily on rotoscoping, hoping to produce characters that blurred the line between animation and live-action. This was particularly important in the battle scenes, in part because of the difficulty Bakshi would otherwise have faced in animating individual motions for each warrior, and in part because of the rotoscope's ability to duplicate and overlap images filmed at different times—enabling Bakshi to quickly fill the frame with a dense population. But time and budget constraints, along with a poorly structured screenplay that tried to condense all three books into a two-hour running time, made Bakshi's experiment a failure.

In the mid-1990s, Peter Jackson proposed and won approval from New Line Pictures to produce a three-part adaptation of Tolkien's work. His origins in low-budget horror/comedy aside, Jackson's successful experimentation with digital special effects in films such as *Heavenly*

Creatures (1994) and *The Frighteners* (1996) convinced him that *The Lord of the Rings* was feasible in production terms. (Massive, one of the effects technologies that would be essential to creating Middle Earth's armies, was developed during this period for Jackson's 2005 remake of *King Kong*.) Like the filmmakers that had come before him, Jackson faced the problem of portraying a large cast of non- and semi-human characters plausibly and consistently enough to carry not one, but three movie installments.

I have already mentioned the host of special effects techniques by which the majority of performances in the trilogy were achieved. But the most significant example of augmented performance in the film is surely that of Gollum. From the beginning, Jackson and his co-producers believed that the only way to realize Gollum would be as a "pure" special effect of some kind; not merely a Level 1 or 2 augmentation of human performance, but a complete substitution of a digital player for a "real" actor. As such, their initial development of the character proceeded entirely in preproduction design. Conceptual artist John Howe and others drew hundreds of sketches to refine Gollum's look; once an acceptable design was chosen, sculptors created a maquette. This was then scanned by laser to produce a 3D computer model, which Jackson intended to composite into live-action plates shot on location. The one realm in which it was felt that an actual actor could contribute to the performance was that of voice. Andy Serkis won the role, but after watching his audition tape, Jackson decided that the actor's physical actions—including the crouching position and contorted face Serkis assumed while voicing Gollum—would enrich the performance of the digital model [Figure 3.2]. In the several years of shooting that followed (all three movies were filmed simultaneously), the system for shooting Gollum evolved through trial and error. Serkis performed the role on location, but only during rehearsals; for the actual shot, he stayed off-camera, saying his lines while the other actors mimed around an empty space into which the digital creature would later be inserted. Later, Serkis re-performed the role from the top, this time wearing a motion-capture suit and acting on an empty stage. Computer technicians captured the physical attributes of Serkis's performance and used these data to guide their animation of Gollum.

Strikingly, Gollum's design underwent revision based on the specific characterization that Serkis brought to the part. The maquette was res-

Figure 3.2. Andy Serkis performing as Gollum in the *Lord of the Rings* trilogy (2001–2003), showing a similar use of production discourse to that of Figure 3.1.

culpted to better reflect Serkis's own features, and corresponding changes were made to the 3D computer model. Recalling the process by which King Kong evolved from a bit player to a lead character as producers grew more confident in Willis O'Brien's special effects, Jackson and the film's other screenwriters, Fran Walsh and Philippa Boyens, taking note of the emotional nuances Serkis was bringing forth, wrote additional pages to flesh out the Gollum's back story and psychology. These new scenes included a pivotal moment in *The Two Towers* when Gollum's split personality plays itself out as a dialogue between his two halves. The resulting character is a composite not just of Serkis and a digital model, but of the small army of writers, artists, designers, and technicians who labored on the performance. Gollum's motions are based on Serkis's, but animators take over whenever the character must do something "impossible," such as crawl up a steep mountain wall. Similarly, animators were primarily responsible for Gollum's facial expressions and eye movements, but worked from reference footage of Serkis's own features.

The conclusion we can draw from this is that Gollum represents a complex intermingling of technologies, skills, and traits. His nature encompasses both the material objects and hardware involved in his design, the human beings who contributed movement and expression to his characterization, and the ephemeral display of pixels on screen.

And yet as a digital character, Gollum represents for many the coming of a new kind of actor, one that threatens to undermine the principles of authenticity and reference on which performance, and the cinematic medium itself, is based. The specifically digital performer—or more accurately, the artificial performer whose performance involves digital imagery in large part—has become a lightning rod for a larger argument about the tradeoffs and relative merits of "old" and "new" media.

Assessing the Synthespian

Since the late 1990s, concerns about the genuineness of performance achieved with the help of special effects have figured prominently in debates over the use of photorealistic virtual actors or synthespians. A product of computer-generated imagery, synthespians mark, for many theorists, not simply the apotheosis of a certain kind of visual engineering, but a threat to the very notion of reference and authenticity on which the notion of "real" performance is built. Writing in an issue of *Screen* devoted to special effects, Barbara Creed sums up the situation this way:

> Through special effects (animation, miniaturization) it was once possible to create objects and things which did not exist, but which did have referents in the real world—objects, drawings, clay figures. Now it is possible to create computer-generated objects, things, and people that do not have referents in the real world but exist solely in the digital domain of the computer. In other words, film has been freed from its dependence on history and on the physical world. Central to these changes is the possibility of creating a virtual actor, of replacing the film star, the carbon-based actor who from the first decades of the cinema has been synonymous with cinema itself. In the future, living actors may compete with digital images for the major roles in the latest blockbuster or romantic comedy.[55]

For Creed, this pool of "posthuman talent" is not limited to above-the-title stardom; she points out that digital actors have been playing bit parts for years, as extras tucked into the corners of the frame or glimpsed in long-distance crowd shots, in movies like *Titanic* (James Cameron, 1997) and *Eyes Wide Shut* (Stanley Kubrick, 1999).[56] But it is primarily the synthespian's "star turn" that concerns Creed, and much of her essay is devoted to exploring the question of the cyberstar's ability to hold spectators' attention or invite their identifications despite the fact that it is a simulacrum (in Jean Baudrillard's specific sense of a copy without a referent). Her argument relates the alleged flatness of the digital image to a corresponding deficit in synthespian affect, and thus its impression of psychological truth. The digital image "appears to lack depth; it has a plastic look," she writes, going on to ask, "To what extent will the virtual nature of the star's image induce in the spectator a sense of depthlessness in his/her relationship with the figure on the screen?"[57]

Creed's conclusion—that "the synthespian does not have an Unconscious"[58]—reflects a larger unease about the sanctity of the cinematic medium itself. The figure of the synthespian has become a crisis point for our conventional understanding of the movies: redefining in fundamental ways an industry whose every stage, from preproduction to editing, sound design, distribution, and exhibition, is increasingly informed by digital technology. Indeed, one side effect of the discourse around synthespian performance has been to retroactively frame the era of analog cinema in the stark terms of a lost golden age, by opposing it to its digital successor. As Creed puts it, "Celluloid cinema dramatically altered the relationship of the individual to reality; the computer-generated image is about to change that relationship once again and in equally profound ways."[59] The basis for this charge is the digital image's supposed lack of reference—its disconnection from the real world.

While Creed sees that disconnection as proof that digital images will always retain a certain depthlessness, other writers argue that computer graphics have shifted cinema into a realm of absolutely convincing simulation. In his conference presentation "The End of Animation History," Mark Langer argues that with digital technology, "photoreal animation is now indistinguishable for the overwhelming majority of viewers from live-action cinema."[60] Citing as evidence a variety of special effects, such as the dinosaurs in *Jurassic Park* and the removal of Gary Sinese's legs for his performance as a Vietnam veteran in *Forrest Gump* (Robert Zemeckis, 1994), Langer asserts that the "indexical relationship between the image and the thing that it represents is gone, or at least fast-vanishing."[61] Langer's and Creed's positions weave a number of separate issues (animation, special effects, acting, indexicality, the unconscious) into a single narrative of cinema's imminent collapse

before an onslaught of digitality. Both writers see the increasing preva-
lence and sophistication of digital imaging as a troubling development.
Langer, for example, notes the fin de siècle trend toward movies—many
making heavy use of digital special effects—like *Being John Malkovich*
(Spike Jonze, 1999), *The Matrix* (the Wachowski siblings, 1999), *Fight
Club* (David Fincher, 1999), and *Memento* (Christopher Nolan, 2000),
in which the boundaries between fantasy and reality blur or even shat-
ter. He links these thematic concerns to our collective arrival "at a point
in cinema history when animation and live-action are collapsing into
one another": a moment at which the zeitgeist has, both through and
because of our image-manipulating abilities, entered a state of perpetual
hallucination.

> What we are seeing in the collapse of the boundary between animation
> and live-action is something that is happening in many areas of our
> culture. This is the destruction of the border separating simulation and
> reality, or the one that exists between the non-material world and the
> material world. . . . I'd argue that all of these have their roots in an ever
> expanding cultural anxiety about the fact that it is no longer possible to
> distinguish between representations of real events or simulations of those
> events.[62]

Crucially, both writers center their critique of digitality on the figure
of the synthespian. For Creed, the degree of control and perfectibil-
ity afforded by the virtual actor imperils the artistic potential of the
medium. "The potential for the cyberstar to epitomize a digitized form
of beauty that is flawless," she writes, "will, combined with the seamless
nature of the digital image flow, create a clean plastic cinema based on
organizational modes of creativity rather than on a play of improvisation
and intuition."[63] For his part, Langer cites the digital performers of *Final
Fantasy: The Spirits Within* (Hironobu Sakaguchi, 2001) as a sign that
the age of perfect simulation is nearly upon us. Ironically, he begins by
noting his own resistance to the synthespians onscreen:

> When I saw *Final Fantasy* last summer, the scene where the characters
> smooch resulted in cries of "eeuw!" from the audience. I'm hypothesizing
> that part of this audience discomfort came from the imperfect reproduc-

tion that the film's 'hyperreal' animation displayed. The characters existed in a liminal position between animation and live-action that made the display of human emotion difficult for the audience to accept. But what will happen when photoreal animation is perfected?[64]

Leaving aside the logical gap here—that Langer is basing his prediction of "perfect" photorealism on a case of "imperfect" reproduction—I wish to stay with the example of *Final Fantasy* and use it as a means of exploring the arguments set forth about digital acting in particular, and augmented or special-effects-dependent performance more generally. For what is at stake in this conversation about synthespians is precisely our ability to evaluate claims of technological change within the film medium—to identify what is and is not actually occurring at the interface between cinematic and digital modes of production. Although computers have indisputably brought to moviemaking much that is new, they are just as indisputably being put to work within existing frameworks and established logics of representation, storytelling, and performance that date back to the earliest days of cinema. Naremore, for example, argues that "CGI seems to undermine documentary authority in the entertainment film. It brings movies closer to the spirit of comic books and animation, it makes some tricks less easily detectable, and it threatens a certain discourse about realism and humanism in the cinema."[65] But even as he claims that "digital effects clearly have their own phenomenology and their favored images,"[66] he acknowledges that whatever novelty computer graphics may actually possess, their practical use is circumscribed by longstanding logics of industry and representation. "In Hollywood, however, [digital effects] tend to be used for exactly the same purposes as older technology like matte shots, optical printers, and rear or front projection—that is, to achieve magical transformations or to combine verisimilar images in order to produce a kind of invisible collage."[67]

The care with which we should approach the digital/cinema "divide," then, is in direct proportion to the power of discourses of technological change to shape our perceptions—to function, that is, as all discourses do, in ideological ways that steer our understanding toward certain "commonsense" conclusions while making other possibilities difficult, if not impossible, to visualize. In short, a closer examination of augmented performance provides an opportunity to cut past what Sean Cubitt has termed "the rhetoric of the unprecedented" surrounding contemporary special effects (a category that includes synthespians and has additionally come to emblematize both the digital revolution and high-tech filmmaking overall).[68]

I have already noted one way in which the discourse of digitality works to naturalize a certain conception of cinema: namely, by contrasting the current or coming state of the art ("a clean plastic cinema") with a more authentic and spontaneous art of the past (based, in Creed's words, on "a play of improvisation and intuition"). Although we could certainly debate the notion that cinema, particularly in its Americanized studio variety, was ever *not* a product of "organizational modes of creativity," the distinction drawn by Creed between artifice and intuition helpfully points us toward a more meaningful definition of synthespian performance style—one that takes into account not just the virtual actor's surface appearance, but its expressive technique.

Based on a popular, long-running series of videogames and developed jointly by Japanese software company Square and Columbia Pictures, *Final Fantasy: The Spirits Within* was not, of course, the first feature-length film to make exclusive use of digital actors. That trail had been blazed six years earlier, in *Toy Story* (John Lasseter, 1995). In fact, Pixar, the company that produced *Toy Story*, had by 2001 released several of its best-known features, including *A Bug's Life* (John Lasseter, 1998), *Toy Story 2* (John Lasseter, 1999), and *Monsters, Inc.* (Pete Docter, 2001). Another studio, DreamWorks, released *Antz* (Eric Darnell and Tim Johnson) in 1998. For the most part, all were box-office successes. *Final Fantasy* differed from the children's films in its attempt to simulate actual human beings rather than toys, insects, and monsters.

To some extent, this shift reflected an expansion of the computer's rendering power, as the relatively simple surfaces of fur, plastic, and chitinous shell demanded less processing power and programming time than the textures of human skin and fabric. But I suggest that it is impossible to consider technological factors apart from genre, and the dramatic expectations conditioned by generic frameworks. Pixar's movies, like many children's films, are built around colorful and exaggerated performance, often by animals or fantastic creatures. In *Toy Story*, *A Bug's Life*, and *Monsters, Inc.*, the acting is magnified to an extreme: characters flail their arms, shake each other by the throat, and fling their bodies around the screen with abandon. This is accompanied by exaggerated facial expressions "readable" from a great distance, along with vocal mannerisms full of color, emphasis, and rat-a-tat delivery. The cartoon aesthetic speaks of the Pixar films' ancestry in animation rather than (as in the case of *Final Fantasy*) live action. But whatever the cause, the performances in *Final Fantasy* are based on an entirely different aesthetic. Like actors in a movie for "grown-ups," the film's synthespians are intended to be psychologically nuanced, naturalistic, and spontaneous. In short, *Final Fantasy* gave us the first digital Method actors.

Naremore observes that movie acting has historically been structured around two contrasting notions of performance.[69] The naturalistic school, articulated by Konstantin Stanislavsky and elaborated by actor and teacher Lee Strasberg, holds that "good acting is 'true to life' and at the same time expressive of the actor's authentic, 'organic' self"; it emphasizes "spontaneity, improvisation, and low-key psychological introspection," and devalues "anything that looks stagy."[70] This stands in contrast to the exaggerated, mannered approach to acting associated with the modernist theater of Bertolt Brecht.

> The antirealistic Brechtian player is more like a comic than a tragedian, concerned less with emotional truth than with critical awareness; instead of expressing an essential self, she or he examines the relation between roles on the stage and roles in society, deliberately calling attention to the artificiality of the performance, foregrounding the staginess of spectacle, and addressing the audience in didactic fashion.[71]

The naturalistic mode thus treats "performance as an outgrowth of an essential self," while the antirealistic mode "implies that the self is an outgrowth of performance."[72] The former is a representational philosophy in line with cinema's implicit promise, per André Bazin, to present an objective recording of events taking place before the camera; the latter is a presentational philosophy descending from the arena of theater. In a sense, then, the difference that Naremore has pinpointed embeds within itself a sedimentary layer marking the transition from one medium (theater) to another (cinema). This difference reflects a logic of historical succession put forth by David Jay Bolter and Richard Grusin, who argue that any given medium, as it emerges, oscillates between an invisible "immediacy" and a self-conscious "hypermediacy."[73] More to the point, the contrasting performance styles echo a distinction often drawn about special effects: that they function in both a "marked," intended-to-be-noticed fashion, as well as a less obvious, "unmarked" mode meant to pass below the radar of conscious perception. Hence, as I suggested in the opening to this chapter, "performance" can be a way to speak about the spectacular and illusory powers of cinema, not to mention the medium's overall strategies of cloaking or highlighting its operations.

Under this rubric, *Final Fantasy* can be seen to adhere to a naturalistic aesthetic, the verisimilar counterpart to Pixar's histrionic performance style. Director Sakaguchi made realism a priority, centering the action on Earth rather than on an alien planet and building his narrative around a scientific rationale for the human soul.[74] The performance of Aki Ross (voiced by Ming-Na), as well as those of her costarring synthespians, is marked throughout *Final Fantasy* by a kind of distracted introspection and hesitancy. This is accomplished partly through facial expression and partly through a soft, redundant manner of speaking that, according to Naremore, characterizes naturalistic acting:

> To achieve the effect of spontaneity, [actors] preface speeches with meaningless intensifiers or qualifiers—a technique especially apparent on television soap operas, where nearly every remark is prefaced with "look," "now," or "well." Naturalistic actors also cultivate a halting, somewhat groping style of speech: instead of saying "I am very distressed," the actor will say "I am dis- . . . very distressed." By the same logic, he or she will start an action, such as drinking from a glass, and then pause to speak before carrying the action through.[75]

For example, in the first extended conversation between Aki and Gray (voiced by Alec Baldwin), which takes place as the two ride an elevator platform, the couple's banter takes the form of frustrated, defensive, half-articulated utterances redolent of soap opera angst. Aki and Gray shoot sidelong glances at each other, flinch from each other's touch, and whirl away in anger [Figure 3.3]. These actions also carry them away from a straightforward presentational style in which actors face the camera in the full-frontal or three-quarter profile favored by classical theater (as well as Pixar movies). As Naremore notes, "The chief mark of realistic psychological drama from the late nineteenth century onward has been the tendency of the actors to turn away, moving out of the strong or shared positions, facing one another on the diagonal so as to make the stage seem less 'rhetorical,' more 'natural.'"[76]

Another interesting phenomenon is the evolution of certain performances over the course of *Final Fantasy*'s development. Dr. Sid (voiced by Donald Sutherland), who was created fairly late in the production, benefited from the learning curve the animators had already climbed. He is among the most individualized and convincing performers in the movie, due in part to the character's aged appearance. According to animation director Andy Jones, "One of the things that helped Sid with his realism is the amount of detail [the animators] were able to add to his skin. . . . Adding more detail, more age spots, more stuff like that makes characters look even more real."[77] But the quality of Sid's performance was also a function of the advanced techniques to which his animators had access. The complex relationship among computer technology, "old-school" animation methods, and the generation of

Figure 3.3. "Method" acting in *Final Fantasy: The Spirits Within* (2001).

character is evident in this extended quote from Steven L. Kent and Tim Cox's *The Making of Final Fantasy: The Spirits Within*.

> When it came to facial control, just as it was with blemishes, Dr. Sid was *Final Fantasy*'s most complicated character. "Sid's animator, Louis Lefebvre, added some personal controls to help animate the face," says Character Artist Francisco Cortina. "Sid is my personal favorite, but he does have a few extra controls. With our system of facial animation set-up, we have the ability to add extra shapes or controls to do certain things. In Sid's case, there are a few more controls, such as jiggling, in his throat." Most of the characters in *Final Fantasy: The Spirits Within* have approximately 100 control points, but more than one dozen additional controls were added to help with Sid. "We put in a lot of vibrations in the skin of his neck," says Jones. "Sid is a much older character. His skin is a lot looser. When Sid talks, we'd import the wave file of the speech itself and see how the wave form looks, and use that to drive the animation of his neck. You may notice that when Donald Sutherland (the voice actor for Dr. Sid) speaks, his neck kind of vibrates a little based on his vocal cords. Little things like that are what make Sid look so real—that along with Louis's (Character Animator Louis Lefebvre) attention to facial details, such as lips and eye movements."[78]

Here again, the chain of evidence is carefully laid out—this time in the professional discourse of a making-of book—tying the minutest of details (Sid's neck wattles) to a real-world referent (Sutherland). This has the dual effect of invoking the real actor, both through his voice's "presence" in Sid, and through an apparently objective mechanism of translation—the audio file and its associated wave form—which "drove" the neck animation. (A Bazinian perspective might argue that, although here the medium's guarantee of authenticity has been transferred onto a mechanism more specific than the light-gathering camera, the implicit promise of machine-guaranteed verisimilitude is preserved.)

It could, of course, be objected that this level of scrutiny misses the forest for the trees. It is one thing to speak of realistic neck wattles, and quite another to speak of a compelling, involving character—like, for example, Sutherland's performances in *Klute* (Alan J. Pakula, 1971) or *Don't*

Look Now (Nicholas Roeg, 1973)—who can sustain an audience's interest for the duration of a feature film. At what point do pixels give way to personality—when does pure processing power equal performance? The search for such distinctions tends to bog down in a kind of Zeno's Paradox. Just as it can be argued that it is logically impossible for an arrow to hit its target (having to first cover half the distance to the bull's-eye, then half that distance, then half again and so on), there seems to be no valid way to draw a line between tiny details of expression and the overall performance to which they add up. The historical examples discussed in the first part of this chapter hint that there is no single point of technological sophistication at which artificial bodies burst into plausible performance. Indeed, the earliest examples of cel and stop-motion animation imply that it takes little more than motivated-seeming movement to encourage audiences into seeing thoughts, intentions, and emotions that aren't really there.

The desire to pinpoint authenticity in augmented performance also speaks to ongoing efforts within industrial discourses to make the labor of special effects visible to audiences, award committees, and other parties for whom such work must be continually foregrounded. Even the most obviously unreal bodies, that is, risk eliding the work that goes into their performance; actor's names and voices tend to be promoted over the designers and technicians whose contributions were also essential. Hence the chain of evidence serves another, at times contradictory role: rather than connecting the content of an acting feat to an originary essence, it can be used to underscore the very complexity and "unnaturalness" of screen characters. Playing an important part in the industrial scenarios through which we collectively imagine the work of special effects to take place, the augmented performer's relationship to the "real" is also a site of struggle over the visibility and value of labor.

A similar calibration of audience perception involves the manner in which augmented performances function within the fantastic-media franchise. By deemphasizing the photographic presence of a human actor in favor of graphic elements that can be re-created within multiple texts and media platforms, these characters can continue to exist as elements of an ongoing diegesis, essentially outliving the actors who might have originated them. (The iconic Frankenstein monster has been played by several different individuals over its "lifespan," as has, more recently, the Marvel Comics character Hulk; interestingly, neither character's recastings have generated commentary on the level of James Bond, Batman, or the Doctor in *Doctor Who*.) The traits of appearance and motion that identify the special-effects-augmented screen body can be transcoded into different forms of media, as when the creatures of *Lord of the Rings* appear in Middle Earth videogames. Augmented performance thus encourages the transubstantiation of bodies across ontological divides, live action giving way to the drawn and painted, the stop-motion-animated, and the digitally rendered avatar. Essentially, the more "costumed" and "cloaked" the performance, the more readily it can travel and reproduce, the basic condition of possibility for the franchise text. In the linking role it plays among texts, the augmented performer is part of a design network; in its transformation of existing elements into newly authored ones, it is partakes of previsualization; and as a particularly quotable element, it migrates. In order for the augmented body to function at all, however, it must successfully sandwich performative layers, from the machinic to the organic, into the recognizability and expressiveness of the movie star.

As an example of how augmented performers modulate awareness of labor and transmedial travel alongside their permutations of natural and artificial, consider another form of contemporary digital stardom, the dog. As stated previously, we are used to high-profile turns by hybrids of human and synthetic performance. Such top-billed performances are based on elaborate rendering pipelines, to be sure, but their celebrity and notoriety are at least as much about the uniquely identifiable star personae attached to these magic mannequins: a higher order of compositing, a discursive special effect. As much processing power as it takes to paint the sutured stars onto the screen, an equivalent amount of marketing and promotion—those other, Foucauldian technologies—is required to situate them as a specific case of the more general march toward viable synthespianism. But what of the humble cur and the scaled-down visual effects needed to sell its blended performance? The five puppy stars of *Space Buddies* (Robert Vince, 2009) are real, indexically photographed dogs with digitally retouched jaw movements and eyebrow expressions; child voice actors supply the final, intangible, irreplaceable proof of character and personality. (The actual threshold of completely virtual performance remains believable speech synthesis.)

The canine cast of *Beverly Hills Chihuahua* (Raja Gosnell, 2008), while built on similar principles, are ontologically closer to the army of Agent Smiths in *The Matrix Reloaded*'s burly brawl: fur textures wrapped over 3D doll armatures and arrayed in Busby-Berkeleyish mass ornament. They are, in short, digital dogs-bodies, and as we wring our hands over the resurrection of Fred Astaire in vacuum-cleaner ads and debate whether Ben Burtt's sound design in *Wall-E* (Andrew Stanton, 2008) adds up to a Best Actor Oscar, our screens are slowly filling with the special-effects-driven stardom of animals. It is odd that we are not treating them as the landmarks they are, despite their immense profitability, popularity, and paradoxical commonplaceness.

In truth, the dogs-body has been around a long time, selling audiences on the dramatic "realism" of talking animals. From Disney's Pluto to *The Jetsons*' Astro, Saturday morning's Scooby Doo to the Muppets' Rowlf, K-9 of *Doctor Who* and *The Sarah Jane Adventures* to Dynomutt and Gromit, dogs have always been animated beyond their biological station by technologies of the screen; we accept them as narrative players far more easily than we do more elaborate and singular constructions of the monstrous and exotic. The latest digital tools for imparting expression to dogs' mouths and muzzles were developed prosaically in pet-food ads: clumsy stepping stones that now look as dated as LBJ's posthumous lip-synching in *Forrest Gump*. These days, it is the rare dog (or cat, bear, and fish) onscreen whose face hasn't been partially augmented with virtual prosthetics. Ultimately, this is less about technological capability than the legal and monetary bottom line: unlike human actors, animal actors can't go ballistic on the lighting technician, or write cumbersome provisions into their contracts to copyright their "aura" in the age of mechanical reproduction. The beasts of show business exist near the bottom of the labor pool: just below that other mass of bodies slowly being fed into the meat-grinder of digitization, stunt people, and just above the nameless hoards of Orcs jam-packing the horizon shots of the Middle Earth films. Jean Baudrillard, in *The System of Objects*, observes that pets hold a unique status as "an intermediate category between human beings and objects."[79] It is a quality they happen to share with special-effects bodies, and for this reason we are likely to encounter menageries in the multiplex for years to come.

Conclusion: Our Puppets, Ourselves

"What is a monster?" asks Michel Tournier in *The Ogre*. "Etymology has a bit of a shock up its sleeve here: 'monster' comes from *monstrare*, 'to show.' A monster is something that is shown, pointed at, exhibited at fairs, and so on. And the more monstrous a creature is, the more it is to be exhibited."[80] In this most basic sense, the artificial bodies of cinema have always been performative—there to put on a kind of show. These bodies in turn required major manipulation, in the form of practical and optical trickery, to achieve their spectacular performances. Hence augmented performance brings together generic concerns (the horror and science-fiction film) with a spectatorial economy of display, not to mention an actual economy of special-effects production that spans budgetary resources, technological advances, and the tools and techniques of a labor force. With all of these dimensions operating simultaneously, it is not surprising that artificial performers "show" themselves beyond their parts onscreen, playing a "starring role" in discourses that surround and support the movie industry, promoting a story of cinema's ever-renewable ability to amaze and terrify us.

Considered in this light, the most recent evolution of the artificial performer—the fully digital character—could be considered "monstrous" in a sense that belies its outwardly "natural" appearance. Despite the efforts that go into the pursuit of photorealistic substitutes or diegetic integration, the reality of augmented performance continues to be undermined by relentless coverage of the methods and materials that make up the synthetic actor. But why should this be any less true of artificial performers than of real ones? As I suggested at the start of the chapter, Judy Garland, like many Hollywood stars, was rarely allowed a single unproblematic identity. Instead, the layers of her persona—her own "constructed" nature—were laid bare by the star system, gossip journalism, and tell-all exposés. My assertion that augmented performance has always been "real" can be inverted to argue that "real" performance has always been artificial. Put more bluntly, screen bodies, whether they are Garland's or Gollum's, have always had their share of monstrosity, in the sense that they exist to be seen—and to be understood as constructs, composites of human beings and different kinds of manipulation.

The augmented performers of cinema play a vital role in what Victoria Nelson has called "the great twentieth-century puppet upgrade."[81] Nelson's book-length survey of western culture's fascination with animate and inanimate replicas of the human form argues that the concept of puppets underwent a profound change in the early 1900s: "From thousands of years as performers and mechanical curiosities to a strikingly telescoped development in brand-new bodies: for a hundred or so years as androids, for seventy-five as robots, for thirty-odd as cyborgs, and for a mere decade as the virtual-reality constructs or "avatars" that might best be described as ethereal Neoplatonic daemons."[82]

Nelson's emphasis throughout is on the spiritual: the dreams and desires projected over the centuries by the human race onto its mechanical doubles. In modern times, this projection has taken the form of "an unconscious belief in the divinity of machines," its most potent expression those machines "made in our own image."[83] Given this focus, it is understandable that her analysis of contemporary puppetry remains centered on representation. In fact, she designates the 1883 publication of Carlo Collodi's *The Adventures of Pinocchio: Story of a Puppet* as "a consolidation of the trend . . . toward a new popular genre of stories *about* puppets in contrast to puppet performances themselves."[84] She examines a number of tropes in the characterization of puppet nature drawn from the movies, including "killer puppets" like Chucky in *Child's Play* (Tom Holland, 1988); "rebel robots" like the false Maria in *Metropolis* (Fritz Lang, 1927) and Peter Weller's character in *Robocop*; "ungrateful golems" and "clumsy clones"; "agile androids"; and "immortal cyborgs."

But the exclusive focus on the representational sphere leaves out another class of puppets, themselves complex amalgams of technologies ranging from hinged mechanism, animated artwork, and robotics to animatronics and CGI. These are the technological bodies used to produce special effects and give fantastic performances—many of which, ironically, constitute the cinematic golems, clones, and androids that are the focus of Nelson's study. In other words, representations of artificial bodies nearly always depend upon the artificial bodies of practical and optical special-effects devices. The fictionalized blending of the organic and technological that is the cyborg must, prior to its onscreen realization, be created as a composite of living and artificial forms: the marriage of an actor's voice to a drawn or painted body; the mapping of movement through motion capture onto a digital armature; the simulation of physical nature such as weight, surface texture, and reflectivity.

Nelson reminds us that "knowing the mechanism of the puppet will never explain to you how it becomes the phantom."[85] But it seems clear that without an understanding of the material component of augmented performance, we miss an important piece of the puzzle. This gap marks critical analyses of monsters, robots, and other fantastical creatures through a symptomatic tendency to slide from a creature's outward appearance to its character and meaning, without pausing to note the ways in which that character is itself a construction dependent on the evolution of special-effects methodologies. William Paul, for example, notes a shift in the representation of transformation between *The Wolf Man* (1941) and *An American Werewolf in London* (John Landis, 1981). In the first film, he writes,

> Change is signaled by a gradual (but discontinuous) metamorphosis in the extremities: overlapping shots of increasingly hirsute hands and feet with claws and a comparably hairy face. This werewolf walks upright like a man and keeps his clothes on like a gentleman. The handling of the transformation makes it easy enough to see the underlying allegory about the beast in man since this beast still appears to be a man. He never loses contact with his human side.[86]

By contrast, the metamorphosis in *An American Werewolf* is "far more complete—at once terrifying and thrilling."

> Of equal importance to the thoroughness of the body's revolution here is the way it happens . . . it seems to take place from the inside out. Some of this is accomplished through erupting sound effects that accompany the change, but it is particularly striking in one shot of David's backbone, which bursts from its indented normal position to form a kind of arch, as if trying to rip itself free from its human body.[87]

Paul relates the difference between the two sequences to cultural shifts between the 1940s and the 1980s, concluding that the later transformation is "congruent with a period in which the hidden had to be exposed, or, to use my formulation about the body, the internal had to be made external."[88] While the analysis is apt, an equally important factor in the shift were advances in makeup techniques that made it possible for the werewolf to emerge from the human form more graphically and explicitly in the 1981 film. Created by Rick Baker, the "change-o-head" system

> involved using life-masks of actors and manipulating or distorting them from behind with rods or inflatable bladders to look as if major changes were happening under the skin. For *Werewolf*, Baker used the technique for the whole body so that the character's face, legs, feet, arms, hands and back are all seen stretching and rippling as if the bones below are reorganizing themselves.[89]

At the same time, we should be cautious not to adopt an approach that emphasizes technology to the exclusion of all other factors. In studying special effects, a fetishistic desire to know how things were done is an inviting trap, one that is all the more slippery for seeming to reveal boundless information in the form of DVD documentaries, fan magazines, and newspaper stories. In practice, this information can channel critical awareness away from significant connections and reinforce, in both overt and covert fashion, a technological folklore friendly to the industry. No better of example of this exists than the allegedly revolutionary nature of digital visual effects, with its promise that special effects are "better than ever"—as well as its dystopian flipside, the threat that CGI spells the end of authentic cinema.

Earlier in this chapter, I described the first known special effect: the use of a dummy to simulate the execution of Mary, Queen of Scots. Naremore links the beheading to a shot in *A.I. Artificial Intelligence* (Steven Spielberg, 2001) in which a female robot's face unfolds to reveal the mechanism underneath. "In one sense the trick shot of Sheila's face isn't unusual," Naremore writes, "because movies have always enjoyed splitting actors apart."[90] I would suggest that, in an equally important sense, movies have also enjoyed *putting actors together*, assembling them from separate shots and, in the case of augmented performance, separate layers of being: different bodies that are themselves composites of referential realism. Perhaps it is this fundamentally composite quality that grants characters built through augmented performance their mobility across not just sequels and franchise installments but across different media platforms. Certainly it no coincidence that their population explosion occurred as a new transmedia ecology was taking shape, born of film's intersection with digital tools, the Internet, and social media, through which the replication and evolution of special effects through quotation and parody was about to undergo a major phase shift.

4

Microgenres in Migration

Special Effects and Transmedia Travel

When the paranormal detective series *Fringe* premiered on Fox in 2008, sharp-eyed observers noted that one of its standout visual devices—expository text floating in three-dimensional space within the frame, so that labels such as FBI HEADQUARTERS, NEW YORK CITY seem to hover amid the buildings of Manhattan like solid, letter-shaped clouds—was not entirely unprecedented. In fact, diegetically integrated three-dimensional text had by that time been inscribing itself across our screens for almost a decade, starting with the David Fincher films *Fight Club* (1999) and *Panic Room* (2001), later moving into videogames such as the title sequence of *Borderlands* (2009), and popping up more recently in the form of airborne text messages in the BBC TV series *Sherlock* (2010–present). The trajectory of this stylistic element is only partly explainable in terms of underlying creators and designers—in each instance being produced by different companies working in different media—or technologies such as match-moving (a form of motion tracking used to embed computer-generated elements into photographic frames, which as a cinematographic technique is only tangentially relevant to the mise-en-scène of digital gaming). In accounting for its replication from one milieu to another, we must instead think about how such signature imagery, once it has been imbued with narrative and other meanings in the public eye, can sometimes become a trope in itself: copied, quoted, mocked, or otherwise referenced iteratively across media instances and platforms. Viewed in this light, the 3D words floating through *Fringe* and other media spaces serve simultaneously as evidence and metaphor of the larger circulatory life enjoyed by special effects, which "migrate" across our media texts, screens, and platforms.

Previous chapters examined how the special effects of *Star Trek* and *Star Wars* functioned within the confines of those franchises to establish and expand textual access to their storyworlds, while augmented performance evolved from its origins in animation and animatronics to become an accepted class of screen labor in *The Lord of the Rings* and *Hobbit* trilogies. Although these intellectual properties germinated in an analog era of special-effects design whose integration with episodic TV, film sequelization, literary adaptation, and paratextual production marked halting and uncertain steps toward the modern fantastic transmedia franchise, all have become profitable powerhouses of popular culture that continue to release new installments under the respective signs of their intellectual property. In doing so, they have capitalized on the resources of a thoroughly digitalized entertainment culture whose generation and deployment of material depends absolutely on the computerization of media content: a revolution these franchises and their kin played a decisive role in fomenting.

By contrast, this chapter considers the circulation of special effects within larger transmedial economies: realms in which branded fictions and their bubble universes interact with and shape each other, along with more fleeting and ephemeral involvement from the sorts of texts in which special effects germinate, mutate, and spread—even when they are not recognized as doing so, as is often the case with television commercials, video games, and animation. And it is within the viral growth media of YouTube, Facebook, Tumblr, and other sites for the sharing of still and moving images that special effects have begun to reproduce and evolve more quickly than ever before, their attention-getting designs forming popular nuclei for the creation of new content both in the professional domains of feature film, videogame, and commercial production and in amateur, grassroots venues such as fan films and mobile-device apps. This circulation of special effects and their behavior as a discrete and scaled-down form of genre is thus very much a phenomenon of digital culture, related not just to new tools for image capture and manipulation but to platforms for distributing such content—along with interactive media formats, such as videogames, that present it to players in new ways.

When this movement of material is coordinated as a means of unfolding a single storyworld across multiple media, it is referred to as transmedia storytelling. Henry Jenkins's definitive example of this practice is the *Matrix* trilogy (the Wachowski siblings, 1999–2003), a cluster of feature films and narrative extensions built around the saga of Neo, subject of a cruelly immersive and restrictive digital regime, and his battle against the synthetic realm that conceals from him and his fellow revolutionaries the truth of their existence.[1] At every stage in *The Matrix*'s public trajectory—advance buzz, promotional teasers and trailers, theatrical exhibition, rental afterlife, and product tie-ins—its distinctive visual aesthetics figured centrally, none more emblematically than a special effect called "bullet time," which portrayed the altered physical reality of combat in a virtual environment.

In this chapter, however, I want to move one step beyond bullet time's role as a kind of narrative glue holding together the various texts of the *Matrix* experience to bring into focus its larger migrational lifespan. For the itinerary of bullet time did not stop with *The Matrix*. As the franchise's most recognized signifier and most quoted element, the special effect spread to other movies and generic contexts, cloaking itself in the vestments of Shakespearean tragedy (*Titus* [Julie Taymor, 1999]), high-concept television remake (*Charlie's Angels* [McG, 2000]), caper film (*Swordfish* [Dominic Sena, 2001]), satirical fantasy (*Shrek* [Andrew Adamson and Vicky Jenson, 2001]), teen adventure (*Clockstoppers* [Jonathan Frakes, 2002]), and cop/buddy film (*Bad Boys 2* [Michael Bay, 2003]). Furthermore, this migration crossed formal boundaries into animation, TV ads, music videos, computer games, and Internet fan films, suggesting, as with *Fringe*'s floating text, that it was bullet time's *look*—and not its underlying technologies or associated authors/ owners—that played the determining role in its proliferation.

Like most flavors of the month, bullet time eventually succumbed to the very ubiquity that marked its success. Put to work as a sportscasting aid in the CBS Super Bowl and parodied not once but twice on *The Simpsons*, the once-special effect died from overexposure. When the Wachowskis returned amid much hype to top themselves in the 2003 sequels *The Matrix Reloaded* and *The Matrix Revolutions*, critics and audiences responded with scorn: they had seen it all before, everywhere else. The rise and fall of bullet time—less a singular special effect than a named and stylistically branded package of photographic and digital techniques—echoes the fleeting celebrity of another special effect, the "morph," ten years earlier. Both played out their fifteen minutes of fame across a Best Buy's–worth of media screens. And both hint at the recent emergence of unusual classes and behaviors of generic objects: aggregates of imaging technologies and narrative meanings that circulate with startling rapidity—and startling frankness—through transmedia networks.

The short-lived cultural career of bullet time qualifies it as what I will call a *microgenre*: a compact synthesis of imagery and narrative elements whose relationship, once established, becomes formulaically recognizable to audiences. The difference between special effects like bullet time and larger genres such as the western or the melodrama stems not just from the speed of their diffusion and evolution but from their branded nature. Intentionally designed by filmmakers to pair a striking visual with a particular set of narrative meanings, bullet time took a technology that had been circulating since the early 1980s and minted it anew, not unlike the alchemy, explored in Chapter 2, by which George Lucas forged originality from familiarity in the first *Star Wars*. The difference is that, once set loose, bullet time spread so quickly and become so pervasive that audiences tired of it. This suggests that bullet time functioned not only as a brand, carrying the commercial signature of its mothership text, *The Matrix*, but also as an entity in the public domain, remaining available for appropriation and commentary until it was finally emptied of its appeal.

As I am defining it here, the migration of special effects, while inseparable from transmedia storytelling, also exceeds it. The replication of certain special effects can be harnessed as a producerly strategy for knitting together narrative and ludic elements in different media only because special effects already function in themselves as liberated transmedia signifiers—marking by their very fecundity the branching pathways and interconnections of convergent media networks in which almost any element can be copied, shared, and transformed. In seeing the migration of special effects like bullet time as a contemporary phenomenon, however, it is important not to neglect the analog roots from which such practices arose, including the sharing and reuse of special-effects "assets" in exploitation and low-budget cinema and TV storytelling.

Swap That Shot: A Brief History of Citation

In "The Sky Is Falling," an episode of the TV adventure series *Voyage to the Bottom of the Sea* (1964–1968), the crew of the submarine *Seaview* encounters an alien spaceship deep underwater.[2] Saucer-shaped, the mysterious craft hovers outside the human command center, flashing its lights through the windows [Figure 4.1]. The unexpected meeting pictured here reflects another, specifically *industrial* encounter taking place at the same time (indeed, in the precise moment of the frame's recording) but along a different axis—one that angles toward a lineage of other texts in other media, realized at other stages in the artistry, craftsmanship, and labor of special and visual effects. Close-eyed fans of science-fiction cinema may suspect they have seen this saucer before, and they would be right: it first appeared in *The Day the Earth Stood Still* (Robert Wise, 1951), where it took part in a memorable triad of genre iconography including the gentle "invader" Klaatu (Michael Rennie) and a towering robot named Gort (Lock Martin).

From a narrative standpoint, of course, the saucers in *Voyage to the Bottom of the Sea* and *The Day the Earth Stood Still* are not meant to be the same. The two media texts do not share a diegesis; characters and events from one storyworld do not carry over into the other. Neither

Figure 4.1. A cameo by Klaatu's flying saucer in *Voyage to the Bottom of the Sea* (1964).

are the movie and TV episode, filmed more than a dozen years apart, in any kind of prequel-sequel relationship to each other. In answering the question of how Klaatu's saucer, which once glided through the skies of Washington, DC, wound up at the bottom of the sea, we would be better off looking at how the texts in question were *made*, for as it turns out, both *Day* and *Voyage* were produced by Twentieth Century Fox. Moreover, footage from *Day* is used in the aerial montage that opens "The Sky Is Falling," suggesting that the recycling of materials and artifacts among studio-owned properties was not unusual at the time.

Tracking the saucer's strange flight path could start, of course, with its broadest dimensions: it represents one instance of a larger catalog of UFO and saucer imagery common in the middle of the twentieth century, not just in cinema but sensational journalism; science fiction art and illustration like those adorning paperbacks, pulps, and digests such as *Amazing Stories* (1926–2005), *Galaxy* (1950–1980), and *Analog* (1930–present; originally published as *Astounding Science Fiction and Fact)*; and children's toys and models. Drilling down into the industrial particulars of *Voyage to the Bottom of the Sea*, attention might shift to Twentieth Century Fox and its labor practices in the 1950s and 1960s—a political economy of the studio special-effects shop during a decade that saw not only a complex symbiosis between movies and television, but a boom in science-fiction and horror filmmaking that placed new demands on the engineering of fantastic visuals. From there, historians of design might consider the saucer through the careers of various individuals who shaped its itinerary, including Frank Lloyd Wright (who consulted on its design it for *Day*) and Irwin Allen, the producer whose brand, before he turned to disaster movies in the 1970s, was a string of TV series like *Voyage*, *Lost in Space* (1965–1968), *The Time Tunnel* (1966–1967), and *Land of the Giants* (1968–1970). Alternatively, fans of science-fiction hardware and the special-effects practices that produce them might focus on the saucer itself as a kind of fetishized object, realized across a number of different forms: a miniature or model, a full-size set, or a matte painting.

Whatever avenue we choose to pursue, the point is that special effects have long possessed histories, identities, and continuities that extend beyond the onscreen shots and scenes in which we first encounter them. The life story of a given special effect involves its designers and creators, its authors and audiences, as well as networks of appropriation, involving citation, homage, and outright rip-off, that copy and mutate them from one instance to another over time. Certainly special effects function, as numerous writers have observed, to convince us that something is taking place onscreen, "tricking" our eyes and ears: as Vivian Sobchack writes of science-fiction film in particular, special effects primarily work to "pictorialize the unfamiliar, the nonexistent, the strange and the totally alien—and to do so with a verisimilitude which is, at times, documentary in flavor and style."[3] By contrast, other types of effects seek to pass beneath conscious notice, serving not as eruptions of spectacle but as a subtle embroidery of film's impression of narrative and spatial seamlessness. Questions about special effects' textual labor, from illusion to integration, have largely dominated film and media studies' engagement with this subset of cinematic practice. But when one concentrates instead on the *artifactual* nature of special effects—acknowledging them as constructs of technology and technique, with their own makers, influences, genres, and trajectories—new problems and opportunities for theorization swim into view, appearing before us like flying saucers of exotic and unexpected origin.

Multiple forces have conspired over time to suppress this consciousness by reinforcing the idea of the cinematic text as a stand-alone object. Marketing initiatives work to singularize movies as products or events to be experienced for the cost of a ticket, rental/streaming fee, or home-media purchase, discursively constituting a bounded text through the "it" in "See it now" or "Own it now." Legal discourses cooperate in conferring the status of trademark and intellectual property that works as a text's prophylactic envelope, defining it as a unique object, discouraging the production of certain kinds of copies and policing new creations that threaten, through similarity, to confuse or co-opt the identity of the "original." Finally, discourses of authorship and auteurism establish texts as artworks springing from the talent and creativity of individuals—themselves constructs of legal, ideological, and economic codes that come together to produce cultural subjects.

At the same time, cinema has always been citational at its heart. Against the seeming singularity of the film text stands its essentially duplicative nature: strung together from multiple images, each differing from each other by minute degrees, the medium's very substrate depends on a kind of machinic multiplicity. Movies exist, after all, in identical, theoretically infinite prints that lend themselves to wide distribution and simultaneous exhibition in scheduled rotation: the public event of a screening marks merely a scheduled replay. Although the first weeks and months of a movie's release follow strictly planned and controlled patterns of scarcity and limited access, these strictures relax over time as films attain ever greater levels of availability, moving from theatrical to home markets while being recoded to different formats such as VHS, DVD, and Blu-ray along the way. Widening contact along the perimeter of an ever-expanding cultural circuit may come at the cost of a narrowing audience—with mainstream viewership here understood as that constituted precisely in its initial encounters with a text's launch—and diminishing financial returns. But through the logics of both the long tail, which forecasts ceaseless revenue from cultural products in tapering but enduring demand, and the subcultural staying power of texts that win an audience's devotion, many films live on, far past the ostensibly singular moment of their arrivals, in the multiple existences that make up what Barbara Klinger has termed their "ancillary afterlife."[4]

Other aspects of special effects' travel have remained more or less consistent across the analog/digital divide: as a tool of marketing and publicity, the spectacular special effects that appear in peak moments of a film text—its high points of action, drama, terror, or wonder—have inevitably been showcased in poster art, lobby cards, photographic stills, trailers, television spots, and other promotional paratexts that crystallize and direct public consciousness of a film before its release. The exploding White House of *Independence Day* (Roland Emmerich, 1996) was one of its most prominent poster images; another, showing a huge alien mothership hovering over the skyscrapers of New York, was equally representative of the special effects used throughout the movie. *2001: A Space Odyssey* (Stanley Kubrick, 1968) featured among its marketing materials artwork of the Pan Am "Orion" Clipper leaving the two-tiered cylindrical space station in orbit around the Earth, and another showing spacesuited astronauts on the Moon with an Aries shuttle landing behind them. These artists' visualizations—preproduction paintings like those that would be vital to selling *Star Wars* to Twentieth Century Fox a few years later—joined photographic posters such as one showing the "Star Child" model from the film's climax. Whether in the form of direct frame enlargements or, more commonly, artwork summarizing the film's most spectacular creations, special effects often constitute the outré core of films' promotional campaigns, even when showing scenes that don't match anything in the movie (for example, the poster for *Forbidden Planet* [Fred M. Wilcox, 1956], which shows the gentle Robby the Robot menacingly cradling Altaira [Anne Francis]).

During the movies' analog era—meaning essentially from the medium's inception in the 1890s to the decade of the 1990s, when digital technologies reached a tipping point in their transformation of the cinematic mode of production—the "travel" of special effects among separate films took two forms: restaging key images and scenarios, and reusing shots and elements wholesale. The first method is most strongly associated with early cinema, or what Tom Gunning has called the "cinema of attractions." There, an emphasis on the staging of spectacle tacked back and forth between innovation and repetition; for every primal scene such as the train rolling up to its platform in the Lumières' *Arrival of a Train at La Ciotat* (1895), a host of other "train" films re-presented the foundational moment with minimal variations. A more direct recycling of materials arrived with the exploitation films of the 1920s–1950s. Eric Schaefer notes that this corpus of low-budget, quickly made movies trafficked in attractions both as elements of fictional and so-called documentary movies, in both of which eruptions of shocking or astounding imagery worked at odds with the surrounding context: "The centrality of spectacle in exploitation films," Schaefer writes, "tended to disrupt or override the traditional cause-and-effect chain in narrative, while it also permitted filmmakers to be slack with classical devices like continuity editing. As a result, the forbidden sights stood out in relief from the shambling wreck of the diegesis."[5] Frequently, the flawed integration of exploitative spectacle was the result of blunt splicing from other productions, where reuse was driven by economic factors that made the borrowing of resource-intensive elements a cost-saving measure. As Schaefer observes, the makers of "B" and lower pictures padded their productions through the liberal use of stock and recycled footage to insert establishing shots and scenes such as chases and natural disasters that were beyond their own means to create.[6]

Special effects by definition consist of cost-saving if paradoxically elaborate and (in relative terms) expensive substitutions for the profilmic "realities" they appear to convey; in his study of 1950s B pictures, Blair

Davis notes the reuse of "action scenes or special effects shots" from picture to picture, such as images of a collapsing Washington Monument—painstakingly animated by Ray Harryhausen—that were transplanted from their original home in *Earth vs. the Flying Saucers* (Fred F. Sears, 1956) to *The Giant Claw* (Fred F. Sears, 1957).[7] With the rise of television in the post–World War II United States, many movie studies began to produce content for the nascent medium of TV, placing new production demands on the in-house practical effects, opticals, and miniatures departments that dominated the special effects industry at the time. Frequently, this early convergence of cinema and television was visibly symptomatized by borrowings like the reuse of Klaatu's saucer from *The Day the Earth Stood Still* discussed above. In another, more extensive set of borrowings, production artifacts from *Forbidden Planet* were repurposed in multiple episodes of *The Twilight Zone* (1959–1964): both interior and exterior sets of the C-57D spaceship appear in episodes "Third from the Sun" and "Elegy," and one of the ship miniatures is memorably hacked to bits by Agnes Moorhead at the end of "The Invaders"; the movie's flight uniforms and blaster props make their way into "The Little People"; technological objects from the underground Krell complex dress the sets of "Execution"; the ground-effect vehicle that transports Commander Adams (Leslie Nielsen) to the home of Dr. Morbius (Walter Pidgeon) roams through "The Rip Van Winkle Caper"; a process shot showing the C-57D in flight, flipped, concludes "The Monsters Are Due on Maple Street"; and another celebrated episode, "To Serve Man," features not just the C57-D exterior set but footage from *The Day the Earth Stood Still* and *Earth vs. the Flying Saucers*.[8]

The *Forbidden Planet* asset enjoying the longest aftermarket career, of course, is Robby the Robot. Designed jointly by A. Arnold Gillespie, Mentor Huebner, and Robert Kinoshita, Robby consisted of a mechanical suit with a human operator (Frankie Darro) inside; his voice, timed to a display of flashing lights beneath his transparently domed head, was recorded postfilmically by Marvin Miller. As a narrative agent composed of human and artificial elements, Robby can be seen as something of a synthespian *avant la lettre*: somewhere between an animated character and a prop, he prefigures not just R2-D2 and C-3PO but Darth Vader, Chewbacca, and Yoda in his ability to recur agelessly across decades of media installments. But unlike the *Star Wars* characters, who remained (until the death of Kenny Baker in 2016) largely tied to their hidden human performers, Robby's post–*Forbidden Planet* stardom consisted of appearances by the elaborate complex of his suit, which marched through productions ranging from the motion picture *The Invisible Boy* (Herman Hoffman, 1957) to episodes of TV series *Lost in Space, Columbo, Mork and Mindy,* and *The New Adventures of Wonder Woman.*[9] While Robby remains one of the most obvious cases of special effects' travel in the analog era, the mode of migration he signifies is merely a more emphatic and character-focused version of borrowings such as those enumerated on the website *Den of Geek,* whose "50 Assets Hollywood Re-used" listicle cites strange-bedfellow sharings of special effects between *The Son of Kong* (Ernest Schoedsack, 1933) and *Citizen Kane* (Orson Welles, 1941); *Torn Curtain* (Alfred Hitchcock, 1968) and *Earthquake* (Mark Robson, 1974); and *A Night to Remember* (Roy Ward Baker, 1958) and *Time Bandits* (Terry Gilliam, 1981).[10]

The cultural competencies required to note and collate these phenomena tend to fall outside traditional academic perspectives that reduce special effects to problems of realism versus illusion. Such arguments portray spectatorship as a contest between credulity and skepticism, with successful special effects striking just the right balance between plausible photorealism and conceptual impossibility. "For many viewers," writes Barry Keith Grant, "the value of (that is to say, the pleasure derived from) science-fiction movies is determined by the quality (synonymous with believability) of the special effects. For these viewers, nothing destroys the pleasure of a science-fiction movie more than seeing the 'seams' of a matte shot or glimpsing the zipper on an alien's bodysuit."[11] In a similar vein, Albert La Valley notes that "too often in science fiction films, we can see the bad matte line (watch the tiger in *Forbidden Planet*), the poor rear projection, and the miniatures which detonate like a bunch of matchsticks (which they often are). The tricks do not work and the plot is interrupted."[12]

The problem with this reasoning is that it idealizes the moment of first contact with special effects, ignoring the archival and comparative work that spectators do before and after viewing. By discarding the notion that a special effect might be revisited over the years, evaluated anew from one viewing to another, traditional media studies has trouble engaging with the way special effects *date.* More noticeably than other filmic elements, effects preserve specific aggregates of narrative and technological practice like insects in amber. These snapshots undermine the discourse of "newness" in which special effects seek to fool the eye in the most up-to-date manner possible. But states of art change over time; audiences in different decades can disagree. Richard Rickett points out the double logic of this aging, which robs past effects of their initial, intended appeal while driving innovation in the present. "As the moving pictures developed," he writes, effects "grew increasingly sophisticated to match changing audience expectations. What thrilled in one decade seemed quaint and creaky in the next. The animated dinosaurs of *The Lost World* (1925) would have made audiences of the 1950s laugh, just as the monsters of the '50s held no terror for viewers in the '80s."[13] Michele Pierson's more nuanced take on the phenomenon is worth quoting at length:

> Images of the incredible shrinking man in flight from a cat many times his size or in mortal combat with a tarantula declare themselves tricks through their sheer impossibility. The wonder of these effects lies in speculating about how they were achieved or *alternatively, and more satisfyingly, in being able to identify their improvement on older methods* of combining images filmed at different times (e.g., the filming of live action in front of a screen on which another film is being projected). What made traveling mattes an improvement on older techniques for combining film images was their ability to mask their techniques of illusion more effectively. But like any special effect that functions in this way *their effectiveness was quickly dulled by repetition.*[14]

Laura Mulvey has coined the term "clumsy sublime" to refer to the ways in which Classical Hollywood's creaky-looking special effects, such as the process shots that place actors in front of rear-projected background imagery, can over time invite appraisal and appreciation in their own right, as what was originally intended to be invisible becomes unmissable and technological shortcut cures into stylistic flourish.[15] Similarly, Julie Turnock notes the way in which the evolution of special effects becomes visible in the same fashion that other stylistic formations age, arguing that "much like we can today see through the 'realisms' of *The Bicycle Thieves* and name their component parts, previous effects styles are likewise more noticeable in hindsight."[16] Ultimately, no effect stands immune to the passage of time and the changing competencies of audiences, whose appreciation of the latest spectacular production is predicated on their familiarity with—and shifting critique of—its ancestors.

One of the foundational texts on cinematic science fiction, Sobchack's *Screening Space*, begins its chapter "Images of Wonder" with an admonition that both acknowledges and dismisses the complex work of special-effects reception.

> Although a great deal has been written about the images in science fiction (SF) films, most often that writing has been more descriptive than analytic. . . . Instead, discussions of the visual surface of the films have usually seemed to degenerate into a delightful but critically unproductive game film enthusiasts play: "Swap that Shot" or "The Robot You Love to Remember." Although there is absolutely no reason to feel guilty about swapping nostalgically remembered images like baseball trading cards, it does seem time to go beyond both gamesmanship and nostalgia toward a discovery of how SF images—in content and presentation—function to make SF film uniquely itself.[17]

Here Sobchack's otherwise impeccable analysis displays its own form of datedness; by rhetorically distancing itself from (and policing the practice of) effects aficionados' "gamesmanship and nostalgia," her characterization of "swap-that-shot" exchanges misperceives the meaningful engagement with popular texts that later studies of fandom would illuminate.[18] When avid readers compare and critique narrative elements—plots, settings, characters—and production contexts—auteurs, techniques, economics—they draw upon specialized archives and indexing systems developed through their own idiosyncratic histories of textual travel: itineraries of nomadic raids on privately owned media territories. Fan communities, as well as unauthorized knowledge bases, rely precisely on such "delightful but critically unproductive" activities. In addition, the dismissal of cross-textual readings pushes special-effects scholarship into an ahistorical formalism, neglecting the activity of audiences who follow effects work as a technical and aesthetic category in itself. These audiences fall outside the simple

binaries thrust upon them—immersion in the image versus appreciation of movie magic—just as special effects themselves demonstrate
stylistic continuities and developmental arcs unaddressed as yet by any
critical vocabulary. In short, characterizing special effects only as effects,
and viewers only as amnesiac consumers of spectacle, renders ironically
invisible the actual process of special effects' production and reception:
an industrial logic of citation/circulation, and a corresponding spectatorial logic of comparisons and continuities.

The lack of academic attention to these dynamics stands in contrast
to—and is perhaps in part a reaction against—the excessive focus on
industrial histories in popular and professional discourses. As a regular
phase in a fantastic blockbuster's marketing, shots and scenes notable
for their heavy use of spectacular effects are anatomized and explained
in publications such as *Cinefex* and *American Cinematographer*, or online in forums such as the *Visual Effects Headquarters* archive, providing
the industrial "disclosures" that are central to the public constitution of
special effects. These local histories, tied to the design and execution of
specific effects, center equally on the human figures of artists and technicians and on the techniques they use to create their illusions, lending
an implicit air of the magician's trade to visual effects work. In general,
such narratives touch but fleetingly on similar special effects in other
films: for example, the portrayal of Superman's power of flight in *Man
of Steel* (Zack Snyder, 2013) might mention the way the same effect was
achieved in *Superman Returns* (Bryan Singer, 2006) or, more distantly,
Superman: The Movie (Richard Donner, 1978), but this would be primarily to frame in laudatory fashion the more advanced and convincing effects work in the Kryptonian hero's latest screen incarnation. The use of
history is equally loose and formulaic in retrospectives on special effects
that appear in overviews of the field such as Christopher Finch's *Special
Effects: Creating Movie Magic* (1984) and Richard Rickett's *Special Effects:
The History and Technique* (2007), both of which begin with chapters on
early cinema, pioneers like Méliès, and optical toys such as the Zoetrope
and Phenakistoscope. Although reasonable starting points in discussing
a category of cinematic practice that dates back to the medium's origins,
the rhetorical impact of this organizational choice is to legitimize screen
illusion as an inherent—and inherently entertaining—aspect of film,
and to establish a self-flattering telos for the industry: one that in Janus-

headed fashion legitimizes contemporary effects production by linking it to a venerated, artisanal past, while simultaneously demonstrating the superiority of today's techniques over older methods.

The trajectories of travel, celebrity, and parody that actually shape the movement of special effects through the visual landscape represent another, less remarked phenomenon of special effects' historical existence. If local narratives of effects production peer backward along the timeline—in essence, reverse-engineering the moment of screen appearance—narratives of migration reach forward in time, tracking repeated usages of or references to the effect in subsequent texts, as well as outward, to consider the trends that cause certain special effects to become temporarily dominant across a range of media forms and formats. This approach adopts a fundamentally fragmentary perspective on the special effect's place in storytelling contexts: while not disconnecting effects completely from the framework of narrative meanings that inevitably color their lifespan, it acknowledges that effects can detach from their textual containers to circulate into new settings and situations. The pros and cons of these dynamics are very much evident in the case of bullet time's transmedial career.

Everything New Is Old Again

> Maybe it was the moment when Trinity leapt in the air and froze, legs akimbo, fingers like talons, a bird of prey in black vinyl, while the camera arced around her in normal time: that was when movies as we knew them changed . . . [or] the scene that the filmmakers called bullet time: the camera revolved around Neo as he twisted backward—almost parallel to the ground—to dodge a gunshot, his long coat fluttering beneath him, the bullets soaring by in slow motion like beads of mercury, leaving shimmering traces in the air. . . . We learned that anything was possible in the movie *The Matrix*. Thanks to free minds in concert with technological bravura, space, time, and motion had become love slaves of the filmmakers' visual fancies.[19]

Written and directed by the Wachowskis as a follow-up to their debut feature, *Bound* (1996), *The Matrix* premiered in U.S. theaters on March 31, 1999, the opening salvo in a contest of expensive, effects-laden blockbusters fueling Hollywood's summer season. Set in a vast neural-interactive simulation regulated by malign computer intelligences and populated by subjects so immersed in a shared dreamworld that they have come to accept it as reality, *The Matrix* gained attention for its dense storyline, its brazen generic borrowing, and in particular the flavor and sophistication of its visual effects. In the eyes of critics, the film's hodge-podge of intellectually provocative and audience-pleasing elements served primarily to string together moments of bullet time: shots with slowed action in one part of the frame while one or more elements within the frame, or the framing itself, move at relatively normal speed [Figure 4.2].[20]

Formally, bullet time appears to be an extended take during which the camera moves in a circle, revolving around an actor held in central focus as the surrounding action unfolds at differential rates of time. Sound effects reflect this "slowdown" as ambient noise drops to a lower, sludgy register, only to resume normal speed as the distortion ends. The mise-en-scène contains numerous floating elements—bullets, spent ammunition, air pressure rings, water droplets—whose slowed or stilled trajectories enhance the shot's uncanniness: dislocations of time and space composited within an unbroken moment. Narratively, bullet time marks escalating breaches in the rules that govern the Matrix. Freed by their knowledge that reality is, in fact, a computer simulation, the protagonists *will* the suppression of gravity or the bending of time, rewriting

Figure 4.2. Bullet time in *The Matrix* (1999) marked the technique's codification as a microgenre.

the cybertextual world in which they are trapped. The effect thus carries the weight of demonstrating resistance to the power of simulation, rendering visible a growing mastery over preprogrammed blindness.[21]

These sequences won praise in compensatory proportion to their second-class narrative status, helping the film achieve, in David Denby's words, "a brazenly chic high style—black-on-black, airborne, spasmodic. The warring characters, hanging from invisible strings, fly through the ether at one another and then fight in a speeded-up, rhythmic version of kung fu that has the clickety-clack excitement of tap dancing."[22] Janet Maslin's review in the *New York Times* was similar: "The martial-arts dynamics are phenomenal (thanks to Peter Pan–type wires for flying and inventive slow-motion tricks)."[23] If some journalists struggled to analogize the movie's visuals and intuit the trickery behind them, others gained information (and ethos) directly from the filmmakers. In a *Newsweek* article titled "Maximizing the Matrix," a two-page spread chronicled the making of the star special effect—complete with step-by-step breakdowns and behind-the-scenes photographs—explicitly linking it to the movie's appeal while tutoring potential viewers in their appropriate reaction:

> Five minutes into *The Matrix*, a leather-clad woman squares off against the local police. As they open fire, she dodges their bullets by running *up* one wall and down the next. Then, as she jumps into the air in front of one of her opponents, she freezes in midair while the camera circles around her. While the other cops look on in shock, she lashes out with a kick that knocks her man down, lands as gracefully as a cat and disappears into the shadows. Without fail, the audience cheers wildly—and it's the kind of response that has propelled *The Matrix* to the year's biggest opening.[24]

In a year dominated by state-of-the-art digital filmmaking, *The Matrix* took home Academy Awards in every category for which it was nominated (Film Editing, Sound, Sound Effects Editing, and Visual Effects), beating out the juggernaut *Phantom Menace* in Sound, Sound Effects, and Visual Effects.[25] Bullet time anchored *The Matrix*'s promotional campaign[26] and quickly became a shorthand signifier for the film itself.

According to visual effects supervisor John Gaeta, bullet time's development began with the Wachowskis' detailed vision of dystopian virtual reality. In script treatments, storyboards, conceptual art, digital animatics, and the finished feature, *The Matrix*'s design shows the Wachowskis to be, like George Lucas, profligate borrowers and synthesizers: magpies of pop culture, drawing inspiration from literary science fiction, *manga* and *anime* (Japanese graphic novels and animation), and kung-fu movies whose signature use of slow-motion, wire-based martial-arts brawling is perhaps the dominant link in *The Matrix*'s pedigree of aesthetic kinship.[27] For the bullet time sequences, Gaeta worked from the Wachowskis' demand for a specific logic of action—what a *Wired* cover story rather disingenuously terms "a visual effect that didn't exist yet."[28] It would show "opponents diving at one another in hyper-slow-motion with guns blazing, pummeling each other while unloading their clips. Meanwhile, the camera covering the action would be running at speeds between 300 fps [frames per second] and 600 fps, making 360-degree moves around the combatants as they spiraled through the air."[29] Gaeta's task was to reverse-engineer this previsualized imagery, bringing together existent and emerging technologies to produce the target illusion.

Initial proposals for finding "a method of manipulating time so the camera can be moving while all of the high-speed stunt action is happening"[30] tended toward the extreme—for example, placing a camera on a rocket-propelled track—but Gaeta opted instead for a solution that merged photographic and digital elements.[31] As realized by the Manex Visual Effects company, bullet time utilized more than one hundred still cameras arrayed in a circle of variable height (the "flight path" of the finished shot) aimed inward at an actor situated before a green screen. Their positions registered by laser, each camera was tripped sequentially as action occurred, generating a set of individual frames that were then digitally stitched together to make a 360-degree image. Computers compensated for minor differences between individual lenses, minimizing what would otherwise be a distracting strobe effect. Finally, the resulting animation of twisting, turning actors was composited against a background whose rotation corresponded to the arc of what is essentially a virtual composite camera.[32] This process, which Gaeta dubbed "Flo-Mo,"[33] had its physical counterpart in Manex's custom-built hardware, an array of cameras resembling "a highly flexible watchband."[34]

Although this history suggests that Gaeta originated bullet time, Flo-Mo and the shots it produces are only a few of the aliases under which the effect has traveled. In the work of multiple authors, in multiple decades, in multiple mediums, bullet time in fact predates *The Matrix*. Such appearances included motion pictures as diverse as Joel Schumacher's *Batman and Robin* (1997) and Vincent Gallo's *Buffalo 66* (1998). At those junctures, the effect floated freely among contrasting narrative situations as filmmakers, echoing Steven Spielberg, sought vivid and appropriate "applications for this art form/technology." To judge from one pair of films, bullet time nearly stabilized as a shorthand for faster-than-light travel; both *Lost in Space* (Stephen Hopkins, 1998) and *Wing Commander* (Chris Roberts, 1999) invoke the effect when spaceships zoom into "hyperspace," suspending astronauts in midair for a few seconds before their craft emerge into normal space-time. Though developed by two different effects houses, the frozen moment/hyperspace sequences in the movies play almost identically, down to the use of a nearly silent soundtrack. (*The Matrix* was apparently the first to accompany bullet time with slowed-down whooshing sounds, reminiscent of a record album played at low speed.) Had the special effect's fortunes played out differently, one of these might have become its accepted generic home: not leather-clad rebels in combat against a prison of simulated reality, but starship crews experiencing the reality-bending effects of hyperspace.

During these early years, bullet time's names were legion: Time-Slice, Timetrack, the Muybridge Effect, multicam, virtual camera movement, time-suspension, the frozen-moment effect, and *temps mort* ("dead time")—a plethora of terms, techniques, and authors that becomes more understandable when we consider special effects as microgeneric units following their own unique logics of development, diffusion, and aging. Effects confound claims of authorship, circulating beyond the boundaries of copyright and intellectual property. While a specific *means* might be patentable—for example, the physical materials of camera and film mechanism, or software used to generate 3D graphics—there is no way to protect an *end* that is nothing more or less than a *look*. The history of special effects (and cinematography overall) is rife with instances of differing approaches used to produce the same, or similar, results. This ambivalence characterizes cinematic enunciation at its most basic and technical; while titles, characters, and dialogue might fall under legal protection, how does one copyright a zoom or pan? Or the chiaroscuro lighting of *film noir*? Or the rhythms of cross-cutting—even something as specific as the trickery Jonathan Demme and editor Craig McKay use in the climax of *The Silence of the Lambs* (1991)? The more closely we scrutinize a technique, the more apparent it becomes that there is no one way to achieve it—an insight which, if unfriendly to the interests of textual landholders, nonetheless beats in the heart of cinematic evolution and variegation. A multiple-path model structures hierarchies of production and taste, opening spaces for amateur, low-budget, and high-end filmmaking even as it imposes on each a specific cultural and industrial location. I will consider just two of bullet time's alternate existences here: Tim Macmillan's Time-Slice and Dayton Taylor's Timetrack.[35]

Tim Macmillan, a British painter and photographer, received his bachelor's degree in fine art at the Bath Academy of Art in 1982. Interested in the intersection between Cubism and contemporary imaging technologies, he began experimenting with what he initially called frozen-time photography. While his early efforts involved handmade photographic emulsions and photograms, he later devised mechanisms similar to Gaeta's: multiple camera rigs using a single length of 16-millimeter film threaded through a long channel and exposed simultaneously to achieve "a perpendicular tracking shot through a space . . . while the viewer experienced a move through space, time was frozen."[36] Over the next twenty years, Macmillan continued to develop his technologies and signature look, doing work in TV commercials and feature films as well as art installations and directing his own films for the BBC. In 1997, he established his own company, Time-Slice Films Limited.[37]

Viewed today, Macmillan's initial experiments harken back to the photographic breakdowns of animal motion pioneered by Eadweard Muybridge and Etienne-Jules Marey (whose names frequently surface in discussions of bullet time). Early 1980s Time-Slice videos such as "Jump" and "Dog" run only a few seconds, freezing man and canine in midair while the point of view revolves around them. By the late 1980s and early 1990s, Macmillan's version of frozen time was popping up in BBC promotional spots and television features. And beginning in 1996, the effect spread to music videos and television ads in countries outside the United Kingdom, contributing to a critical mass that led to bullet time's first multinational exposure in a TV ad for the Gap ("Khakis Swing," 1997[38]). During this time, Macmillan's technological base evolved through a series of increasingly sophisticated camera setups—the Macro Rig, Insect Rig, Linear Rig, and so on—enabling higher resolution and larger scales of film track and image capture. These developments were reflected screenside in ambitious permutations of the frozen-time aesthetic, such as a Del Monte ad (2000) in which a man strolls through a static beach scene: seagulls with blurred wings hang in the air like Christmas ornaments and statue-like soccer players strain to block a motionless incoming ball, which the main character, smiling wryly, ducks beneath.

Macmillan is, of course, aware of bullet time's proliferation in the hands of other authors. His website laconically notes "the emergence of a plethora of similar camera rigs or arrays. As the concept disseminates through film and television and as the software needed to compile, track, stabilize, and interpolate between the adjacent frames improves, we are now experiencing a tidal wave of the frozen-time effect in TV commercials and feature films."[39]

In the face of this tidal wave, Dayton Taylor, another bullet-time innovator, sought authorship status in both public and legal forums, selling his story to magazines such as *American Cinematographer* and *Scientific American* while pursuing legal protection for his apparatus.[40] Inspired by Chris Marker's experimental film *La Jetée* (1962) as well as Industrial Light and Magic's work on *Indiana Jones and the Temple of Doom* (Steven Spielberg, 1984), Taylor experimented with still and motion-picture photography as an undergraduate at the University of Colorado in the mid-1980s.[41] Taylor was intrigued by the metaphysical implications of the match cut, a staple of continuity editing that links disparate shots around shared graphic, spatial, or kinetic elements. Taylor built a simple master-slave camera setup that captured one instant (a man exhaling cigarette smoke, for example) from two different angles. He describes himself as falling in love with the resulting visual complex: "I found the pairs of pictures my cameras took to be fascinating because the uncanny simultaneity was so evident in them. I shot hundreds of pictures with this pair" of cameras, choosing subjects that I felt would emphasize the uniqueness of the simultaneity of the images: objects in the air, people in motion, etc."[42] For the next several years, Taylor refined and extended his techniques, constructing prototypes of multiple-camera rigs, "a modular system comprising an unlimited number of tiny 35mm still cameras which all shared a common stripe of film."[43] Taylor is noteworthy for his dogged pursuit of a patent for the Timetrack system, a goal which, in his words, "forced me to focus on exactly what the invention was, and what it was not. . . . Through the process of putting my ideas into words and drawings I discovered what the essence of my invention actually was."[44] The resulting patent, applied for in December 1994, was approved in August 1997. It describes a "system for producing time-independent virtual camera movement in motion pictures and other media," calling for "an array of cameras . . . deployed along a pre-selected path with each camera focused on a common scene."[45]

Detailing a history of similar inventions, Taylor cites a range of alternative "multiphotographic systems for producing three-dimensional images," comprising more than a dozen patents issued between 1965 and 1993. Such footnotes suggest that bullet time's history deepens and ramifies the more closely we examine it. (Indeed, if we include Muybridge and Marey in the mix, the effect's history becomes coextensive with that of cinema itself.) They also suggest the ultimate *inability* of the patent process to ensure monopolistic control over anything other than a particular configuration of technology, leaving bullet time available to anyone who wishes to duplicate its surface attributes. But unfixable authorship/ownership has not stopped the efforts of one filmmaker after another to put in a claim for the invention of bullet time in the public mind. An article on Timetrack published in 1997 emphasizes the unique challenges posed by this visual arms race:

> [Dayton Taylor has] managed to rope in a handful of investors, including Steven Seagle, who writes for the *Sandman* comic books. He's landed a few advertising jobs from clients who like the effect. And thanks to the mediations of Roger Ebert, he's caught the eye of the potentate of high himself, Steven Spielberg. Of course, what this wave of enthusiasm amounts to will depend a great deal on what Timetrack becomes. A letter from Spielberg to Ebert, included in Taylor's press kit, illustrates the point well; between encomiums, the director finds himself wracking his brain "trying to think about applications for this art form/technology." Unless Taylor can suggest some meaningful reasons to use his brainchild sometime soon, it could easily go the way of technologies like Q-Sound. (And don't tell me you remember Q-Sound.)[46]

Bullet time's fate links considerations of economics (roping in investors) and popularity (finding clients who like the effect). Even at this early stage, two years before *The Matrix*, migration was working to knit together different media (television, comic books, cinema). And it seems clear that specific implementations of the effect helped determine its fortunes, threatened constantly by obsolescence and irrelevance (going the way of Q-Sound) until it found its stylistic home and widespread audience consciousness. Turning, then, from bullet-times-that-might-have-been, I will now address this stabilization more directly. How did *The Matrix* manage to achieve it? How did this alter bullet time's trajectory across multiple media screens? And what happened to rob the effect of its appeal?

As codified in *The Matrix*, bullet time was not only visually arresting but almost irresistibly stylish. Along with designer sunglasses and tight-fitting leather, the effect involved, in Jeffrey Sconce's words, "looking cool while you duel. . . . Ostensibly a dystopic film about the 'horrors' of virtual imprisonment, *The Matrix* nevertheless contributes to the reigning romance of cyberspace by presenting virtuality as a hipster playground of high-action and high-fashion."[47] Like any hot new style, bullet time spread, following an established logic in which newly minted effects get incorporated into other, competing texts seeking to trade upon the original's attention-getting appeal.

This borrowing, which grants effects their citational lifespan, is by no means limited to specific genres, even to specific mediums. Imagery travels anywhere that screens or stories exist to support it. During a period extending from 1999 to 2003, bullet time, with its complex articulation of objects within liquid transformations of time and space, seemed to be everywhere—adopted and adapted to the point of cliché as a stylized staging of action in film, television, cartoons, videogames, even broadcast sporting events.[48] TV shows on which bullet time put in guest appearances include two episodes each of *The Simpsons*[49] and *Angel*.[50] More broadly, the forensic detective series *C.S.I.* (1999–2015) clearly drew visual inspiration from bullet time's "go anywhere" virtual camera, making frequent use of through-the-keyhole zooms, microscopic closeups, false-color images, and slow-motion replays. But it is in the rapidly shifting soil of advertising, music videos, and videogames—among the most ephemeral and sensorially immediate of forms—that bullet time took root and blossomed. Ads for everything from Apple Jacks and Taco Bell to BMW and Citibank Visa combined slowed or stopped time with freely roaming cameras.[51] And the *Max Payne* videogame series (2001–2013) features a mode that makes the special effect interactive. Invoked with a mouse- or button-click, *Payne*'s bullet time enables players to dodge or fire bullets with pinpoint accuracy while their onscreen avatars—clad, like Neo, in black leather—leap and dive, *Matrix*-fashion. Each of these instances had its own creators and its own means of achieving the target illusion, a key factor in bullet time's ability to adapt and transmit itself across media and genre boundaries.

Furthermore, the special effect moved unimpeded by intellectual property law. Techniques and conventions circulate within an unregulated field of citation, a field in which copyright applies feebly if at all. As Jane M. Gaines points out in *Contested Culture*, names and likenesses are at least potentially protected against unauthorized reproduction; I can't make and distribute a movie about Indiana Jones or Anakin Skywalker without risking a lawsuit.[52] As argued earlier, Lucasfilm can't copyright a zoom, a rack focus, or a blue-screen shot. Yet ownership of a kind can still be established at the level of stylistic signature and a form of brand consciousness. Any cinematographer can choose to shoot in deep focus, but it is principally Gregg Toland's work on *Citizen Kane* with which the technique is associated. Similarly, if the label *bullet time* for a short while adhered without argument to *The Matrix*, it did so not through some unique and originary essence, but through the synthesis of existing technologies and a narrative that cemented certain textual and visual meanings in the public mind. (Hence the importance of *The Matrix*'s framing material: the shots and narrative content that precede and follow the effect, assigning it a particular set of affordances such as "kung fu cyberpunk.") It was *The Matrix*'s proprietary packaging of signifiers that caught on in the public imaginary, corralling bullet time's meanings and kicking off a chain of citation that would end, four years later, in archness and decay. (Once formalized, bullet time became formulaic.) In the moment of its branding, bullet time's historical traces were retroactively organized under *The Matrix*'s authorial force field. Pre-*Matrix* appearances of the effect were for a time spoken of colloquially as *Matrix* moments, or—more precisely but no more logically—as developmental steps toward *The Matrix*.

As suggested earlier, special effects evade restrictions imposed by copyright law. In this respect, they remain as available for quotation/homage/rip-off as any other unregulated element of cinematic production. But circulation never occurs absolutely freely; audiences and critics play the game of "swap that shot," drawing connections and uncovering continuities, carving out space for critical evaluation of an element's myriad deployments. In short, bullet time's extensive history of travel did not go unremarked in a meta sense. Playing out the special effect's tension between synchronic and diachronic dimensions, audiences grew increasingly conscious of its iterative existence with each "fresh" exposure. Following the first post-*Matrix* wave of citation, references to bullet time took on a reflexive air, acknowledging the joke of their own brazen borrowing; only a year after the release of the first film in the trilogy, bullet time was being invoked more to amuse audiences than to dazzle them. Of the eight films from 2001 and 2002 mentioned earlier, half were outright parodies: for example, during an attack by Robin Hood's merry men in *Shrek*, Princess Fiona leaps into the air, hangs suspended for an instant while she straightens her hair, then eagle-kicks her attackers Trinity-style. The martial-arts parody *Kung Pow: Enter the Fist* (Steve Oedekerk, 2002), indexes *The Matrix*'s key moments during an extended duel between the Chosen One (Oedekerk) and a digitally animated cow. (The money shot shows the Chosen One dodging long squirts of milk from the cow's udders, with the milk whooshing by like bullets.[53]) Just as the original effect anchored *The Matrix*'s promotional campaign, bullet time, along with other signifiers culled from the film's production design—tight leather clothing, expensive sunglasses, the glowing green alphanumerics of computer code—appeared in numerous fan films and Internet parodies.

The migration of bullet time did not escape the attention of critics and fans, groups as quick to mock failure as they are to celebrate success. Some of this criticism targeted *The Matrix*'s own auteurist aura. Responding to a May 2003 *Wired* article on the sequel *Reloaded*, an online fan wrote:

Hate is a strong word that I hesitate to use about someone I've never met, but I have really despised [John Gaeta] since the first time I heard him open his mouth. This was mostly because he really acts like he invented the "bullet time" effect, but really all he and his team did was enhance it from a stopped-time-lapse effect into a variable-time-lapse effect. The stopped-time version was used in TV commercials (and possibly a music video) prior to the first *Matrix*. Gaeta constantly stands on the shoulders of those that came before him (and his team of hard-working artists) and gives them no credit.[54]

As early as 1998, in fact, some commentators had considered the special effect passé. "The frozen moment is not new," pointed out Richard Linnett. "It has become a standard gag, repeated in so many different clips and commercials (including a recent client-direct Gap Spot 'Khaki Swing' by Matthew Rolston of bicoastal Venus Entertainment) that it has created a kind of dizzying overfamiliarity."[55] In the same year, an article titled "Bedtime for Deadtime" predicted the effect's demise.

> I had to be the first to say it: by the end of the year, people will be sick of deadtime. Yes, I know, right now it's the hippest, coolest, most outrageous thing in visual effects. Yes, I know, it's catching on like wild-fire . . . [but] how long is it before the use of deadtime becomes as cliché as the use of morphing? Morphing was breakthrough technology once; now you can get morphing software from a box of Cracker Jacks. I think the crappy deadtime shot is just waiting to flash before my eyes.[56]

The article goes on to sarcastically script the effect's potential use as an uninspired marketing tool: "Does bad credit make you feel like your [sic] . . . FROZEN IN TIME? Our prices are so low they'll make you . . . STOP IN YOUR TRACKS. Does microwave pizza make you feel a little . . . FROZEN?"[57]

If these obituaries now seem premature—after all, bullet time had yet to find its widest audience—post-*Matrix* feedback pulled no punches, targeting any film daring to make unironic use of the effect. "The four-year cribbing of *The Matrix*'s bullet-time flies and flips certainly will continue, but never so egregiously as director Len Wiseman and his cronies have done here," one reviewer wrote of the vampires-and-gunplay film *Underworld* (Len Wiseman, 2003). "They expect us to drool at the cool with absolutely no other goal in mind than to provide visual mimicry of heroes like Neo . . . with a cheaper budget and, worse yet, even cheaper imagination."[58] Even more definitive was a review of *House of the Dead* (Uwe Boll, 2003): "OK, that whole *Matrix* 'bullet-time' stop-motion special effect, where the camera circles a character—midbrawl—to show 360 degrees of slow-motion bullets, kicks and sword-stabs? Officially over. As in overused, worn-out, played. If Tarantino didn't hack it to death in *Kill Bill*, then the makers of *House of the Dead* do."[59] A more considered analysis of the special effect's proliferation came from the *London Times*:

In the summer of 1999 many people left the cinema wishing that all films could be like *The Matrix*. . . . Sadly, their wish came true. *The Matrix*, rather like Neo's stern-jawed nemesis Agent Smith, replicated itself and every action film since has copied, borrowed, or stolen bits of *The Matrix*. . . . Advertising also got in on the *Matrix*-a-like act, with Levi's, Nike, Kellogg's, Bacardi Breezer and even Center Parcs all using familiar special effects to sex up their brands. Then there are the pop videos for Bon Jovi, Christina Aguilera and notably the now defunct boyband A1, who dodged bullets and bent the metaphysics of time and space in *Take on Me*. It has become so bad that the film's sequel, *The Matrix Reloaded*, out this week on DVD, looks like a rip-off of the original.[60]

As this review hints, the ultimate victim of bullet time's aging was the *Matrix* series itself. Taking rampant appropriation both as praise and challenge, the sequels responded by shifting bullet time to the next level. *Newsweek*, for example, reported on the series' cultural influence in a cover story that designated 2003 "the year of *The Matrix*":

Nothing from the movie has been swiped as often as "bullet time," the dazzling FX trick in which the camera appears to whiz 360 degrees around a central image. It was jammed into *Charlie's Angels* and parodied in *Shrek* and *Scary Movie*. If you watched the Super Bowl last year, you saw a crude version of it on Fox, which used the technology (cleverly, for a change) to show big plays from numerous angles. At first, [producer Joel] Silver says, the Wachowskis were tickled by the copycatting, but soon they began noticing fight scenes—like the one in *Charlie's Angels*— that were shot exactly like theirs. "So they decided to create images that no one could copy," says the producer. "There's only two ways to do that: time and money."[61]

The studio emphasized a technology called universal capture or "u-cap" (part of a larger concept, virtual cinematography), which combined high-resolution scans of actors with fully computer-generated sets, synthesizing digital and photographic environments to an unprecedented degree. In the massive wave of publicity attending the first sequel, Gaeta maintained his techno-utopian cant, boasting of the ability to create

> 50 simultaneous events in a fluid, unending shot, whereas each of these events used to take us all day long to get a two-second piece with 40 takes to perfect. . . . And I can have all this action make sense and interrelate, and I can follow it with a God's-eye camera moving at speeds that would tear an ordinary camera apart. The system will escalate martial arts into a now-transcendental super zone. I think there are going to be people in Hong Kong and Asia who will look at this film and just be, like, flipping.[62]

Although *Reloaded* and (to a lesser extent) *Revolutions* were profitable, audiences failed to "flip." Instead, they accused the follow-up films of squandering the promise of the first *Matrix*. Much of the criticism centered on the sequels' employment of special effects, whose abstraction, excess, and artificial cleanliness left audiences confused and unsatisfied. Attempting to "create images that no one could copy," bullet time's popularizers seemed to encounter migration's inverse: their professed aim of origination and authenticity forced them into a new aesthetic territory in which the only forbidden act was the reproduction of "classic" bullet time. By taking effects to the next level, the *Matrix* makers were outdone by their own initial success.

Special Effects, Genres, and Conventions

So far I have described a model of transmedia travel without addressing the question of what, exactly, is doing the traveling—a process? A look? A shot? A sequence? There are two reasons for this. First is the definitional difficulty posed by special effects themselves. As Christian Metz and his successors have argued, there are always multiple ways to map the manipulation of motion-picture imagery, ranging from the overly general to the overly specific. To describe all cinema as *trucage* is philosophically provocative, but fails to explain why certain classes of image are considered more or less "special" than others. That is, within a field of industrial image production, what ends and whose interests are served by labeling one shot as artificial and another as real? At the other end of the spectrum, categorizing special effects according to the processes by which they were achieved (e.g., distinguishing between stop-motion and digital animation, between painted matte shots and front-screen projection) may be appropriate to technical discussions or how-to articles. When it comes to questions of theory and history, however, this approach seems fine-grained to a fault, paying little attention to the plasticity and combinatorial fluidity that drive optical innovation.

More damningly, both taxonomic extremes reinscribe a fundamental misrecognition of the way effects acquire their semiotic identities: the assumption that special effects work only at the level of the *shot*. As the preceding discussion has shown, effects draw meaning not just locally from their constitutive elements (fragments of image composited together to simulate one unbroken take of film), but globally from their surrounding contexts (narrative, mise-en-scène, and genre). Scenes, sequences, even the films in which visuals are imbedded help to dictate special effects' reception; it was not bullet time itself, but *The Matrix*'s particular enframing of it, that stabilized the effect sufficiently to carry it through a series of citations in other forums. This seems clear enough from comments made by David Edelstein, who cites bullet time as *The Matrix*'s defining breakthrough while noting that the "technology wouldn't have such a kick without the Wachowskis' stylistic (and philosophical) underpinnings":[63]

Tales in which the world turned out to be a computer simulation have been told onscreen before, as recently as *Dark City* (1998) and *The Thirteenth Floor* (1999)—neither a hit. A science-fiction screenwriter I know said he'd been stewing over his own simulated-universe project for years when *The Matrix* came out. "What I didn't think of," he said sadly, "was the martial-arts angle." And that's the crux of it. . . . In a funny way, the Wachowskis—who hired Hong Kong's greatest action choreographer, Woo-Ping Yuen—have provided a retroactive explanation for why warriors in Hong Kong movies can fly: They're in a kind of simulation, a Matrix.[64]

In calling attention to the *motivation* of special effects, this perspective pushes us toward a more systemic understanding of their operations. The "moment" of the attraction may indeed win fleeting awe from viewers. But the situation of that moment within a string of others—and the family resemblances linking the moment to similar instances in surrounding media—contributes to a transmedial kinship that plays a central if not determining role in the reception, acceptance, or rejection of a given special effect.

A second reason to avoid the definition of migratory elements is that we ought not limit migration solely to special effects. Is it only spectacle that travels transmedially? Can strings of spectacle, sections of stories "chunk" or "chapterize" into equivalently dynamic agents? Once we begin to disassemble the assumptions that channel analysis toward either end of the scale (at one extreme, the shot; at the other, the completed two-hour film), a host of other metrics for the description of visual and narrative elements swim into view: microunits, macrounits, and everything in between. Bullet time's movement, that is, hints at the movement of other transmedia splinters—the breakdown and recombination of elements whose parent texts, working on behalf of their authors/owners, seek to stabilize those elements into particular packages of meaning and logics of action. Successful stabilization cements a stylistic authorship that remains intact across a trajectory of citations. Such "standing waves" blending narrative, action, and event might include car chases, space battles, musical numbers, bank robberies, sex scenes, monster attacks, courtroom showdowns: any textual subunit that fans might include in their ten-best lists, the "robots they love to remember."

As a Classical Hollywood parallel, consider the emergence and circulation of the so-called "Hitchcock Zoom" [Figure 4.3]. Produced by simultaneously zooming in or out while tracking the camera in the opposite direction, the visual result is a figure held in central focus while the background shifts giddily behind him or her. Like bullet time, the Hitchcock zoom has a discernible, if multiply authored, history. It first came to public notice at a key scene in *Vertigo* (Alfred Hitchcock, 1958), when Scottie Ferguson (Jimmy Stewart)'s dizziness prevents him from pursuing Madeleine (Kim Novak) up a steep staircase. The effect was developed not by Hitchcock but Irmin Roberts,[65] a second-unit cameraman: "Combining a forward zoom with a reverse

Figure 4.3. The Hitchcock zoom in *Vertigo*—a microgenre of Classical Hollywood.

track, the cameraman instinctively came up with what became known as the 'vertigo shot'—one of the most innovative and imitated effects in film history."[66] Like bullet time, the technique migrated, appearing with different names (trombone shot, contra-zoom) in different films (a partial trajectory includes *Marnie* [1964], *Le Samourai* [1967], *Jaws* [1975], *Goodfellas* [1990], *Safe* [1995], and *Panic Room* [2002]). And like bullet time, the Hitchcock zoom eventually ended up a tired cliché. One online satire of filmmaking staples includes the following sardonic guidance on "trombone zooms: Most notably used in *Vertigo* and *Jaws*. Sometimes known as a trombone shot, this always looks good. Use it as often as you can. It is particularly useful when a character gets a piece of bad news as it visually denotes that their world has altered."[67] The rapid and evidently predictable aging of transmedial subunits such as bullet time and the Hitchcock zoom further make the case for their classification as *instances of genre on a compressed and accelerated scale*, undergoing rapid aging over a span of months and years, rather than decades. The phenomenon of generic development is a fixture, if not a fixation, of genre theory. John G. Cawelti writes that "one can almost make out a life cycle characteristic of genres as they move from an initial period of articulation and discovery, through a phase of conscious self-awareness on the part of both creators and audiences, to a time when the generic patterns have become so well-known that people become tired of their predictability."[68] Similarly, Steve Neale paraphrases a model of development put forth by Thomas Schatz, wherein genres pass through stages of experimentation (in which conventions get established), classicism (in which conventions achieve formal transparency), and refinement (in which conventions become formally "opaque" and "self-conscious").[69] The study of genre is, of course, a contentious field, and the arguments for and against notions of development, evolution, and aging are too numerous to rehearse here. But the fact remains that more particularized conceptions of genre might help transmedia studies to discern generic operations and transformations in higher resolution and greater historical specificity. Cawelti claims that the late stages of generic development mark the point at which "parodic and satiric treatments proliferate and new genres gradually arise."[70] If this is so, then the migration of microgenres offers a productive means of reconceptualizing the nagging problems of genre study: how genres arise, intermingle, and fade, only to give rise to new genres or exciting reinventions of old ones.

In the conclusion to his overview of the field, Neale argues that "most critics and theorists have in practice nearly always used the concept of genre as a way of avoiding detailed study of anything other than selective examples of Hollywood's art. . . . [Genre criticism] has also constructed structural models and evolutionary schemas as a way of avoiding rather than conducting socio-cultural and historical analysis."[71] From this, he reasons that "studies are needed of unrecognized genres like racetrack pics, of semi-recognized genres like drama, of cross-generic cycles and production trends like overland bus and prestige films, and of hybrids and combinations of all kinds."[72] While I agree with Neale that historically rooted analyses can only benefit our understanding of genre, I also believe in the worth of structural, evolutionary, and scalar approaches, especially those derived from the emerging field of new media studies. Lev Manovich proposes scalability as an essential aspect of new-media objects:

> Different versions of the same media object can be generated at various sizes or levels of detail. The metaphor of a map is useful in thinking about the scalability principle. If we equate a new media object with a physical territory, different versions of this object are like maps of this territory

generated at different scales. . . . Different versions of a new media object may vary strictly quantitatively, that is, in the amount of detail present: For instance, a full-size image and its icon.[73]

Applying this concept to genre opens up new conversations about iconography—a genre's preferred and symbolically laden imagery—and conventions—standardized units of plot, theme, or technique. *Genre* becomes an attribute locatable everywhere from a single frame (establishing shot of a prairie town) to an extended scene (a gunfight in a dusty street), from a short sequence (lawman brings order to an unruly populace) to an entire film (*Stagecoach* [John Ford, 1939]). The microgeneric object brings together cinematographic techniques and semantic content, binding them into packages whose meanings are known to (though not necessarily shared by) both producers and audiences. In this sense, the microgenre seems little different from genre itself. Microgenres are distinguished only by their *specificity* and by the *speed* with which they play out their public life, moving—with something of the uncannily blended fast- and slow-motion of bullet time—from experimentation to classicism to refinement and parody in the space of a few years.

Histories of cinematic style provide another way of conceptualizing migration. Barry Salt and David Bordwell have authored encyclopedic surveys of Classical Hollywood's stylistic norms—the rise of continuity editing, for example, or the increasing use of close-ups and cutaways.[74] For both writers, the history of style skeptically undercuts master narratives of film development (e.g., the Bazin-derived notion of an inexorable march toward realism), providing a corrective to the high theory that came to dominate film studies in the 1970s. By examining aesthetic tendencies in light of changes in technology, stylistic studies explore the repetitions and variations structuring the 100-year history of cinema:

> What leap most readily to the eye are the differences: one shot versus several; single versus multiple camera positions; fairly flat versus relatively deep compositions; distant views versus closer ones; spatial and temporal continuity versus discontinuity. Can we pick out plausible patterns of change running from our earliest image to our most recent one? Are there overall principles governing these differences? . . . Our images provide mere traces of trends, hints of complex and overlapping developments.

> For now they serve to highlight simple facts too often forgotten. The way movies look has a history; this history calls out for analysis and explanation; and the study of this domain—the history of film style—presents inescapable challenges to anyone who wants to understand cinema.[75]

For these authors, special effects, like any cinematographic technique, emerge and reproduce themselves within an environment of competing alternatives: optical printing enables traveling mattes, which supersedes the use of superimpositions and forced-perspective miniatures. This "problem/solution" model proposes a kind of industrial and aesthetic database of techniques, continually subject to innovation and available to any creator.[76] "No filmmaker comes innocent to the job," Bordwell writes. "Task and functions are, more often than not, supplied by tradition. For any given stylistic decision, the artist can draw on the solutions bequeathed by predecessors. Most minimally . . . the artist can just replicate devices that have proved successful."[77] Bordwell goes on to note that the lifespan of such devices or (to use E. H. Gombrich's term) schemas is shaped by an ongoing process of review and modification. Some devices stay the same over time, while others are tweaked—or transformed outright.

> Replication, revision, synthesis, rejection: these possibilities allow us to plot the dynamic of stability and change across the history of style. For example, since every film demands a multitude of technical choices, we should expect that most choices will replicate or synthesize traditional schemas. Revising or rejecting an inherited schema always demands fresh decisions, and unforeseen problems can swiftly proliferate. Since the virtues of a new schema can be discovered only through trial and error, the strategic filmmaker will innovate in controlled doses, setting the novel element in a familiar context that can accustom the viewer to the device's functions. For such reasons, in any film very few schemas are likely to be revised and rejected.[78]

Does bullet time qualify as such a schema? In one sense, yes. If the "problem" in that instance is taken to be the filmmaker's desire to capture slow-motion action with a freely moving camera, then the "solution" offered by bullet time merged multiple-camera rigs and postproduction digital processing to produce the target imagery. Once established, bullet time appeared in one production after another as a broadly avail-able technique. As it replicated, it underwent revision at the hands of multiple innovators (Macmillan, Taylor, Gondry, Gaeta, et al.), each of whom brought different technologies, stylistic goals, and economic con-siderations to the table. Eventually, one version of the effect became the norm. "Once we recognize as well that alternative devices are available—there is always another way to do anything—we can see that schemas often compete with one another. They will be judged by their ease, their comparative production economy, and their ability to fulfill functions deemed important to the task at hand. Over time one set of schemas can beat its rivals and win a prime place."[79]

The strength of the problem/solution model is that it accounts for both multiple authorship and the unregulated reproduction of tech-niques. (We might consider these to be migration's minimum conditions of possibility.) Its weaknesses, however, are just as profound. First, it does not sufficiently explore the logic by which techniques *decline*—when a given solution, having won widespread acceptance, becomes overfamil-iar and exhausted. Relatedly, the model is mute on the subject of parody, pastiche, and satire, perhaps due to Bordwell's abhorrence of postmod-ern theory. The lineages of bullet time and the Hitchcock zoom demon-strate that as techniques become conventions, they grow increasingly vulnerable to self-conscious quotation and ironic rereadings—surely a crucial aspect of the replication-revision-synthesis-rejection cycle by which extant solutions give way to emergent ones. Second, the model confines itself to schema that seem both artificially precise and absurdly broad: camera distance, shot length, depth staging, composition. Al-though it hints at larger constellations of techniques and meaning, the model seems reluctant to engage with more compelling syntheses such as the tendency to use cross-cutting in sequences of suspense or pursuit. (To risk a biological metaphor, it is like describing the human body ex-clusively in terms of cells, ignoring larger structures such as bones and organs.) Third, the problem/solution model glosses over potential mis-matches between producers' and audiences' perspectives. The adequacy of any convention is never assured; rather, moments of stylized short-hand function as *offerings* from the film's creators to its audience (an audience which, to compound the complexity, includes other films and filmmakers). Audiences are free to accept or reject these offerings—a trite montage sequence, a predictable "saw it coming a mile away" twist ending, a miscast romantic couple with no discernible chemistry—and the deliberations that they engage in constitute a principal pleasure of spectatorship and fandom. The fate of any given schema, then, rests not only with its intended efficacy, but the use to which it is put in audiences' viewing histories.

I do not raise these points to condemn histories of style, anymore than I wish to reify some excessively formalistic notion of genre. Rather, I suggest that migratory thinking offers a way to reconcile the two approaches into a dynamic, descriptive model of contemporary media behavior, composed equally of fixed/owned/stabilized territories and unfixable/citable/publicly held lands. Genre is, almost by definition, that which cannot be copyrighted. One can own a text—and use the law to prevent other texts from too closely approximating it—but one cannot own the field of cultural meanings and archetypes bound up in "the western," "the horror film," and so on, any more than one can regulate the use and reuse of iconography and conventions specific to those genres. By considering media texts as flows of migratory elements at differing scales and speeds, we bring together formal and cultural perspectives to see texts in both their synchronic and diachronic dimensions, as timeless systems and historically rooted practices.

Conclusion: Microgenres in a Digital Age

In an argument that parallels some of my thinking on microgenres, Leon Gurevitch has argued that digital "attractions"—show-stopping deployments of visual effects such as the panoramic flyby of the luxury ship embarking on its fateful voyage in *Titanic* (1997)—mark the conjunction of sensorially oriented spectacle and the promotional logics that have long underlain commercial filmmaking.[80] Building on Tom Gunning's characterization of early cinema as dominated by a logic of theatrical display that was later subsumed to the storytelling priorities of Classical Hollywood, Gurevitch suggests that contemporary uses of CGI, particularly as showcased in shots and set pieces intended to be appreciated in their own right as feats of visual engineering, break free from their narrative trappings in order to promote the films in which they appear—indeed, to function as proof of the medium's overall illusionistic prowess.

This fragmentation is made possible not just by the digital technologies used to generate spectacular sequences but by the media platforms on which such content circulates, a process by which "the computerization of culture reconfigures traditional film forms under the logic of the database and the archive."[81] Gurevitch writes,

> Favorite moments in film are uploaded and downloaded on YouTube to be viewed in short segments that correspond to the length of spot ads or the actualities that dominated early film history (themselves promotional forms in their own right). Cognizant of this, film makers construct set piece special effects sequences that can operate as digital attractions across a range of platforms that ultimately promote the feature film itself.[82]

In this model, special effects circulate among the domains of narrative films, commercial advertisements, and promotional videos available on the websites of visual-effects houses to showcase their own companies. Examples of such circulatory elements include not just bullet time but the impossibly accomplished zooms that open *Fight Club* (1999) and *Moulin Rouge* (Baz Luhrmann, 2001), digitally animated water shapes in *The Fellowship of the Rings* (Peter Jackson, 2001) and Jonathan Glazer's *Surfer* ad (1999), and gravity-defying fights staged in treetops in both a Levi's commercial and *Crouching Tiger, Hidden Dragon* (Ang Lee, 2000).[83]

While Gurevitch's concept of the "cinemas of transactions" usefully connects instances of special effects with their underlying technological and commercial bases, its adherence to the attractions model effectively rules out the significance of story—and by implication story*worlds*—as important factors by which certain special effects achieve enough recognizability to ensure their coherence across the various platforms on which they manifest. Indeed, by focusing exclusively on "the transferable function of these digital attractions," the cinemas of transactions perspective intentionally disregards the genealogical relationships by which special effects develop and dissipate semantic identities over their cultural lifespan.[84] By choosing synchronic precision over diachronic scope in this way, the analysis also risks collapsing all visual effects into digital practices, and hence obscuring the analog dimensions of both their historical development and current manufacture: the flyby shot in *Titanic*, to take one example, is a complex assemblage of elements including a live-action background plate of the ocean and physical actors standing on deck.

The repetition of special-effects shots and sequences has also been framed in terms of what Kristen Whissel terms the *digital emblem*, "a cinematic visual effect that operates as a site of intense signification and gives stunning (and sometimes) allegorical expression to a film's key themes, anxieties, and conceptual obsessions."[85] These visually mannered instances of storytelling, which include the staging of fight scenes in terms of intensified verticality and battle sequences involving huge masses of colliding armies or "digital multitudes," derive their unique status from the way they visualize, albeit in metaphorical ways, structural binaries such as the conflict between residual and emergent historical epochs or the individual versus the collective. More relevant to their functioning as microgenres is the way they recur in recognizable patterns across different movies; as Whissel writes, "Contemporary films deploy these effects in surprisingly consistent ways in order to interrogate and emblematize the concepts and themes with which they are concerned, often regardless of genre or nation of origin."[86] The digital emblem thesis provides an intriguing counterpoint to the cinemas of transactions, since it is often a film's grandest and most dramatic shots and sequences that circulate in promotional arenas; they serve in this sense as both conceptual and commercial emblems. The digital emblem is also useful as a way of interpreting the narrative and thematic dimension of spectacular special effects without entirely neglecting the industrial "narratives" that gave rise to them:

> Recent writing on cinematic digital multitudes tends to focus on the technologies used to create them, the software programs devised to increase their visual complexity and photorealism, and the time and money saved by replacing thousands of live extras with computer-generated substitutes. Less attention has been paid to the way in which, once rendered, the digital multitude has functioned as an effects emblem across a broad range of contemporary films, enabling the compelling rearticulation of certain thematic obsessions regarding historical time, on the one hand, and the nature of collectivities, on the other, through a surprisingly consistent set of formal conventions.[87]

These formal conventions, however, remain in Whissel's analysis a phenomenon exclusive to the movies; although patterns of visual-effects usage may become emblematic by virtue of their repetition across a variety of texts, those texts are all, in the end, confined to the single medium of cinema. Another, perhaps more subtle limitation is the interpretive emphasis on allegory that, in reading special effects as encoded expressions of structural binaries, neglects the other labor they do in constructing and branding storyworlds and establishing impressions of authorial originality while mediating forces that would destabilize those constructs.

Both of these models, however, foreground the importance of computer technologies to special effects' migration, and open up a host of questions about how the digital transformation of not just cinema but all visual media has led to a transmedia environment characterized by new forms of networked and interconnected content. The dominance of software tools such as the 3D design program Autodesk Maya created an industry standard for developing and sharing digital "assets"—data files for the description of characters, vehicles, buildings, indeed entire environments—while other components and plug-ins enable the animation, staging, and lighting of those assets along with particle, cloud, and pyrotechnic effects. As mentioned earlier, special effects' travel in the analog era was confined to elements borrowed wholesale by one production from another: snatches of stock footage; a reused prop, matte painting, or miniature. While certainly mobile enough, the "chunks" of those predigital assets were simply too large and undigested to serve as anything more than blunt appropriations. By contrast, a code-based special-effects cinema is object-oriented down to the finest grain of its texture. Digital infrastructures make it trivial to share content across productions, tweaking that content as needed; the rise of franchises based on consistent and ever-growing storyworlds populated by increasingly effects-dependent performers (as discussed in the previous chapter) seems a natural outgrowth of this shared algorithmic substrate. Because television has undergone a similar transformation, special-effects assets have the potential to travel freely between movies and TV; as for videogames, their status as the first truly "born digital" medium puts them (or rather their mode of production) at the center rather than the periphery of transmedial special effects.

It is indeed a grand vision, this transmedial melting pot in which digitality has smelted into one universal alloy the formerly disparate domains of live action, animation, and special effects, to say nothing of the differences between cinema, television, and videogames. Against its totalizing rush, we should ground ourselves in the fact that distinctions among the various ontologies of moving-image media remain prominent, if not longer quite as free of debate—consider, for example, the controversy over whether *Avatar* (James Cameron, 2009) should have been considered an animated or live action film for the purposes of the Academy Awards. As touched on in the problem/solution model discussed above, successful migration of special effects is the exception rather than the rule; only a select handful of effects usages achieve sufficient critical (or popular) mass to be recognized as microgenres, and thus to initiate the kinds of feedback loops in which content creators draw on those templates.

What, then, accounts for failed migration—what conditions limit or selectively guide the migration of special effects microgenres across texts? The Hitchcock zoom achieved its mobility across texts by working at the level of the camera lens; as a manipulation of framing and depth of field, it could be applied to many different kinds of visual material. Bullet time's spread can be explained in much the same way, with its subject matter ultimately less important than its formal presentation. In microgenres that have become prominent in the last decade, *content* seems to be a defining element of their identity: think, for example, of car crashes staged from within the vehicle, looking out the driver's or passenger's side window as an oncoming truck collides from an unexpectedly perpendicular angle; or of the trope by which a character leaps from a great height to land, thunderously, on one knee. In the latter case, the body is almost always monstrous or superpowered, hence a special-effects-dependent or "augmented" performance, as discussed in Chapter 3. My point in bringing it up here is to demonstrate that while these emergent microgenres may seem tightly tied to the action they frame, the precedent of bullet time (and the Hitchcock zoom before it) suggests that these local semantic trappings will soon dissipate, freeing what is essentially an evolution of cinematographic form to become a naturalized and tacit weapon in visual media's representational arsenal.

In the digital milieu, the grammars that emerge from microgeneric evolution might seem to range across communities of practice more freely than in the analog era. Mobile apps such as Action Movie FX and FXGuru enable iPhone and Android devices to add visual effects to videos shot by the user, promising amateurs the ability to emulate the work of industrial effects houses. YouTube and Vimeo channels showcase special-effects demos and short narrative features executed by non- or semi-professionals using more advanced, but still consumer-level, tools. As the discussion of *Star Trek* fan productions in Chapter 1 suggested, however, even the most polished digital visual tricks executed at these levels reflect a history of amateur filmmaking in which special effects multiplied, mirroring their big-screen models.

The organization of special effects into microgenres may seem to reinforce our conception of them as sealed, stable units—as artifacts with a fixed essence. But in fact, their migratory behavior flows from their composite and relational nature; they are "sandwiches" of techniques, technologies, and narrative that briefly cohere, then break apart to take up new roles in different textual homes. Microgenres such as bullet time mark not just the latest catchy visual, but also the corresponding movement of materials and personnel through networks of labor and capital. They mark ongoing points of contention and agreement between producers and audiences. They set the agenda for the replication of cultural products across a wavefront of industrialized iteration. Ultimately, they condense and localize the interweavings of media, technology, and storytelling, merging the ineffable and the pragmatic. Like any good special effect, microgenres hover at the edge of our conceptual horizon, tantalizing us with their elusive reality, their impossible solidity.

Conclusion

The Effects of Special Effects

It seems inarguable that cinema has in the last few decades developed a bad case of what Scott Bukatman calls "CGI-tis": a toxic surge of digital visual effects and the plastic irrealities they can create—indeed, are creating at an overcranked level, on multiple fronts simultaneously.[1] This sense of being overwhelmed by contemporary special effects surely stems not just from how they might dominate the running time of a given film, but how they have come to permeate our visual and media culture, serving as assets in functions as diverse as promotion and marketing, insider and fan blogs, fan filmmaking, and fabrication/collecting, to say nothing of other media—principally television and videogames—in which special effects and their interactive kin are now commonplace.

In response to CGI-tis, antibodies have arrived in the form of a promise to return, or at least pay homage, to an older way of making movies. This grasping for authenticity can be found in the rotating sets built to simulate dream gravity in Christopher Nolan's *Inception* (2010), Colin Trevorrow's promise to include animatronic dinosaurs in *Jurassic World* (2015), and an emphasis across many of the promotional materials for *The Force Awakens* (J. J. Abrams, 2015) that the new *Star Wars* film would employ some physical sets, props, and creatures like those used throughout the Original Trilogy. As much a promotional strategy as a mode of production, these initiatives, by enshrining a particular conception of the analog, ironically collapse a key opposition between "real" and "unreal" effects as they were understood prior to the digital era. For most of cinema's celluloid existence, physical, practical, and mechanical effects staged live before the camera were understood to be ontologically distinct from animation, matte paintings and traveling mattes, and miniature work done after the end of principal filming. Back then, the term "special effects" was reserved for the former, "visual effects" for the latter. Revisited from the standpoint of the digital, with its inevitable associations to virtuality and weightlessness, the special/visual differences of analog filmmaking have alloyed into a single sense of hands-on manipulation, a mode of manufacture almost artisanal in its use of material tools, whether they be wind machines, latex costumes, small-scale models, or optical printers. The once ephemeral realm of postproduction has hardened into a play of artifacts coordinated by design documents, what I have elsewhere described as *object practices* based on *build code*.[2]

I sometimes think of our desire to recuperate filmmaking's analog past as inverting our fascination with the Singularity—that hypothetical, fateful juncture of technological evolution at which our machines will surpass us in intelligence and power.[3] Although imagined often (usually with a substantial assist from special effects!) as a dystopian dawn of godlike artificial intelligences that will at best ignore us and at worst seek to exterminate us, as a thought experiment the Singularity is notable for its conceptual opacity: the assumption that, whatever form the future takes, even our most educated and reasonable predictions about it are likely to be wrong, given how transcendently irrevocable such a historical rupture will be. Remembering the analog in the time of the digital is like peering backward across just such an epochal shift, trying to see beyond a Singularity that has already occurred. Both eras manifest a radical alterity in relation to each other; it may be as impossible to see the past accurately as it is to see the future.

In part, this book has been an effort to interrupt that sense of impossibility. By reestablishing connections between characteristic blockbuster forms of the late analog and early digital eras, I hope to have shown how many of today's industrial strategies and aesthetic practices are logical outgrowths, if in mutated and exponentially metastasized states, of their predecessors. Moreover, I have tried to demonstrate that the storytelling practices and special-effects behaviors most associated with modern entertainment media—sprawling yet coherent fictional worlds, casts of artificial characters to inhabit them, and special effects that both work within and migrate across platforms and properties—enjoyed long and formative gestations in analog times. When digital production methodologies began to take root, their initial points of entry were in emerging franchises of the fantastic whose worlds, characters, and events required the design and manufacture of systematic unrealities, and whose cor responding budgets and industrial infrastructures made possible the first incursions of digitality. In this sense, the special-effects-dependent transmedia empires of today have less to do with the computer's take-over of cinema than with how digital tools evolved to serve essentially analog agendas.

This satisfying alliance of two apparently opposed trends is on ample display in *The Force Awakens*, which is made up of analog and digital pieces and bits, blended successfully—to judge by box office and critical response alike—into a marriage of currency and nostal-gia. Think of that movie's special effects, then, as carrying out a kind of sleight-of-hand, distracting us with a staged fight between old and new, "real" and "fake." The victor doesn't matter, because the point is to get us to watch the movie, to pay attention, to dispute and evalu-ate. Two kinds of prestidigitation transpire in the special effects of *The Force Awakens*—and by extension those in a number of impor-tant franchises of the fantastic, including Star Trek, Harry Potter, The Hunger Games, Transformers, and the Marvel Cinematic Universe—at once drawing attention to themselves and deflecting it as they conjure into existence worlds and characters consistent and distinctive enough to extend across media.

Throughout this book I have avoided making strong ideological claims, for fear of tarring special effects with a version of the mind-bending power they have always and unfairly been credited with in rela-tion to spectatorial credulity. Although very young children, people with dementia, or individuals who have somehow never seen a movie or tele-vision show may be completely "fooled" by a special effect or so repelled by its artifice as to reject it entirely, it is extremely difficult to imagine most viewers being so transparently accepting or rigidly closed off. In-stead, we tend to acknowledge and evaluate special effects—both in the moment of viewing and in the diffused time-spaces of promotion and reception—as, precisely, special; if their portrayal of unrealities failed to tip us off to their presence, the paratexts surrounding them work re-lentlessly to publicize the labor and ingenuity that went into their con-struction, inviting our scrutiny of them as feats of artistry, engineering, and the sensational magic that is still among cinema's most potent and defining powers. While special effects may present baffling conundrums of belief when considered abstractly or theoretically, in practice they are like most other attributes of the medium, designed to entertain and engross on multiple levels.

Yet the same coevolution of technology and entertainment that produced the digital revolution and fantastic transmedia franchises alongside each other has also fused them together in the public mind, so that critical conversations about special effects too readily fall into predictable ruts, pocked with paradoxes. Special effects are "better than ever" because of their sophistication and ubiquity, but also "worse than ever" for precisely the same reasons; they have robbed cinema of its material essence, but also promise to restore that essence; they interrupt and dilute storytelling but also enable new and wonderful kinds of stories to be told. These contradictions seem fated never to be resolved; like the primary perceptual problem identified by Christian Metz in relation to special effects, they fix our attention precisely because of their undecidability, existing for the pleasure of our disavowal. If this book has an ideological mission, it is simply to step back and ask what phenomena come into view when we stop accepting special effects at face value—putting aside, at least temporarily, concerns about their believability, their relationship to traditional narrative formats, or their role in much larger debates about digital manipulation and indexical truth.

Since 2000, a wave of scholarship has addressed special effects with increasing technical and historical specificity. Julie Turnock, Lisa Purse, Stephen Prince, Lisa Bode, Dan North, Shilo T. McClean, Kristen Whissel, Jason Sperb, Jenna Ng, Michael S. Duffy, Aylish Wood, Jessica Aldred, and others have contributed valuably to an emerging field of special-effects studies. Although their work shares as its spark a preoccupation with the digital moment, their investigations cover divergent ground, ranging from questions of performance in the age of motion capture to the unique phenomenologies of digital imagery, the software and hardware tools that have become standard workhorses in the industry, and the intersection of visual effects and independent, experimental film artists. To a person, their writing acknowledges the importance of maintaining strong connections to the analog past. Meanwhile, the theorization of digital cinema, animation, and the formal characteristics of videogames brush against special effects as objects of inquiry even when not explicitly identified as such.

Were its canvas infinitely large, this book would more completely explore those cognate fields. I regret in particular the exclusion of perspectives from production studies and software studies that are clearly central to comprehending the world of visual effects today. Similarly, I regret that so little time was spent on the state of the industry itself. Now a global enterprise, visual effects houses around the world collaborate on large film projects, their work coordinated by hyperadvanced versions of the various control systems, such as animatics, which George Lucas used to channel the creative output of the *Star Wars* production team in the 1970s. The cloud-based sharing of assets such as animation models and data captured from real-world reference goes hand in hand with systems of managerial oversight that make it possible for decision-making production hubs to monitor and shape in real time the labor of artists, designers, coders, and animators dispersed across the planet: an information infrastructure without which today's transmedia franchises would not be possible. But the emergence of such networks to support the elaborate pipelines of storyworld and character manufacture has come at the cost of a stable financial foundation. As the 2013 closure of the award-winning Rhythm and Hues company after twenty-five years of award-winning work in films such as *Babe* (George Miller, 1995) and *Life of Pi* (Ang Lee, 2013) starkly demonstrates, visual effects houses are increasingly being forced into bankruptcy by tax subsidy laws, work-for-hire contracts, and bidding regimes that make the farming-out of effects work a cutthroat business with shrinking profit margins.

Finally, I hope in future work to address more directly the issue of gender in relation to both the fandom and profession of special effects. Aficionados of film technology who follow special effects and their artists are a readership, as Michele Pierson notes in her study of the fanzine *Photon* (1963–1977), with ambitions to one day join the industry.[4] The amateur special effects films that once served as their apprenticeship now, with the assistance of digital tools, function as calling cards to a profession made up predominantly of men—and my own position, as a cis white male whose fascination with special effects extends back to boyhood, has not escaped my notice. More work needs to be done on the social and cultural dynamics around effects work at both the amateur and professional levels, not least because special effects supply much of the content of our cultural imaginary.

Toward this more comprehensive description of special effects, we must start by embracing them as complex and multidimensional objects whose significance and impact goes far beyond the moments in which they flash by onscreen. Their technical manufacture, so fervently documented by fan magazines, professional journals, DVD/Blu-ray extras, and YouTube videos over the years, and the cast of technicians, designers, and artists involved in their production represent one facet of this complicated lifespan. Another can be found in the types of storytelling that have emerged in tandem with special effects' development: inherently transmedial, world-based, and populated by characters whose augmented nature grants them unusually extended and expansive screen presence. All these phenomena are worth investigating, not only because they mark the apotheosis of a certain market logic in which increasingly systematic franchises can potentially live forever through reboots and recastings, but also because these juggernaut entertainment machines constitute dynamic spaces for the staging of conflicts between amateurs and professionals, a generational succession of poachers and producers who supply the human labor on which these franchises depend. On an even larger scale, special effects mark the convergence of different media forms—cinema, television, and videogames most obviously, but also comic books and graphic novels, board and tabletop gaming, and new fabrication technologies such as 3D printing. A diverse and disparate field, these domains come together around the assets of fantastic franchises: detailed and photogenic unrealities produced through discoverable processes, based on shared popular archives, shareable on social media, and thus essential parts of the contemporary mediascape.

ACKNOWLEDGMENTS

Thanks to my earliest advisers and graduate-student friends: Ken Hillis, Greg Siegel, Chris Dumas, Jacob Smith, and Jim Kendrick. Thanks also to the members of my dissertation committee: Barbara Klinger, Chris Anderson, James Naremore, Joan Hawkins, and Michele Pierson; colleagues Chris Cagle, Dan North, Michael S. Duffy, Julie Turnock, Lisa Purse, and Lisa Bode; and heroes Scott Bukatman, Angela Ndalianis, Vivian Sobchack, and Mark J. P. Wolf. I am grateful as well to my fellow Swarthmore faculty members Patricia White, Sunka Simon, Tim Burke, and Will Gardner. I dedicate this book with love to my family, Katie, Zachary, and Trevor; my parents, Stan and Dorothy; and my siblings Paul, Tom, Joan, and Mary.

Most of all, thanks to Henry Jenkins, a sterling exemplar, steadfast friend, and consummate coach.

NOTES

INTRODUCTION

1 Chuck Tryon, "Digital 3D, Technological Auteurism, and the Rhetoric of Cinematic Revolution," 184. See also Charles Acland, "The End of James Cameron's Quiet Years."

2 All data come from Box Office Mojo, www.boxofficemojo.com.

3 Rounding out the top ten franchises are Shrek and James Bond. The former, digitally animated, could itself be considered an extended deployment of special effects, while the long-running spy saga, although set in a world that is recognizably a version of our own, has always showcased settings, stunts, ingenious props, and eye-popping mayhem created through special effects.

4 Michele Pierson, *Special Effects: Still in Search of Wonder*, 93.

5 Christian Metz, "*Trucage* and the Film," 664.

6 Henry Jenkins, *Convergence Culture: Where Old and New Media Collide*, 95–96.

7 Apart from *The Animated Series* (1973–1974), only a handful of novels, such as James Blish's *Spock Must Die* (1970) and Theodore M. Cogswell and Charles A. Spano Jr.'s *Spock, Messiah!* (1976), marked new fictions set within the Trek universe, and even these were of dubious canonical standing.

8 Henry Jenkins, "Transmedia 202: Further Reflections."

9 Metz, "*Trucage*," 657–75.

10 Although in subsequent releases the 1977 film was rechristened *Star Wars—Episode IV: A New Hope* to reflect its place in a multichapter sequence, I have chosen to refer to it by its original, two-word title except where the later numbering is relevant.

11 Dan North, *Performing Illusions: Cinema, Special Effects and the Virtual Actor*, 12.

12 Jesper Juul, *Half-Real: Video Games between Real Rules and Fictional Worlds*.

13 Pierson, *Special Effects*; Jonathan Gray, *Show Sold Separately: Promos, Spoilers, and Other Media Paratexts*.

14 Michel Foucault, *The Order of Things: An Archeology of the Human Sciences*, xv.

15 Albert J. La Valley, "Traditions of Trickery: The Role of Special Effects in the Science Fiction Film," 143.

16 See, for example, *Every Frame a Painting*, https://www.youtube.com/user/everyframeapainting.

17 Christopher Finch, *Special Effects: Creating Movie Magic*, 23.

18 Ibid., 20–21.

19 Ibid., 30.
20 Ibid., 32. See also Katharina Loew, "Magic Mirrors: The Schüfftan Process."
21 David Bordwell, Janet Staiger, and Kristin Thompson, *The Classical Hollywood Cinema: Film Style and Mode of Production to 1960*, 148.
22 Ibid.
23 Ibid., 243.
24 Ibid., 311.
25 Ibid., 93.
26 Ibid., 94.
27 Ibid., 125.
28 Ibid., 126.
29 Ibid., 128.
30 Ibid., 135.
31 Ibid., 147.
32 Ibid., 221.
33 Finch, *Special Effects*, 36.
34 Ibid., 39.
35 Peter Ettedgui, *Production Design and Art Direction*, 8.
36 Ibid.
37 Angela Ndalianis, *Neo-Baroque Aesthetics and Contemporary Entertainment*, 4–5.
38 Ibid., 2–3.
39 Ibid., 159.
40 Ibid., 151.
41 Ibid.
42 Ibid., 189.
43 Ibid., 181.
44 Julie Turnock, *Plastic Reality: Special Effects, Technology, and the Emergence of 1970s Blockbuster Aesthetics*.
45 Ibid., 109.
46 Ibid., 146–78.
47 David Trend, *Worlding: Identity, Media, and Imagination in a Digital Age*.
48 Carlos A. Scolari, Paolo Bertetti, and Matthew Freeman, *Transmedia Archeology: Storytelling in the Borderlines of Science Fiction, Comics, and Pulp Magazines*; see also Avi Santo, *Selling the Silver Bullet: The Lone Ranger and Transmedia Brand Licensing*.
49 Derek Johnson, *Media Franchising: Creative License and Collaboration in the Culture Industries*, 115–22.

CHAPTER 1. THAT WHICH SURVIVES

1 John Meredith Lucas, "That Which Survives," *Star Trek*, season 3, episode 17, directed by Herb Wallerstein, aired January 24, 1969.
2 Heather Urbanski, *The Science Fiction Reboot: Canon, Innovation, and Fandom in Refashioned Franchises*, 44–54.

3 Matt Hills, *Fan Cultures*, 137.

4 See, for example, *Third Person: Authoring and Exploring Vast Narratives*, edited by Pat Harrigan and Noah Wardrip-Fruin; Mark J. P. Wolf, *Building Imaginary Worlds: The Theory and History of Subcreation*; Frank Rose, *The Art of Immersion*; and *Storyworlds across Media: Toward a Media-Conscious Narratology*, edited by Marie-Laure Ryan and Jan-Noël Thon.

5 "Appendix: Timeline of Imaginary Worlds," in Wolf, *Building Imaginary Worlds*, 288–346.

6 Francesca Coppa, "A Brief History of Media Fandom," 41–59.

7 obsession_inc., "Affirmational Fandom vs. Transformational Fandom."

8 Matt Hills, "From Dalek Half Balls to Daft Punk Helmets: Mimetic Fandom and the Crafting of Replicas."

9 Henry Jenkins, *Textual Poachers: Television Fans and Participatory Culture*.

10 Susan R. Gibberman, *Star Trek: An Annotated Guide to Resources on the Development, the Phenomenon, the People, the Television Series, the Films, the Novels, and the Recordings*, xi.

11 Ibid.

12 Quoted in Stephen E. Whitfield, *The Making of Star Trek*, 40.

13 Derek Johnson, *Media Franchising: Creative License and Collaboration in the Culture Industries*, 116.

14 Ibid., 117.

15 "Database," *Startrek.com*, n.d., accessed September 12, 2005. The complete definition reads as follows:

> As a rule of thumb, the events that take place within the live action episodes and movies are canon, or official *Star Trek* facts. Story lines, characters, events, stardates, etc. that take place within the fictional novels, the Animated Adventures, and the various comic lines are not canon. There are only a couple of exceptions to this rule: the Jeri Taylor penned novels "Mosaic" and "Pathways." Many of the events in these two novels feature background details of the main *Star Trek: Voyager* characters. (Note: There are a few details from an episode of the Animated Adventures that have entered into the *Star Trek* canon. The episode "Yesteryear," written by D. C. Fontana, features some biographical background on Spock.)

16 Joel Engel, *Gene Roddenberry: The Myth and the Man behind Star Trek*, 122–23.

17 Whitfield, *Making of Star Trek*, 75.

18 Herbert F. Solow and Yvonne Fern Solow, *The Star Trek Sketchbook: The Original Series*, 3.

19 Paul Schneider, "Balance of Terror," *Star Trek*, season 1, episode 14, directed by Vincent McEveety, aired December 15, 1966; George Clayton Johnson, "The Man Trap," *Star Trek*, season 1, episode 1, directed by Marc Daniels, aired September 8, 1966; Jerry Sohl, "The Corbomite Maneuver," *Star Trek*, season 1, episode 10, directed by Joseph Sargent, aired November 10, 1966.

20 Gene L. Coon (writer) and Fredric Brown (story), "Arena," *Star Trek*, season 1, episode 18, directed by Joseph Pevney, aired January 19, 1967.

21 William Lister Krewson, "Master Craftsman," 78.

22 Solow and Solow, *Star Trek Sketchbook*, 168.

23 Ibid., 2.

24 Lee Cronin, "Spock's Brain," *Star Trek*, season 3, episode 1, directed by Marc Daniels, aired September 20, 1968.

25 Quoted in Whitfield, *Making of Star Trek*, 79.

26 Herbert F. Solow and Robert H. Justman, *Inside Star Trek: The Real Story*, 27.

27 Whitfield, *Making of Star Trek*, 84. Interestingly, the question of "which way is up" plagues the *Enterprise* to this day—images of the ship are still flipped from time to time when printed in publications whose typesetters and proofreaders are perhaps unacquainted with *Trek*.

28 Whitfield, *Making of Star Trek*, 80.

29 "Early Warp Vessels," 34–41.

30 Solow and Justman, *Inside Star Trek*, 41. The figure provided by Whitfield (*Making of Star Trek*, 124) is even higher: $630,000.

31 Roddenberry, "Star Trek Proposal," 12.

32 Ibid., 10.

33 Solow and Justman, *Inside Star Trek*, 134–35. Italics in original.

34 Ibid., 175.

35 Ibid., 111.

36 Quoted in Daniel Fiebiger, "Special Visual Effects," 64.

37 Jan Alan Henderson, "Where No Show Had Gone Before," 36.

38 Ibid., 37.

39 Ibid., 39.

40 Solow and Justman, *Inside Star Trek*, 254.

41 Ibid., 253.

42 Ibid. Norman Spinrad, "The Doomsday Machine," *Star Trek*, season 2, episode 6, directed by Marc Daniels, aired October 20, 1967.

43 Solow and Justman, *Inside Star Trek*, 253.

44 Gene Roddenberry, "The Menagerie," *Star Trek*, season 1, episodes 11 and 12, directed by Marc Daniels and Robert Butler, aired November 17 and 24, 1966.

45 Solow and Justman, *Inside Star Trek*, 250–51.

46 Ibid., 251.

47 Gene Roddenberry, "Writer-Director Information," 1.

48 Joan Winston, *The Making of the Trek Conventions*.

49 Engel, *Gene Roddenberry*, 117–21.

50 Arthur H. Singer, "Turnabout Intruder," *Star Trek*, season 3, episode 24, directed by Herb Wallerstein, aired June 3, 1969.

51 Quoted in Solow and Justman, *Inside Star Trek*, 418–19.

52 Winston, *Making of the Trek Conventions*, 23.

53 Ibid., 25–26.

54 Ibid.
55 Ibid., 47.
56 Ibid.
57 Greg Tyler, "Karen Dick."
58 Paul Newitt, "An Interview with Franz Joseph."
59 Ibid.
60 Ibid.
61 Ibid.
62 Ibid.
63 Gerry Williams and Penny Durrans, "These Will Be a Reality Sooner Than You Think."
64 Newitt, "An Interview with Franz Joseph."
65 Ibid.
66 Williams and Durrans, "These Will Be a Reality Sooner Than You Think."
67 "Paper Back Talk," 210.
68 Bob Rehak, "Transmedia Space Battles: Reference Materials and Miniatures Wargames in 1970s *Star Trek* Fandom," 325–45.
69 Joan Marie Verba, *Boldly Writing: A Trekker Fan and Zine History, 1967–1987*, 17.
70 Lynn Simross, "Fotonovel: The Movie-Picture Book," OC_B1.
71 Shane Johnson, *Mr. Scott's Guide to the Enterprise*; Rick Sternbach and Michael Okuda, *Star Trek: The Next Generation Technical Manual*; Herman Zimmerman, Rick Sternbach, and Michael Okuda, *The Deep Space Nine Technical Manual*. For other examples, see "List of *Star Trek* reference books," *Wikipedia*, n.d.
72 Dick Hebdige, *Subculture: The Meaning of Style.*
73 Judith and Garfield Reeves-Stevens, *Star Trek Phase II: The Lost Series*, 12.
74 Ibid., 45.
75 Ibid., 29.
76 Ibid., 27.
77 Ibid., 104–5.
78 Ibid., 69.
79 David Alexander, *Star Trek Creator: The Authorized Biography of Gene Roddenberry*, 460.
80 Kay Anderson, "*Star Trek: The Wrath of Khan*: How the TV Series Became a Hit Movie, at Last," 52.
81 Alexander, *Star Trek Creator*, 460. Italics in original.
82 Quoted in Anderson, "How the TV Series Became a Hit Movie," 53–54.
83 Jenkins, *Textual Poachers.*
84 Ibid., 9–10.
85 Ibid., 10.
86 Ibid., 11.
87 Camille Bacon-Smith, *Enterprising Women: Television Fandom and the Creation of Popular Myth*, 67.
88 See, for example, Heather R. Joseph-Witham, *Star Trek Fans and Costume Art* (Jackson: University Press of Mississippi, 1996); Lincoln Geraghty, *Cult Collectors:*

Nostalgia, Fandom, and Collecting Popular Culture (New York: Routledge, 2014); Kurt Lancaster, *Warlocks and Warpdrive: Contemporary Fantasy Entertainments with Interactive and Virtual Environments* (Jefferson, NC: McFarland and Company, 1999); Bob Rehak, "Materializing Monsters: Aurora Models, Garage Kits, and the Object Practices of Horror Fandom," *Journal of Fandom Studies* 1, no. 1 (2013): 27–45.

89 Jenkins, *Textual Poachers*, 16–24.

90 Jeffrey Sconce, "*Star Trek, Heaven's Gate*, and Textual Transcendence," in *Cult Television*, edited by Sara Gwenllian-Jones and Roberta E. Pearson (Minneapolis: University of Minnesota Press, 2004), 200.

91 Sara Gwenllian-Jones, "Virtual Reality and Cult Television," in *Cult Television*, edited by Sara Gwenllian-Jones and Roberta E. Pearson (Minneapolis: University of Minnesota Press, 2004), 83–84.

92 Ibid., 86.

93 Alan N. Shapiro, *Star Trek: Technologies of Disappearance* (Berlin: Avinus Verlag, 2004), 9. Italics in original.

94 Ibid., 10–11.

95 Chris Gregory, *Star Trek: Parallel Narratives* (New York: St. Martin's Press, 2000), 2.

96 Shapiro, *Technologies of Disappearance*, 15.

97 Sconce, "Star Trek, Heaven's Gate, and Textual Transcendence," 215.

98 Gregory, *Parallel Narratives*, 128.

99 David Howard and Robert Gordon, *Galaxy Quest* (screenplay), May 4, 1999.

100 Ibid.

101 Verba, *Boldly Writing*, 23.

102 Bacon-Smith, *Enterprising Women*, 67.

103 Jonathan Gray, *Show Sold Separately: Promos, Spoilers, and Other Media Paratexts*, 187.

104 Ferdinand de Saussure, *Course in General Linguistics*.

105 The ship's full designation is *NTE Protector*—"NTE" standing for "Not The *Enterprise*."

106 Alan McKee, "How to Tell the Difference between Production and Consumption: A Case Study in *Doctor Who* Fandom," in *Cult Television*, edited by Sara Gwenllian-Jones and Roberta E. Pearson (Minneapolis: University of Minnesota Press, 2004), 167–85.

107 Ibid., 171.

108 Ibid., 172.

109 Ibid., 179.

110 "FAQ," *Star Trek New Voyages*, accessed July 27, 2006.

111 Ibid.

CHAPTER 2. USED UNIVERSES AND IMMACULATE REALITIES

1 Julie Turnock, *Plastic Reality: Special Effects, Technology, and the Emergence of 1970s Blockbuster Aesthetics*.

2 Marcus Hearn, *The Cinema of George Lucas*, 106.

3   Quoted in ibid., 106.

4   Chuck Tryon, "Digital 3D, Technological Auteurism, and the Rhetoric of Cinematic Revolution," 184.

5   Dale Pollock, *Skywalking: The Life and Films of George Lucas*, 142.

6   Ibid., 134.

7   Ibid., 142. Italics in original.

8   Kristen Brennan, "*Star Wars* Origins."

9   Hearn, *Cinema of George Lucas*, 18.

10 John Baxter, *Mythmaker: The Life and Work of George Lucas*, 110.

11 Ibid., 140.

12 Hearn, *The Cinema of George Lucas*, 80.

13 Ibid., 37.

14 Jim Collins, *Architectures of Excess: Cultural Life in the Information Age*, 126.

15 Ibid.

16 Baxter, *Mythmaker*, 110.

17 Hearn, *Cinema of George Lucas*, 52.

18 Pollock, *Skywalking*, 134–35.

19 Ibid., 135.

20 Hearn, *Cinema of George Lucas*, 83–84.

21 Pollock, *Skywalking*, 136.

22 Ibid.

23 Ibid.

24 Ibid., 146.

25 Ibid., 147.

26 Quoted in Hearn, *Cinema of George Lucas*, 83.

27 Ibid., 83–84.

28 Ibid.

29 Quoted in Pollock, *Skywalking*, 149.

30 Quoted in Hearn, *Cinema of George Lucas*, 83–84.

31 Quoted in Pollock, *Skywalking*, 149.

32 Ibid., 150.

33 Paul Mandell, "Joseph Johnston," 78.

34 Paul Mandell, "John Stears," 64.

35 Quoted in Pollock, *Skywalking*, 197.

36 Steve Neale, *Genre and Hollywood*, 39.

37 Jonathan Gray, *Show Sold Separately: Promos, Spoilers, and Other Media Paratexts*, 175–206.

38 Carol Titelman, ed., *The Art of Star Wars*.

39 Quoted in Pollock, *Skywalking*, 153–54.

40 Quoted in Hearn, *Cinema of George Lucas*, 89.

41 Baxter, *Mythmaker*, 175.

42 Ibid.

43 Hearn, *Cinema of George Lucas*, 89.

44 Jim Smith, *George Lucas* (London: Virgin Books, 2003), 76–77.

45 Pollock, *Skywalking*, 157.

46 Ibid., 171–72.

47 Paul Mandell, "John Dykstra," 11.

48 Mandell, "Johnston."

49 Patricia D. Netzley, *Encyclopedia of Special Effects*, 8.

50 Ibid., 171.

51 Collins, *Architectures of Excess*, 126.

52 Neale, *Genre and Hollywood*, 248.

53 Angela Ndalianis, "Special Effects, Morphing Magic, and the 1990s Cinema of Attractions," 251–71; Michele Pierson, *Special Effects: Still in Search of Wonder*.

54 Don Shay, "30 Minutes with the Godfather of Digital Cinema," 62.

55 Ibid.

56 Ibid., 65.

57 Quoted in Mark Cotta Vaz and Patricia Rose Duignan, *Industrial Light & Magic: Into the Digital Realm*, 108.

58 David Bordwell, Janet Staiger, and Kristin Thompson, *The Classical Hollywood Cinema: Film Style and Mode of Production to 1960*, 249.

59 Ibid.

60 Will Brooker, "Return to Mos Eisley: The Star Wars Trilogy on DVD."

61 Jody Duncan, *Mythmaking: Behind the Scenes of Attack of the Clones*, 13.

62 Ibid., 214.

63 Shay, "30 Minutes," 66.

64 Pierson, *Still in Search of Wonder*, 95–96.

65 Ibid., 96.

66 Shay, "30 Minutes," 66.

67 Will Brooker, *Using the Force: Creativity, Community, and Star Wars Fans*, 76.

68 Brooker, "Return to Mos Eisley."

69 Ibid.

70 See Jason Sperb, *Flickers of Film: Nostalgia in the Time of Digital Cinema*.

71 Obi-Swan, "Obi-Swan's Revenge of the Ranch! SITH DVD Reviewed!!"

72 Brooker, "Return to Mos Eisley."

73 Jacob Bryant, "George Lucas Says He Sold 'Star Wars' to 'White Slavers.'"

74 Greil Marcus, *The Manchurian Candidate*, 14. Italics added.

75 Ibid., 39–40.

76 Pollock, *Skywalking*, 189.

77 Tom Gunning, "The Cinema of Attractions: Early Film, Its Spectator, and the Avant-Garde," 56–62.

78 Thomas Schatz, "The New Hollywood," 29–30.

79 Peter Biskind, *Easy Riders and Raging Bulls: How the Sex-Drugs-and-Rock'n'Roll Generation Saved Hollywood*, 343.

CHAPTER 3. CHAINS OF EVIDENCE

1 Christian Metz, "*Trucage* and the Film," x.

2 Lisa Bode, *Making Believe: Screen Performance and Special Effects in Popular Cinema.*

3 Dan North, *Performing Illusions: Cinema, Special Effects, and the Virtual Actor*; Angela Ndalianis, "Baroque Facades: Jeff Bridges's Face and *Tron: Legacy*," 154–65; Lisa Purse, *Digital Imaging in Popular Cinema.*

4 Aljean Harmetz, *The Making of The Wizard of Oz*, 188–204.

5 Ibid., 250–51.

6 Ibid., 217–18.

7 Ibid., 253–54.

8 Ibid., 168–71.

9 Ibid., 178.

10 Alfred Kinsey et al., *Sexual Behavior in the Human Male*, 639, 656.

11 Richard Rickett, *Special Effects: The History and Technique*, 10.

12 Ibid., 12.

13 James Naremore, "Love and Death in *A.I. Artificial Intelligence*," 265–66.

14 Ray Morton, *King Kong: The History of a Movie Icon from Fay Wray to Peter Jackson*, 38–39.

15 Erik Barnouw, *The Magician and the Cinema.*

16 Michelle Pierson, *Special Effects: Still in Search of Wonder*, 11.

17 Ibid.

18 Matthew Solomon, "Twenty-five Heads under One Hat: Quick-Change in the 1890s," 3.

19 Ibid., 4.

20 Rickett, *Special Effects*, 13.

21 Ibid., 13.

22 See the Introduction's discussion of this image as an example of preproduction art.

23 Barbara Maria Stafford and Frances Terpak, *Devices of Wonder: From the World in a Box to Images on a Screen*, 268.

24 Ibid., 272–73.

25 Donald Crafton, *Before Mickey: The Animated Film 1898–1928*, 7.

26 Rickett, *Special Effects*, 136–37.

27 Ibid., 137.

28 Ibid.

29 Crafton, *Before Mickey*, 113.

30 Ibid.

31 Rickett, *Special Effects*, 137.

32 Crafton, *Before Mickey*, 317.

33 Ibid., 338.

34 Ray Harryhausen claims that the shift to anthropomorphic dimensional animation turned "the process from a novelty into the embryo of an art form" (Ray Harryhausen and Tony Dalton, *Ray Harryhausen: An Animated Life*, 9).

35 Rickett, *Special Effects*, 150–51.

36 Morton, *King Kong*, 20–21.

37 Cynthia Erb, *Tracking King Kong: A Hollywood Icon in World Culture*, 13.

38 Morton, *King Kong*, 22–25.

39 Ibid., 34.

40 Ibid., 35.

41 Quoted in *RKO Production 601: The Making of Kong, Eighth Wonder of the World*.

42 Quoted in Harryhausen and Dalton, *An Animated Life*, 10.

43 Quoted in *RKO Production 601*.

44 Harryhausen and Dalton, *An Animated Life*, 24.

45 Jennifer Benidt, "The Terminator," 4–23.

46 Ibid., 18.

47 Rickett, *Special Effects*, 204.

48 Quoted in ibid., 227.

49 Stephen Prince, "True Lies: Perceptual Realism, Digital Images, and Film Theory," 28.

50 Ibid., 32.

51 Ibid., 29.

52 Ibid., 33.

53 Ibid.

54 "Beatles Plan for Rings Film."

55 Barbara Creed, "The Cyberstar: Digital Pleasures and the End of the Unconscious," 80.

56 Ibid., 79.

57 Ibid., 84.

58 Ibid., 84.

59 Ibid., 80.

60 Mark Langer, "The End of Animation History."

61 Ibid.

62 Ibid.

63 Creed, "The Cyberstar," 85.

64 Langer, "The End of Animation History."

65 Naremore, "Love and Death in *A.I. Artificial Intelligence*," 264–65.

66 Ibid., 266.

67 Ibid.

68 Cubitt, "Special Effects Today," 116.

69 James Naremore, *Acting in the Cinema*.

70 Ibid., 2.

71 Ibid., 3.

72 Ibid., 19.

73 David Jay Bolter and Richard Grusin, *Remediation: Understanding Media Change*.

74 Jody Duncan, "*Final Fantasy*: Flesh for Fantasy," 34.

75 Naremore, *Acting in the Cinema*, 44.

76 Ibid., 37.

77 Quoted in Steven L. Kent and Tim Cox, *The Making of Final Fantasy: The Spirits Within*, 147.

78 Ibid., 148.

79 Jean Baudrillard, *The System of Objects*, 89.

80 Michel Tournier, *The Ogre*, 3–4.

81 Victoria Nelson, *The Secret Life of Puppets*, 249.

82 Ibid., 249.

83 Ibid., 251.

84 Ibid., 253.

85 Ibid.

86 William Paul, *Laughing Screaming: Modern Hollywood Horror and Comedy*, 384.

87 Ibid.

88 Ibid.

89 Rickett, *Special Effects*, 300.

90 Naremore, "Love and Death in *A.I. Artificial Intelligence*," 265–66.

CHAPTER 4. MICROGENRES IN MIGRATION

1 Henry Jenkins, *Convergence Culture: Where Old and New Media Collide*.

2 Don Brinkley, "The Sky Is Falling," *Voyage to the Bottom of the Sea*, season 1, episode 6, directed by Leonard Horn, aired October 19, 1964.

3 Vivian Sobchack, *Screening Space: The American Science Fiction Film*, 88.

4 Barbara Klinger, *Beyond the Multiplex: Cinema, New Technologies, and the Home* (Berkeley: University of California Press, 2006), 8.

5 Eric Schaefer, *"Bold! Daring! Shocking! True!": A History of Exploitation Films, 1919–1959*, 80.

6 Ibid., 56–73.

7 Blair Davis, *The Battle for the Bs: 1950s Hollywood and the Rebirth of Low-Budget Cinema*, 177.

8 Rod Serling, "Third from the Sun," *The Twilight Zone*, season 1, episode 14, directed by Richard L. Bare, aired January 8, 1960; Charles Beaumont, "Elegy," *The Twilight Zone*, season 1, episode 20, directed by Douglas Heyes, aired February 19, 1960; Richard Matheson, "The Invaders," *The Twilight Zone*, season 2, episode 15, directed by Douglas Heyes, aired January 27, 1961; Rod Serling, "The Little People," *The Twilight Zone*, season 3, episode 28, directed by William Claxton, aired March 30, 1962; Rod Serling, "Execution," *The Twilight Zone*, season 1, episode 26, directed by David Orrick McDearmon, aired April 1, 1960; Rod Serling, "The Rip Van Winkle Caper," *The Twilight Zone*, season 2, episode 24, directed by Jus Addiss, aired April 28, 1961; Rod Serling, "The Monsters Are Due on Maple

Street," *The Twilight Zone*, season 1, episode 22, directed by Ronald Winston, aired March 4, 1960; Rod Serling, "To Serve Man," *The Twilight Zone*, season 3, episode 24, directed by Richard L. Bare, aired March 2, 1962. Interestingly, "Elegy" also includes sound effects later heard as the background beeps and hums on the bridge of *Star Trek*'s *Enterprise*.

9   Barney Slater, "War of the Robots," *Lost in Space*, season 1, episode 20, directed by Sobey Martin, aired February 9, 1966; Steven Bochco, Dean Hargrove, and Roland Kibbee, "Mind Over Mayhem," *Columbo*, season 3, episode 6, directed by Alf Kjellin, aired February 10, 1974; Bruce Kalish and Philip John Taylor, "Dr. Morkenstein," *Mork & Mindy*, season 2, episode 5, directed by Harvey Medlinsky, aired October 7, 1979; Bill Taylor, "Spaced Out," *The New Adventures of Wonder Woman*, season 3, episode 14, directed by Ivan Dixon, aired January 26, 1979.

10 Martin Anderson, "50 Assets Hollywood Re-used," http://www.denofgeek.com/movies/13962/50-assets-hollywood-re-used.

11 Barry Keith Grant, " 'Sensuous Elaboration': Reason and the Visible in the Science-Fiction Film," 22.

12 Albert J. La Valley, "Traditions of Trickery: The Role of Special Effects in the Science Fiction Film," 146.

13 Richard Rickett, *Special Effects: The History and Technique*, 8.

14 Michele Pierson, *Special Effects: Still In Search Of Wonder*, 110. Italics added.

15 Laura Mulvey, "A Clumsy Sublime," 3.

16 Julie Turnock, *Plastic Reality: Special Effects, Technology, and the Emergence of 1970s Blockbuster Aesthetics*, 11.

17 Sobchack, *Screening Space*, 64.

18 See Henry Jenkins, *Textual Poachers: Television Fans and Participatory Culture*; John Tulloch and Henry Jenkins, eds., *Science Fiction Audiences: Watching Doctor Who and Star Trek*.

19 David Edelstein, "Bullet Time Again: The Wachowskis Reload."

20 Rickitt phrases it more succinctly: "Shots in which the camera roams freely around a scene in which the action appears to have been frozen at one moment in time" (Rickitt, *Special Effects*, 185). But as Mark J. P. Wolf has observed, "bullet time" can also designate a variety of cinematic distortions in which real or virtual cameras explore a newly liberated time-space. Sometimes the action is completely frozen while the camera travels at "normal" speed, while in other instances both camera and subject undergo changes in their respective time frames (Mark J. P. Wolf, "Space, Time, Frame, Cinema: Muybridge, Frozen Time, and Beyond").

21 In this sense, bullet time comments not only on the need to question authority, but also on the filmmakers' desire to push the boundaries of representation— bringing their own technological "kung fu" to bear on the problem of wowing jaded audiences. In commentaries and interviews, John Gaeta praises the significance of *The Matrix*'s optical achievements, situating them within a larger history of cinematic innovation:

It's all baby steps toward something much larger that won't be really common-place for a few years. But there are people around the world scratching their heads about a new way to photograph things. And it'll be as revolutionary as when cameras came off sticks and went to cranes, when they came off cranes and went to Steadicams. We're talking about cameras that are now broken from the subject matter, that are virtual. So that's the next phase, that's what computers have introduced to cinematography ("What Is Bullet Time?").

22 David Denby, "The Current Cinema," 194.

23 Janet Maslin, "The Matrix."

24 N'Gai Croal, "Maximizing the Matrix," 64.

25 Other 1999 nominees included *Stuart Little* for Visual Effects; *Fight Club* for Sound Effects Editing; *The Green Mile*, *The Insider*, and *The Mummy* for Sound; *American Beauty*, *The Sixth Sense*, *The Cider House Rules*, and *The Insider* for Film Editing.

26 "The film's Super Bowl trailer hinted that this would be the first movie since *Terminator 2* with truly 'how'd they do that?' special effects" (Croal, "Maximizing the Matrix," 64).

27 Aesthetic and thematic intertexts frontloaded into the *Matrix* sequels were even more dense and varied. The production team for *Reloaded* reportedly drew from a mélange of visual references, including "*Alien, 2001, Vertigo, Apocalypse Now, Koyaanisqatsi*, and *20,000 Leagues Under the Sea*, along with documentary footage of car crashes, robotics manufacturing, nineteenth-century submarines, glassblowers at work, the drilling of the Chunnel, the heavyweight bouts of Rocky Marciano, and the explosion of the *Hindenburg*" (Steve Silberman, "Matrix²," 114).

28 Ibid., 118.

29 Ron Magid, "Techno Babel," 50.

30 Ibid.

31 This and the rest of the technical discussion are drawn equally from the *Matrix* DVD commentary and from Barbara Robertson, "Living a Virtual Existence," 54–59.

32 Dependent on computers for its existence, the bullet time camera is perhaps better described as a phenomenological construct that inverts traditional modes of cinematographic recording. Instead of multiple exposures from a single run of film through a unitary mechanism, bullet time blends many single shots into an apparently unbroken take. It is, in a sense, only the *idea* of a camera, its actual referent an army of lenses.

33 Magid, "Techno Babel," 52.

34 Ibid.

35 Michel Gondry, a director of music videos, TV ads, and feature films, is also credited by some with originating the effect in spots for Smirnoff and Polaroid (1996). His comparatively early use, along with the wide audience his work reached, mark him as a major contender in the origination sweepstakes. Gondry himself,

however, was sanguine when confronted with the work of yet another innovator, the French director Emmanuel Carlier:

> "Sometimes ideas are in the air," says Gondry. "Basically, my technique is simpler than Carlier's. It's just two cameras, one in each hand, and you can do it wherever you want. You take two shots and morph in between. The two methods are complementary. Mine is more fluid in terms of the motion, the other has more layers in it" (Richard Linnett, "The Gondry Effect").

36 TimeSlice Films, "Tim Macmillan—Early Work 1980–1994," January 20, 2010, YouTube, https://youtu.be/ocLJWCnMhTo.

37 For a complete record of Macmillan's productions, as well as a discussion of his camera technologies and underlying philosophy, see his official website at http://timeslicefilms.com/.

38 The Gap ad, directed by Matthew Ralston, featured effects by the production house Steele VFX. Described in March 1999 (one month before the release of *The Matrix*) as "one of the more recognizable of recent commercials by virtue of its visual effects," the ad showed "a group of dancers jitterbugging in khakis. One dancer vaults over the head of another, resulting in an impossible freeze frame that appears to allow the camera to arc around these dancers in 3D space" (Eric Huelsman, "Cool Effects That Make for Hot TV," 45). The article goes on to say that "the net result is a jaw-dropping effect that has since become a hallmark for the visual effects industry" (ibid., 46).

39 Ibid.

40 Gary Stix, "Special Effects: Pictures Worth a Thousand Cameras," 46.

41 Dayton Taylor, "Virtual Camera Movement: The Way of the Future?" 93.

42 Ibid., 94.

43 Ibid.

44 Ibid.

45 U.S. Patent No. 5,659,323. Issued August 19, 1997.

46 David Lindsay, "The Patent Files: Muybridge Squared," 35.

47 Jeffrey Sconce, *Haunted Media: Electronic Presence from Telegraphy to Television*, 204.

48 The January 2000 Super Bowl, aired on CBS, made use of a bullet time variant to replay action on the field.

49 "Insane Clown Poppy" (aired November 12, 2000) used the effect as opening-credit punchline, showing the Simpson family suspended in midair over their couch as the living room rotated around them. Only a few months later, the episode "New Kids on the Bleech" (aired February 25, 2001) featured the guest-starring boy band N'Sync in a leap-freeze-and-rotate dance move called "The Matrix."

50 "A New World" (aired May 6, 2002) and "The Magic Bullet" (aired April 16, 2003).

51 "Stare," directed by John Hoeg, Leo Burnett Advertising Agency; "SQ" and "CQ," directed by Paciwood Music & Entertainment, Foot Cone & Belding Advertising

Agency; "Pure Drive," directed by Michel Gondry, Fallon Worldwide Advertising Agency; "Leon Live," directed by Leon Tai, Paciwood Music & Entertainment.

52 Jane Gaines, *Contested Culture: The Image, the Voice, and the Law.*

53 While the effects for *Kung Pow*'s cow fight were achieved through methods similar to *The Matrix*'s, *Shrek*, an entirely digitally animated feature, rendered bullet time using no photographic elements whatsoever. *Osmosis Jones* (2001), like *The Simpsons*, rendered bullet time in 2D cel animation. This demonstrates again that the special effect, far from depending on any particular underlying technology (e.g., multiple cameras and digital interpolation), *itself* adapts underlying technologies (e.g., hand-drawn artwork) for its realization.

54 Anthony, "Comment on John Gaeta Interview about Third Matrix Movie."

55 Linnett, "The Gondry Effect."

56 Owen Hammer, "Bedtime for Deadtime."

57 Ibid.

58 Nick Rogers, "*Underworld* Represents Underbelly of Hollywood," 16.

59 Roger Moore, "*Dead* Is a Morgue of Clichés," D5. It should be noted that by this point the effect is being credited with appearances it did not even make—*Kill Bill Volume I* (2003) contains no bullet-time shots.

60 Johnny Dee, "Attack of the Clones," 8.

61 Devin Gordon, "The Matrix Makers," 87.

62 Quoted in Edelstein, "Bullet Time Again."

63 Ibid.

64 Ibid.

65 Dan Auiler, *Vertigo: The Making of a Hitchcock Classic*, 66.

66 Ibid. To save costs, the shot was actually accomplished in postproduction, using a scaled-down set. "The miniature model of the tower's interior was built on its side; mounted on tracks, the camera moved back as the lens zoomed in. The effect is startling: The viewer's perspective is stretched in one surreal, dizzying motion, as if one is falling and rising simultaneously" (Auiler, *Vertigo*, 156).

67 Andrew Cousins, "Short Film the Wilderman Way," Netribution Film Network, February 18, 2015, https://www.netribution.co.uk/features/carnal_cinema/53.html.

68 John G. Cawelti, "*Chinatown* and Generic Transformation," 200.

69 Steve Neale, *Genre and Hollywood*, 211–12.

70 Cawelti, "*Chinatown*," 200.

71 Neale, *Genre and Hollywood*, 252.

72 Ibid., 254.

73 Lev Manovich, *The Language of New Media*, 38.

74 Barry Salt, *Film Style and Technology: History and Analysis*; David Bordwell, *On the History of Film Style*. See also David Bordwell, Janet Staiger, and Kristin Thompson's *The Classical Hollywood Cinema: Film Style and Mode of Production to 1960*.

75 Bordwell, *History of Film Style*, 2–4.

76 For a full discussion of the problem/solution model, see Bordwell, *History of Film Style*, 149–57.

77 Ibid., 151–52.

78 Ibid., 154–55.

79 Ibid., 155.

80 Leon Gurevitch, "The Cinemas of Transactions: The Exchangeable Currency of the Digital Attraction," 375–77.

81 Ibid., 369.

82 Ibid.

83 Ibid., 374–75.

84 Ibid., 375.

85 Kristen Whissel, *Spectacular Digital Effects: CGI and Contemporary Cinema*, 6.

86 Ibid., 13.

87 Ibid., 60.

CONCLUSION

1 Scott Bukatman, "Foreword," ix.

2 Bob Rehak, "From Model Building to 3D Printing: *Star Trek* and Build Code across the Analog/Digital Divide."

3 Vernor Vinge, "The Coming Technological Singularity: How to Survive in the Post-Human Era," 1993, https://edoras.sdsu.edu/~vinge/misc/singularity.html.

4 Michele Pierson, *Special Effects: Still in Search of Wonder*, 66–70.

BIBLIOGRAPHY

Acland, Charles. "The End of James Cameron's Quiet Years." In *Media Studies Futures*, edited by Kelly Gates, 269–95. London: Blackwell Press, 2013.

Alexander, David. *Star Trek Creator: The Authorized Biography of Gene Roddenberry*. New York: Roc, 1994.

Anderson, Kay. "*Star Trek: The Wrath of Khan*: How the TV Series Became a Hit Movie, at Last." *Cinefantastique* 12, no. 5–6 (July–August 1982): 52.

Anthony. "Comment on John Gaeta Interview about Third Matrix Movie." *Kottke.org* (October 20, 2003). kottke.org.

Auiler, Dan. *Vertigo: The Making of a Hitchcock Classic*. New York: St. Martin's Press, 1998.

Bacon-Smith, Camille. *Enterprising Women: Television Fandom and the Creation of Popular Myth*. Philadelphia: University of Pennsylvania Press, 1992.

Barnouw, Erik. *The Magician and the Cinema*. New York: Oxford University Press, 1981.

Baudrillard, Jean. *The System of Objects*. Translated by James Benedict. London: Verso, 1996.

Baxter, John. *Mythmaker: The Life and Work of George Lucas*. New York: Avon Books, 1999.

"Beatles Plan for Rings Film." *CNN.com* (March 28, 2002). http://edition.cnn .com/2002/SHOWBIZ/Movies/03/28/rings.beatles/index.html.

Benidt, Jennifer. "The Terminator." *Cinefex* 21 (April 1985): 4–23.

Biskind, Peter. *Easy Riders and Raging Bulls: How the Sex-Drugs-and-Rock'n'Roll Generation Saved Hollywood*. New York: Touchstone, 1999.

Bode, Lisa. *Making Believe: Screen Performance and Special Effects in Popular Cinema*. New Brunswick, NJ: Rutgers University Press, 2017.

Bolter, David Jay, and Richard Grusin. *Remediation: Understanding Media Change*. Cambridge, MA: Massachusetts Institute of Technology Press, 1999.

Bordwell, David. *On the History of Film Style*. Cambridge, MA: Harvard University Press, 1997.

Bordwell, David, Janet Staiger, and Kristin Thompson. *The Classical Hollywood Cinema: Film Style and Mode of Production to 1960*. London: Routledge, 1988.

Brennan, Kristen. "*Star Wars* Origins." *Jitterbug Fantasia* (January 30, 2006). http:// www.moongadget.com/origins/.

Brooker, Will. "Return to Mos Eisley: The Star Wars Trilogy on DVD." *TheForce.net* (September 29, 2004). theforce.net.

————. *Using the Force: Creativity, Community and Star Wars Fans.* New York: Continuum, 2002.

Bryant, Jacob. "George Lucas Says He Sold 'Star Wars' to 'White Slavers.'" *Variety* (December 30, 2015), variety.com.

Bukatman, Scott. "Foreword." In *Special Effects: New Histories/Theories/Contexts*, edited by Dan North, Bob Rehak, and Michael S. Duffy, ix–xii. London: Palgrave/BFI, 2015.

Cawelti, John G. "*Chinatown* and Generic Transformation." In *Film Genre Reader*, edited by Barry Keith Grant, 183–201. Austin: University of Texas Press, 1986.

Collins, Jim. *Architectures of Excess: Cultural Life in the Information Age.* New York: Routledge, 1995.

Coppa, Francesca. "A Brief History of Media Fandom." In *Fan Fiction and Fan Communities in the Age of the Internet*, edited by Karen Hellekson and Kristina Busse, 41–59. Jefferson, NC: McFarland and Company, 2006.

Cousins, Andrew. "Short Film the Wilderman Way." *Netribution Film Network* (February 18, 2015). netribution.co.uk.

Crafton, Donald. *Before Mickey: The Animated Film 1898–1928.* Cambridge, MA: Massachusetts Institute of Technology Press, 1982.

Creed, Barbara. "The Cyberstar: Digital Pleasures and the End of the Unconscious." *Screen* 41, no. 1 (Spring 2000): 79–86.

Croal, N'Gai. "Maximizing the Matrix." *Newsweek* 133, no. 6 (April 19, 1999): 64–65.

Cubitt, Sean. "Phalke, Méliès, and Special Effects Today." *Wide Angle* 21, no. 1 (January 1999): 114–30.

Davis, Blair. *The Battle for the Bs: 1950s Hollywood and the Rebirth of Low-Budget Cinema.* New Brunswick, NJ: Rutgers University Press, 2012.

Dee, Johnny. "Attack of the Clones." *London Times* (October 11, 2003): 8.

Denby, David. "The Current Cinema." *New Yorker* 75, no. 9 (April 26 and May 3, 1999): 192–94.

Duncan, Jody. "*Final Fantasy*: Flesh for Fantasy." *Cinefex* 86 (July 2001): 33–44, 127–29.

————. *Mythmaking: Behind the Scenes of Attack of the Clones.* New York: Del Ray, 2002.

"Early Warp Vessels." *Star Trek: The Magazine* 1, no. 16 (August 2000): 34–41.

Edelstein, David. "Bullet Time Again: The Wachowskis Reload." *New York Times* (May 11, 2003): 2A: 1.

Engel, Joel. *Gene Roddenberry: The Myth and the Man Behind Star Trek.* New York: Hyperion, 1994.

Erb, Cynthia. *Tracking King Kong: A Hollywood Icon in World Culture.* Detroit: Wayne State University Press, 1998.

Ettedgui, Peter. *Production Design and Art Direction.* Woburn, MA: Focal Press, 1999.

Fiebiger, Daniel. "Special Visual Effects." *Cinefantastique* 27, no. 11–12 (July 1996): 64–75.

Finch, Christopher. *Special Effects: Creating Movie Magic.* New York: Abbeville Press, 1984.

Foucault, Michel. *The Order of Things: An Archeology of the Human Sciences*. New York: Vintage Books, 1994.

Gaines, Jane. *Contested Culture: The Image, the Voice, and the Law*. Chapel Hill: University of North Carolina Press, 1991.

Gibberman, Susan R. *Star Trek: An Annotated Guide to Resources on the Development, the Phenomenon, the People, the Television Series, the Films, the Novels, and the Recordings*. Jefferson, NC: McFarland and Company, 1991.

Gordon, Devin. "The Matrix Makers." *Newsweek* 141, no. 1 (December 30, 2002 and January 6, 2003): 80–89.

Grant, Barry Keith. "'Sensuous Elaboration': Reason and the Visible in the Science-Fiction Film." In *Alien Zone II: The Spaces of Science Fiction Cinema*, edited by Annette Kuhn, 16–30. London: Verso, 1999.

Gray, Jonathan. *Show Sold Separately: Promos, Spoilers, and Other Media Paratexts*. New York: New York University Press, 2010.

Gunning, Tom. "The Cinema of Attractions: Early Film, Its Spectator, and the Avant-Garde." In *Early Cinema: Space Frame Narrative*, edited by Thomas Elsaesser with Adam Barker, 56–62. London: BFI Publishing, 1990.

Gurevitch, Leon. "The Cinemas of Transactions: The Exchangeable Currency of the Digital Attraction." *Television & New Media* 11, no. 5 (2010): 375–77.

Hammer, Owen. "Spotlight: Bedtime for Deadtime." *Visual Effects Headquarters* (June 1998).

Harmetz, Aljean. *The Making of The Wizard of Oz*. New York: Hyperion, 1998.

Harrigan, Pat, and Noah Wardrip-Fruin, eds. *Third Person: Authoring and Exploring Vast Narratives*. Cambridge, MA: Massachusetts Institute of Technology Press, 2009.

Harryhausen, Ray, and Tony Dalton. *Ray Harryhausen: An Animated Life*. New York: Billboard Books, 2004.

Hearn, Marcus. *The Cinema of George Lucas*. New York: Harry N. Abrams, 2005.

Hebdige, Dick. *Subculture: The Meaning of Style*. London: Routledge, 1997.

Henderson, Jan Alan. "Where No Show Had Gone Before." *American Cinematographer* 73, no. 1 (January 1992): 34–40.

Hills, Matt. *Fan Cultures*. London: Routledge, 2002.

———. "From Dalek Half Balls to Daft Punk Helmets: Mimetic Fandom and the Crafting of Replicas." *Transformative Works and Cultures* 16 (2014).

Huelsman, Eric. "Cool Effects That Make for Hot TV." *Animation World Magazine* 3, no. 12 (March 1999): 45.

Jenkins, Henry. *Convergence Culture: Where Old and New Media Collide*. New York: New York University Press, 2006.

———. *Textual Poachers: Television Fans and Participatory Culture*. New York: Routledge, 1992.

———. "Transmedia 202: Further Reflections." *Confessions of an Aca-Fan* (August 1, 2011). henryjenkins.org.

Johnson, Derek. *Media Franchising: Creative License and Collaboration in the Culture Industries*. New York: New York University Press, 2013.

Johnson, Shane. *Mr. Scott's Guide to the Enterprise*. New York: Simon and Schuster, 1989.

Juul, Jesper. *Half-Real: Video Games between Real Rules and Fictional Worlds*. Cambridge, MA: Massachusetts Institute of Technology Press, 2005.

Kent, Steven L., and Tim Cox. *The Making of Final Fantasy: The Spirits Within*. Indianapolis: Brady Publishing, 2001.

Kinsey, Alfred, et al. *Sexual Behavior in the Human Male*. Bloomington: Indiana University Press, 1948.

Krewson, William Lister. "Master Craftsman." *Cinefantastique* 27, no. 11–12 (July 1996): 78–79.

Langer, Mark. "The End of Animation History." Paper presented to the Ottawa Student Animation Festival: Teacher's Symposium, Ottawa, Canada, October 19, 2001.

La Valley, Albert J. "Traditions of Trickery: The Role of Special Effects in the Science Fiction Film." In *Shadows of the Magic Lamp: Fantasy and Science Fiction in Film*, edited by George Slusser and Eric S. Rabkin, 141–58. Carbondale: Southern Illinois University Press, 1985.

Lindsay, David. "The Patent Files: Muybridge Squared." *New York Press Weekly* 10, no. 37 (September 10–16, 1997): 35.

Linnett, Richard. "The Gondry Effect." *Shoot* (May 8, 1998): n.p.

Loew, Katharina. "Magic Mirrors: The Schüfftan Process." In *Special Effects: New Histories/Theories/Contexts*, edited by Dan North, Bob Rehak, and Michael S. Duffy, 62–77. London: Palgrave/BFI, 2015.

Magid, Ron. "Techno Babel." *American Cinematographer* 80, no. 4 (1999): 46–55.

Mandell, Paul. "John Dykstra." *Cinefantastique* 6, no. 4/7, no. 1 (1978): 11–17.

———. "John Stears." *Cinefantastique* 6, no. 4/7, no. 1 (1978): 64.

———. "Joseph Johnston." *Cinefantastique* 6, no. 4/7, no. 1 (1978): 77–78.

Manovich, Lev. *The Language of New Media*. Cambridge, MA: Massachusetts Institute of Technology Press, 2001.

Marcus, Greil. *The Manchurian Candidate*. London: British Film Institute, 2002.

Maslin, Janet. "The Matrix." *New York Times* (March 31, 1999).

Metz, Christian. "*Trucage* and the Film." Translated by Françoise Meltzer. *Critical Inquiry* 3, no. 4 (Summer 1977): 657–75.

Moore, Roger. "*Dead* Is a Morgue of Clichés." *[Albany, NY] Times Union* (October 14, 2003): D5.

Morton, Ray. *King Kong: The History of a Movie Icon from Fay Wray to Peter Jackson*. New York: Applause Theatre & Cinema Books, 2005.

Mulvey, Laura. "A Clumsy Sublime." *Film Quarterly* 60, no. 3 (2007): 3.

Naremore, James. *Acting in the Cinema*. Berkeley: University of California Press, 1988.

———. "Love and Death in *A.I. Artificial Intelligence*." *Michigan Quarterly* 44, no. 2 (Spring 2005): 256–84.

Ndalianis, Angela. "Baroque Facades: Jeff Bridges's Face and *Tron: Legacy*." In *Special Effects: New Histories/Theories/Contexts*, edited by Dan North, Bob Rehak, and Michael S. Duffy, 154–65. London: Palgrave/BFI, 2015.

———. *Neo-Baroque Aesthetics and Contemporary Entertainment*. Cambridge, MA: Massachusetts Institute of Technology Press, 2004.

———. "Special Effects, Morphing Magic, and the 1990s Cinema of Attractions." In *Meta-Morphing: Visual Transformation and the Culture of Quick-Change*, edited by Vivian Sobchack, 251–71. Minneapolis: University of Minnesota Press, 2000.

Neale, Steve. *Genre and Hollywood*. London: Routledge, 2000.

Nelson, Victoria. *The Secret Life of Puppets*. Cambridge, MA: Harvard University Press, 2001.

Netzley, Patricia D. *Encyclopedia of Special Effects*. New York: Checkmark Books, 2001.

Newitt, Paul. "An Interview with Franz Joseph." *Trekplace.com* (June 1984). trekplace.com.

North, Dan. *Performing Illusions: Cinema, Special Effects, and the Virtual Actor*. London: Wallflower Press, 2008.

Obi-Swan. "Obi-Swan's Revenge of the Ranch! SITH DVD Reviewed!!" *Ain't It Cool News* (October 6, 2006). www.aint-it-cool.com.

obsession_inc. "Affirmational Fandom vs. Transformational Fandom." *obsession_inc* (June 1, 2009).

"Paper Back Talk." *New York Times* (July 13, 1975): 210.

Paul, William. *Laughing Screaming: Modern Hollywood Horror and Comedy*. New York: Columbia University Press, 1994.

Pierson, Michele. *Special Effects: Still in Search of Wonder*. New York: Columbia University Press, 2002.

Pollock, Dale. *Skywalking: The Life and Films of George Lucas*. Hollywood, CA: Samuel French, 1990.

Prince, Stephen. "True Lies: Perceptual Realism, Digital Images, and Film Theory." *Film Quarterly* 49, no. 3 (Spring 1996): 24–33.

Purse, Lisa. *Digital Imaging in Popular Cinema*. Edinburgh: Edinburgh University Press, 2013.

Reeves-Stevens, Judith, and Garfield Reeves-Stevens. *Star Trek Phase II: The Lost Series*. New York: Pocket Books, 1997.

Rehak, Bob. "From Model Building to 3D Printing: *Star Trek* and Build Code across the Analog/Digital Divide." In *The Routledge Companion to Media Fandom*, edited by Suzanne Scott and Melissa Click (forthcoming).

———. "Transmedia Space Battles: Reference Materials and Miniatures Wargames in 1970s *Star Trek* Fandom." *Science Fiction Film and Television* 9, no. 3 (2016): 325–45.

Rickett, Richard. *Special Effects: The History and Technique*. New York: Billboard Books, 2000.

RKO Production 601: The Making of Kong, Eighth Wonder of the World. *King Kong* DVD. Burbank, CA: Turner Home Entertainment/Warner Home Video, 2005.

Robertson, Barbara. "Living a Virtual Existence." *Computer Graphics World* 22, no. 5 (1999): 54–59.

Roddenberry, Gene. "Star Trek Proposal." March 11, 1964. Manuscript Collections, Lilly Library, Indiana University.

————. "Writer-Director Information." August 30, 1966. Manuscript Collections, Lilly Library, Indiana University.

Rogers, Nick. "*Underworld* Represents Underbelly of Hollywood." *[Springfield, IL] State Journal-Register* (September 25, 2003): 16.

Rose, Frank. *The Art of Immersion.* New York: W. W. Norton, 2012.

Ryan, Marie-Laure, and Jan-Noël Thon, eds. *Storyworlds Across Media: Toward a Media-Conscious Narratology.* Lincoln: University of Nebraska Press, 2014.

Salt, Barry. *Film Style and Technology: History and Analysis.* London: Starword, 1983.

Santo, Avi. *Selling the Silver Bullet: The Lone Ranger and Transmedia Brand Licensing.* Austin: University of Texas Press, 2015.

Saussure, Ferdinand de. *Course in General Lingustics.* Chicago: Open Court Publishing, 1983.

Schaefer, Eric. *"Bold! Daring! Shocking! True!": A History of Exploitation Films, 1919–1959.* Durham, NC: Duke University Press, 1999.

Schatz, Thomas. "The New Hollywood." In *Film Theory Goes to the Movies,* edited by Jim Collins, Hilary Radner, and Ava Preacher Collins, 8–36. New York: Routledge, 1993.

Scolari, Carlos A., Paolo Bertetti, and Matthew Freeman. *Transmedia Archeology: Storytelling in the Borderlines of Science Fiction, Comics, and Pulp Magazines.* New York: Palgrave Macmillan, 2014.

Sconce, Jeffrey. *Haunted Media: Electronic Presence from Telegraphy to Television.* Durham, NC: Duke University Press, 2000.

Shay, Don. "30 Minutes with the Godfather of Digital Cinema." *Cinefex* 65 (March 1996): 58–67.

Silberman, Steve. "Matrix²." *Wired* 11, no. 5 (May 2003): n.p.

Simross, Lynn. "Fotonovel: The Movie-Picture Book." *Los Angeles Times* (September 18, 1978): OC_B1.

Sobchack, Vivian. *Screening Space: The American Science Fiction Film.* New Brunswick, NJ: Rutgers University Press, 1999.

Solomon, Matthew. "Twenty-five Heads under One Hat: Quick-Change in the 1890s." In *Meta-Morphing: Visual Transformation and the Culture of Quick-Change,* edited by Vivian Sobchack, 3–20. Minnesota: University of Minneapolis Press, 2000.

Solow, Herbert F., and Robert H. Justman. *Inside Star Trek: The Real Story.* New York: Pocket Books, 1996.

Solow, Herbert F., and Yvonne Fern Solow, *The Star Trek Sketchbook: The Original Series.* New York: Pocket Books, 1997.

Sperb, Jason. *Flickers of Film: Nostalgia in the Time of Digital Cinema.* New Brunswick, NJ: Rutgers University Press, 2016.

Stafford, Barbara Maria, and Frances Terpak. *Devices of Wonder: From the World in a Box to Images on a Screen.* Los Angeles: Getty Research Institute, 2001.

Sternbach, Rick, and Michael Okuda. *Star Trek: The Next Generation Technical Manual.* New York: Simon and Schuster, 1991.

Stix, Gary. "Special Effects: Pictures Worth a Thousand Cameras." *Scientific American* 275, no. 5 (November 1996): 46.

Taylor, Dayton. "Virtual Camera Movement: The Way of the Future?" *American Cinematographer* 77, no. 9 (1996): 93–100.

Titelman, Carol, ed. *The Art of Star Wars*. New York: Ballantine Books, 1979.

Tournier, Michel. *The Ogre*. Translated by Barbara Bray. New York: Pantheon Books, 1972.

Trend, David. *Worlding: Identity, Media, and Imagination in a Digital Age*. Boulder, CO: Paradigm Publishers, 2013.

Tryon, Chuck. "Digital 3D, Technological Auteurism, and the Rhetoric of Cinematic Revolution." In *Special Effects: New Histories/Theories/Contexts*, edited by Dan North, Bob Rehak, and Michael S. Duffy, 183–95. London: Palgrave/BFI, 2015.

Tulloch, John, and Henry Jenkins, eds. *Science Fiction Audiences: Watching Doctor Who and Star Trek*. London: Routledge, 1995.

Turnock, Julie. *Plastic Reality: Special Effects, Technology, and the Emergence of 1970s Blockbuster Aesthetics*. New York: Columbia University Press, 2015.

Tyler, Greg. "Karen Dick." *Trekplace.com* (1999).

Urbanski, Heather. *The Science Fiction Reboot: Canon, Innovation, and Fandom in Refashioned Franchises*. Jefferson, NC: McFarland and Company, 2013.

Vaz, Mark Cotta, and Patricia Rose Duignan. *Industrial Light & Magic: Into the Digital Realm*. New York: Ballantine Books, 1996.

Verba, Joan Marie. *Boldly Writing: A Trekker Fan and Zine History, 1967–1987*. 2nd ed. Minnetonka, MN: FTL Publications, 2003.

"What Is Bullet Time?" Directed by Josh Oreck. *The Matrix*. DVD. Burbank, CA: Warner Home Video, 1999.

Whissel, Kristen. *Spectacular Digital Effects: CGI and Contemporary Cinema*. Durham, NC: Duke University Press, 2014.

Whitfield, Stephen E. *The Making of Star Trek*. New York: Ballantine Books, 1968.

Williams, Gerry, and Penny Durrans. "These Will Be a Reality Sooner Than You Think." *Subspace Chatter* 8 (October 1976).

Winston, Joan. *The Making of the Trek Conventions*. New York: Playboy Press, 1979.

Wolf, Mark J. P. *Building Imaginary Worlds: The Theory and History of Subcreation*. New York: Routledge, 2012.

———. "Space, Time, Frame, Cinema: Muybridge, Frozen Time, and Beyond." Paper presented to the Society for Cinema and Media Studies Conference, Atlanta, GA, March 5, 2004.

Zimmerman, Herman, Rick Sternbach, and Michael Okuda. *The Deep Space Nine Technical Manual*. New York: Simon and Schuster, 1998.

INDEX

A. I. Artificial Intelligence, 149

Abel, Robert, 51

Abrams, J. J., 1, 25, 65, 72, 193

Abyss, The, 98, 129

Academy Awards, 5, 167

Academy of Motion Picture Arts and
    Sciences, 5. *See also* Academy Awards

affirmational fandom, 28–29, 50, 62, 101

Aldred, Jessica, 196

Alien, 34

Aliens, 97–98

Allen, Irwin, 43, 156

Alphaville, 78

Amazing Stories (magazine), 156

American Cinematographer, 6, 164, 171

American Werewolf in London, An, 148

AMT (Aluminum Model Toys), 34

Analog (magazine), 156

analog era, 4, 7, 29, 108, 152, 159, 161, 189,
    191, 194

Angel, 173

animatics, 75, 85–92, 94–96, 168, 197

animatronics, 92, 109, 111, 114, 117, 126, 128,
    130, 147, 152, 193

Antz, 138

"Arena" (TV episode), 35

Arrival of a Train at La Ciotat, 159

artist-inventor couplet, 94

Art of Star Wars, The, 84

Asimov, Isaac, 77

Astaire, Fred, 145

Astro (character), 145

Autodesk Maya, 189

Avatar (2009 film), 1, 190

Avengers, The, 1

Avengers: Age of Ultron, 1

Babe, 197

Bacon-Smith, Camille, 56, 63

Bad Boys 2, 153

Baker, Rick, 149

Bakshi, Ralph, 131

"Balance of Terror" (TV episode), 34

Ballantine Books, 48, 84

Barwood, Hal, 80

Batman (character), 1, 144

Batman and Robin, 169

Baudrillard, Jean, 135, 145

Bazin, André, 98, 139, 142, 183

Being John Malkovich, 136

Bennett, Harve, 52

Betty Boop (character), 131

Beverly Hills Chihuahua, 145

Biskind, Peter, 103

Blade Runner, 73

blueprint culture, 28, 45, 48–49, 84, 101;
    rise of, 42–49

blueprints, 10, 21, 28, 32–33, 45, 55–57, 59,
    61–64, 82; movie script as, 13. *See also*
    General Plans

Bode, Lisa, 107, 196

Boll, Uwe, 177

Bolter, David Jay, 140

Bond, James (character), 144

Boorman, John, 131

Borderlands, 151

Bordwell, David, 12, 94, 183–185

bottle shows, 29, 40–43

ABOUT THE AUTHOR

Bob Rehak is Associate Professor of Film and Media Studies at Swarthmore College.